Derivatives

This book provides a comprehensive but concise treatment of the subject of Derivatives. It focuses on making essential concepts accessible to a wider audience. It eschews complicated mathematics and uses high school level mathematics to explain the concepts. It describes and explains various derivative instruments, their use and pricing, and the functioning of derivative markets. It uses a large number of examples to elucidate concepts and illustrate their real-life application. A distinguishing feature of the book is that it goes beyond the narrow perspective of derivative traders and investors and takes a broader approach which enhances its appeal to a range of readers.

This book will be useful for students in the fields of economics, econometrics, derivatives, and finance and financial professionals, bankers and investors.

T. V. Somanathan, till recently director at the World Bank, Washington, is currently additional secretary in the Government of India. He has a PhD in Economics (University of Calcutta) and is an ACA (England and Wales), FCCA (London), FCMA (London), FCIS (London), ACS, ACMA (India). He is also a member of the Indian Administrative Service (IAS) and has served in a variety of policy-making positions in state and union governments in India. He is a recipient of several academic awards and distinctions and the author of over 80 published papers and of chapters in several reference books. He co-authored with V. Anantha Nageswaran *The Economics of Derivatives* which was published by Cambridge University Press in 2015.

V. Anantha Nageswaran teaches International Economics and Financial Markets at the Singapore Management University, at Indian Institutes of Management Bangalore and Indore, and at the SP Jain Centre for Management in Singapore. He has a PhD in Finance (University of Massachussetts) and an MBA (IIM, Ahmedabad) and was earlier with Credit Suisse, UBS and Bank Julius Baer in Switzerland and Singapore. He is the co-author, with T. V. Somanathan, of *The Economics of Derivatives*. He has also co-authored the book *Can India Grow?*

Harsh Gupta, chief investment officer of an Indian public markets fund in Mumbai, has an MBA (INSEAD), BA Economics (Dartmouth) and is a CFA and FRM. He has worked as a management consultant at Bain & Company in London and Houston, and for MIT Poverty Action Lab as a Research Associate. He writes about policy issues for *Mint*.

Derivatives

Second Edition

T. V. Somanathan
V. Anantha Nageswaran
Harsh Gupta

CAMBRIDGE
UNIVERSITY PRESS

University Printing House, Cambridge CB2 8BS, United Kingdom

One Liberty Plaza, 20th Floor, New York, NY 10006, USA

477 Williamstown Road, Port Melbourne, vic 3207, Australia

314 to 321, 3rd Floor, Plot No.3, Splendor Forum, Jasola District Centre, New Delhi 110025, India

79 Anson Road, #06–04/06, Singapore 079906

Cambridge University Press is part of the University of Cambridge.

It furthers the University's mission by disseminating knowledge in the pursuit of education, learning and research at the highest international levels of excellence.

www.cambridge.org
Information on this title: www.cambridge.org/9781108416207

First edition first published in 1998 by Tata McGraw Hill
Second edition first published 2018

Printed in India by Akash Press, New Delhi

A catalogue record for this publication is available from the British Library.

Library of Congress Cataloging-in-Publication Data

Names: Somanathan, T. V., author. | Nageswaran, V. Anantha, author. | Gupta, Harsh, 1986- author.
Title: Derivatives / T.V. Somanathan, V. Anantha Nageswaran, Harsh Gupta.
Description: 2nd edition. | Cambridge ; New York, NY : Cambridge University Press, 2017. | Earlier edition: 1998. | Includes bibliographical references and index.
Identifiers: LCCN 2017025020| ISBN 9781108416207 (hardback : alk. paper) | ISBN 9781108402712 (pbk. : alk. paper)
Subjects: LCSH: Derivative securities.
Classification: LCC HG6024.A3 S6628 2017 | DDC 332.64/57--dc23 LC record available at https://lccn.loc.gov/2017025020

ISBN 978-1-108-41620-7 Hardback
ISBN 978-1-108-40271-2 Paperback

Dedicated to

T. V. S

The late Professor Rakhal Dutta, Head of the Department of Economics,
Calcutta University

V. A. N

All the gurus – past, present and future

H. G.

My parents

Contents

List of Tables, Figures and Boxes

Note: The source of all tables and figures not citing a specific source is the authors themselves.

Tables

Figures

Boxes

Foreword

The four decades since the 1970s have been a period of extraordinarily rapid social and technological change, with few spheres of human endeavour left untouched. In the financial markets in particular, where I have had the privilege of being an active participant at all levels, the pace of change has been frenetic, with the growing importance of derivatives being one of the most significant.

In the pre-1970s world of fixed exchange rates, controlled interest rates, limited international trade, administered prices (and in countries like India, price controls and rationing), we hardly needed derivatives. In today's world, where price volatility is a constant feature of markets, derivatives are an integral part of financial markets and essential for sound risk management. Derivatives are no longer confined to the developed countries. Many of the most actively traded derivatives markets are now in emerging economies.

Derivatives are important but they are also complicated. The second edition of this book provides the reader with a sound understanding of the fundamental principles and practices of derivatives markets. It is comprehensive, covering topics ranging from pricing to accounting, while remaining concise. What makes this book stand out is the fact that it is written in plain language, de-mystifies a complex subject, and is easy to understand. At the same time, it does not over-simplify the subject. It provides a clear conceptual framework to each topic, which puts issues in context and makes them easier to comprehend. I am confident it will prove very valuable to a wide variety of readers.

K. V. Kamath
President
New Development Bank

Shanghai, June 2017

Preface to the First Edition

As recently as 1985, futures trading was so obscure in India that even bankers, financial journalists and some professors of finance and economics would ask what it was. Discussions on the subject, with layman or professional alike, would almost always have to begin with a lengthy introduction.

Today, awareness has increased. The gradual globalisation of the Indian economy means that Indian professionals and academics simply cannot afford to be unaware of futures and other derivatives, and their applications in India. Yet, there is no work of reference on the subject for the Indian reader to turn to. This book is a modest attempt to fill that gap.

While covering the whole canvas, the book tries to address the specific needs of diverse groups of readers. For the professional and the student of finance, it provides a detailed study of the manner in which the markets work and how the knowledge can be used to make profits or avoid losses. For the academic and the student of economics, it surveys the theoretical literature, explains methods by which empirical studies can be performed and presents some of the findings of the author's empirical research on Indian futures markets. For the policymaker, regulator and government official, the book examines at length the larger public purpose of derivatives markets, covering the regulatory experience in India, comparing it with experience abroad and suggesting improvements. For the generalist manager, management accountant, internal auditor and board member of a corporate entity, it discusses at length the management of derivative exposures; a job which cannot be left entirely to the specialist (as the spate of expert-led derivative disasters has so painfully shown). For the financial accountant and external auditor, it provides a detailed overview of the accounting treatment of derivative transactions and the issues involved. For the tax practitioner, it examines the taxation of derivatives under the Income Tax Act.

In a book of this nature, there is always a difficulty in balancing the needs of the practitioner with those of the academic. However, the author is hopeful that just the right balance has been struck. Issues primarily of academic interest have been placed in Appendices. Similarly, there is a difficult judgement to be exercised on the degree of complexity to which the text should go, since an attempt to meet the needs of the derivatives super-specialist would detract from the usefulness of the book to others. The approach in the book is to start with the assumption that the reader knows nothing about the subject, and then step by step, reach a level where he has a comprehensive picture of the nature, functions and uses of each derivative security, as well as the economic, regulatory, accounting, taxation and other issues relating to derivatives. To enhance understanding, a large number of worked examples have been included. However, the book does not cover highly complicated trading strategies. It also avoids the use of advanced mathematics and calculus, by explaining concepts narratively, and providing numerical examples that illustrate them comprehensively.

This book owes so much to so many, that their invaluable contribution has been acknowledged separately. Responsibility for any errors, omissions or inadequacies rests entirely with the author. Any views expressed in this book are the personal views of the author and should not be construed as representing the views of the organisation(s) for which the author is currently, or was previously, working. Suggestions for improvement are earnestly solicited.

September 1998   T. V. Somanathan

Preface to the Second Edition

In the 19 years since the first edition of this book appeared, much has changed. There was a time when the Western expert consensus was that financial markets should be largely left alone and that derivatives should be regulated as lightly as possible. That has changed after the global financial crisis of 2008. There is now greater caution about the effects of derivatives on the economy.

Derivatives were relatively insignificant in Indian financial markets in 1998 and were just beginning to recover from decades of severe restrictions, imposed at a time when the government pursued a 'socialistic pattern of society'. Today, India has active derivative markets not only in commodities but also in various financial instruments (so much so that there have been criticisms that equity derivatives trading in India has reached excessive proportions vis-à-vis the cash markets). Meanwhile, the Indian economy too has grown faster than the global average. In short, derivatives are more significant now in Indian markets and Indian markets are more significant in global terms.

Amidst all the changes, one fact remains unchanged: derivatives are an important feature of a modern market economy and are here to stay. They matter not only to developed markets but to emerging markets as well. Therefore, a basic understanding of how these markets work is essential for those who participate in these markets, those who aspire to work in them and those who comment on them, but also for those who seek to study the economy. Students of commerce, business and finance, bankers and accountants, analysts and financial journalists, non-financial economists and managers – all need a basic understanding of the essentials of derivatives markets. Yet, most books on derivatives are geared to specialists and they often take a mathematical approach.

This book aims to enable the general reader – whether student, practitioner, banker, commentator or investor – to gain a basic understanding of the derivatives markets and how they operate. It does not presume any prior knowledge of derivatives. The response to the first edition (which went into nine reprints till 2010) indicated that it succeeded in good measure in attaining that objective. It is the authors' sincere hope that this edition will do the same.

In this edition, the basic style and approach of the first edition – simplicity in explanation, lucidity in exposition of concepts, avoidance of calculus and advanced mathematics,and instead the use of narrative with specific numerical examples to illustrate concepts – have been retained. However, the content has been comprehensively updated and improved. Recent developments in the subject have been incorporated. Many new topics have been added.

The first edition devoted considerable space to issues of relevance primarily to economists and policymakers. This book has reduced emphasis on those issues. The interested reader could however turn to *The Economics of Derivatives* (Cambridge University Press, 2015, by Somanathan and Nageswaran) for a comprehensive treatment of those aspects. Certain issues that are now of merely historical interest (such as the chapter on the *badla* system) have been omitted. This book includes topics that were non-existent or less relevant then (for example, exchange traded funds) and also has a more detailed treatment of several issues (options strategies for instance).

Derivatives are important and useful tools. The authors hope this book will help readers gain a good understanding of these tools as well as the benefits and the risks that they bring and will help users handle derivatives wisely and carefully.

Responsibility for any errors, omissions or inadequacies rests entirely with the authors. Any views expressed in this book are the personal views of the authors and should not be construed as representing the views of the organisations for which the authors are currently, or were previously, working.

T. V. Somanathan

V. Anantha Nageswaran

Harsh Gupta

Acknowledgements

We owe a debt to Qudsiya Ahmed, Anwesha Rana, Aditya Majumdar and Suvadip Bhattacharjee of Cambridge University Press for their outstanding professionalism at various stages in the production of this book. We also thank Ratnesh Jha, Managing Director, Cambridge University Press, South Asia for his invaluable support.

We are deeply grateful to Mr K. V. Kamath for kindly agreeing to write the foreword to this edition.

We are very grateful to Mr Srivatsa Krishna, IAS, Mr P. S. Srinivas, (formerly of the World Bank and currently at the New Development Bank), Mr D. Sampath Kumar (formerly Editor, *Business Line*), Mrs Aarati Krishnan and Ms Rajalakshmi Nirmal (both of *Business Line*), Mr S. Santhanakrishnan (Managing Partner, PKF Sridhar & Santhanam, Chartered Accountants), Dr G. Sreekumar (Chief General Manager, Reserve Bank of India) and Ms Araceli Tria (formerly of the World Bank) for their valuable help in various ways at various stages.

We thank the following for permission to use published material:

- Ms Carolyn Ramsteiner and Thomson Reuters
- Mr Jon Vialoux and Equity Clock (a division of Tech Talk Financial Network/ Equityclock.com)
- Mr Hemant Jha and McGraw Hill Education

Harsh Gupta would like to especially acknowledge Professor Elias Papaioannou, Professor Meir Kohn, Professor Pierre Hillion and Professor Lucie Tepla for his intellectual growth while absolving them of any errors in his conceptual understanding that may have crept in.

Part – I
Introduction

1

Introduction

In the early 1980s, the word 'derivative' was used mainly in chemistry (as in, hydrocarbon derivatives) or mathematics (as in, the second derivative of a function). Today, it is most commonly used in the context of financial markets. This is a reflection of the phenomenal speed with which these new financial instruments have evolved. Derivative markets today have an estimated value of over ₹ 378 crore crores or ₹ 3.78 x 10^{16}. [1] To put this figure in perspective, it is several times larger than the whole world's Gross Domestic Product (GDP)! Once considered exotic instruments used only by the high priests of international finance, these have now become ubiquitous. More and more companies and even some governments are using, or being forced to use, derivatives in a fast-changing world of unprecedented opportunities and unprecedented risks. An understanding of derivatives is thus a necessity for anyone interested in the financial markets.

Definition of derivative

A derivative security (commonly shortened to derivative) is *a security or contract designed in such a way that its price or value is derived from the price of an underlying asset.*

For instance, the price of gold 'futures contracts for October maturity' is derived from the price of gold. The value of a 'September call option' on sugar is derived from the price of sugar. The value of a 'five year interest rate swap' is derived from the prevailing rate of interest. The price of a derivative security is not arbitrary; it is linked to the price of the underlying asset. A rise in the

---

1   According to the Bank for International Settlements, total notional value outstanding on derivative contracts (interest rates and foreign exchange) traded at exchanges (as of March 2016) and over-the-counter (interest rates, commodities, equities and credit default swaps as of second half of 2015) but excluding exchange traded equity derivatives was USD 566 trillion (approx.). Separately, turnover in equity derivatives (single stock and index futures and options) in 2015 reported by the World Federation of Exchanges amounted to USD 346 trillion (approx.).

price of the underlying may lead to a rise (or fall) in the price of the derivative, but in a predictable way. Because the relationship is predictable, transactions in derivatives can be used as a method to compensate for, or offset, the risk of price changes in the underlying asset. Formulae can usually be used to calculate the effect of the price of the underlying in the price of the derivative. However, the relationship is not always precise and the formulae are not always accurate and hence derivatives may not always work exactly as intended.

The simple definition presented above is widely used. However, it does contain errors of inclusion and exclusion.

Firstly, a security does not become a derivative merely because its price is 'derived' from that of another. The cost of a basket of vegetables containing potatoes, carrots and cabbages in a particular ratio is indeed 'derived' from the price of the individual vegetables in the basket. Does that mean that the basket of vegetables is a derivative of potatoes, carrots and cabbages? The answer is no. This is because the basket is simply a collection of those assets. In the financial markets, there are similar notional 'baskets' known as mutual funds. Among mutual funds, there is a special category called 'exchange traded funds' (ETFs) and among them is a sub-class of index funds. Index funds, in their performance, attempt to exactly mimic the performance of an index by holding the same combination of securities or commodities as the index. Mutual funds and such ETFs are generally not treated as derivatives. Thus, to exclude them from the 'conventional' definition, it is necessary to note that a derivative is a security which derives its price from the underlying *without actual ownership of the underlying*.

Secondly, some securities now called, or regarded as, 'derivatives' do not derive their price from the price of some other asset or liability or instrument. Rather, they derive their value from the occurrence or non-occurrence of some event and conceptually are similar to insurance. For instance, 'credit default swaps' are securities whereby,

- one party pays a fixed fee every year; and
- in return, the second party agrees to compensate the first party if there is a default on repayment of a loan by another (third) party.

Similarly, certain types of securities known as 'catastrophe derivatives' have a cash flow which is triggered only when a defined natural disaster (say, a cyclone) occurs. These instruments are actually closer to insurance contracts than to conventional derivatives but are usually classified as derivatives. The definition needs to be expanded to include them.

Thirdly, some types of bets will also fit the simple definition of derivatives. For example, if a person has a wager with another whereby he wins ₹ 100 if the share price of Tata Consultancy Services Limited Motors is more than ₹ 2,500 on a certain date, then this wager might constitute a financial derivative in terms of the simple conceptual definition. Such agreements may however be legally invalid, because betting is seen as socially unproductive or indeed harmful. Pure bets are usually not regarded as derivatives (though some scholars argue that they should be).

For practical purposes, a better definition of derivatives would be that:

> *A derivative is a legally enforceable security or contract designed in a way that its value is derived from the value of an underlying asset (without actual ownership thereof) or from the value of an event which may or may not take place.*

The term 'asset' includes a liability which can be thought of as a negative asset.

While there is now a bewildering variety of derivatives, the most prominent types of derivatives are those known as:

- *forwards* and *futures* which involve the purchase/sale of an asset to be delivered at a future date with a *price fixed now;*
- *options* which give one party a *unilateral right* to buy (or, alternatively, to sell) an asset from another at a price fixed now but *without the compulsion or obligation* to actually do so (i.e., the first party can on its own decide to whether or not to exercise the right); and
- *swaps*, which are contracts where two parties exchange (swap) two different sets of cash flows.

Each of these (and more exotic instruments often involving combinations of these) will be described in detail in subsequent chapters.

Derivatives trading: Exchanges vs. 'over-the-counter'

Many derivatives transactions are carried out through *exchanges*. These are organised and regulated markets (similar to stock exchanges) which provide standardised and well-regulated arrangements for buyers and sellers to transact. Table 1.1 lists the main derivatives exchanges of the world.

Table 1.1: Important derivatives exchanges

	Name of the exchange	Main instruments traded
1	The Korea Exchange	Index futures and options, single stock futures and options, interest rate futures, foreign exchange futures and options, commodity futures
2	Chicago Mercantile Exchange (CME) Group, includes Chicago Board of Trade (CBOT), OneChicago and New York Mercantile Exchange (NYMEX)	Futures and options in agriculture, interest rates, energy, equities, metals, foreign exchange, weather indices, Bitcoin derivatives
3	Eurex (Germany)	Interest rate futures/options/futures on swaps, equity futures/options, volatility futures and options, exchange traded funds (ETF) derivatives, commodity futures and options, total return and dividend -based derivatives, property derivatives
4	New York Stock Exchange (NYSE) Euronext	Equities (stock indices, stock options), stock index futures, commodity futures, interest rate futures, options on ETFs
5	National Stock Exchange or NSE (India)	Stock index futures and options, single stock futures and options, currency futures, interest rate futures. (Commodity options to be launched soon and likely to be traded on NSE, Multi Commodity Exchange or MCX and National Commodity Derivatives Exchange or NCDEX)
6	BM&F Bovespa (Brazil)	Futures in equities, commodities, foreign exchange; stock index options
7	Chicago Board Options Exchange or CBOE (USA)	Index options, index futures, equity options, options on exchange traded notes/products (ETP), credit options
8	NASDAQ OMX Group (USA, Scandinavia)	Stock options/futures/forwards, Index option/futures, ETF options, Dividend Futures, Forwards on Baskets, Binary Options (Over-Under), Gold/Oil and other derivatives

	Name of the exchange	Main instruments traded
9	Multi Commodity Exchange of India (includes MCX-SX)	Commodity futures (metals, bullion, agricultural, energy)and currency futures
10	Moscow Exchange (Russia)	Single stock futures and option, stock index futures, interest rate futures, foreign exchange and commodity futures
11	Intercontinental Exchange or ICE (USA)	Exchange traded futures and options in agricultural products, oil products, natural gas, electricity and other underlyings. Over-the-counter (OTC) instruments in oil products, natural gas, electricity
12	Zhengzhou Commodity Exchange (China)	Commodity futures especially agricultural and chemical product such as wheat, sugar, cotton, rapeseed oil, and petroleum based products
13	London Metal Exchange or LME (U.K.)	Futures and options of a variety of base metals and other commodity products
14	Tokyo Commodity Exchange or TOCOM (Japan)	Futures and other derivatives for agricultural commodities, base and precious metals, energy products
15	Singapore Exchange Limited or SGX	Equity index and options; dividend index, foreign exchange, interest rates and commodities (metals, agricultural, petrochemical and electricity) futures, forwards and swaps

Source: Compiled from exchange websites.

India now figures in the top league in terms of volume of trading of derivatives. In 2015, the NSE was first in the number of stock index option contracts traded and second in the number of single stock futures contracts traded. In currency options, NSE occupied the top position in the world in number of options traded and in terms of turnover, it was placed second.[2] From the 1970s, when even domestic derivative markets were gradually being closed down, the situation has changed so much that the NSE now offers derivatives for buying and selling an American stock market index (the S&P 500 share index). Table 1.2 provides the contract specification for this

---

2 *Indian Securities Market Review 2015,* National Stock Exchange of India, Mumbai, 2015.

contract and illustrates some of the typical features of an exchange-traded futures contract.

Table 1.2: Contract specifications for NSE's S&P 500 index futures contract

S&P® futures contract specifications	
Ticker symbol	S&P500
Contract size	250 units
Notional value	Contract size multiplied by the index level (For example: if the current index value is 1000 then the notional value would be 1000 x 250 = ₹ 2,50,000)
Tick size	0.25
Trading hours	As in equity derivative segment
Expiry date	Third Friday of the respective contract month. In case third Friday is a holiday in USA or in India the contract shall expire on the preceding business day.
Contract months	Three serial monthly contracts and three quarterly expiry contracts in the Mar-Jun-Sep-Dec cycle
Daily settlement price	Last half hour's weighted average price
Final settlement price	All open positions at close of last day of trading shall be settled to the special opening quotation (SOQ) of the S&P 500 Index on the date of expiry. (http://www.cmegroup.com/trading /equity-index/files/SOQ.pdf)
Final settlement procedure	Final settlement will be cash settled in INR based on final settlement price
Final settlement day	All open positions on expiry date shall be settled on the next working day of the expiry date (T+1)
Position limits	The trading member/mutual funds position limits as well as the disclosure requirement for clients is same as applicable in case of domestic stock index derivatives

Source: NSE

While a considerable amount of derivatives trading takes place on exchanges like those listed in Table 1.1, it is also common for derivatives to be transacted 'over-the-counter', i.e., directly without the intermediation of an exchange.

Such transactions are known as 'over-the-counter' (OTC) transactions. Swaps are predominantly traded over-the-counter. Overall, and primarily because of the swap market, the total value of derivatives traded over the counter exceeds that traded on exchanges.

Evolution of derivatives

Forward trading in some form or other is quite ancient. It is not clear where and when the first forward market came into existence. There are reports that forward trading existed in India as far back as 2,000 BCE and also that some forms of forward trading existed in Roman times. Forward trading in a somewhat systematic manner is believed to have been in existence in the twelfth century English and French fairs.

There was forward trading in rice in seventeenth century in Japan. The trade, known as *cho-ai-mai a kinai* (rice-trade-on-book), centred around Dojima, a district of Osaka. The trade in rice grew and evolved to the stage where receipts for future delivery were traded with a high degree of standardisation. In 1730, the market received official recognition from the Tokugawa Shogunate (the ruling class of Shoguns or feudal lords). The Dojima rice market can thus be regarded as the first futures market in the sense of an organised exchange with standardised trading terms.[3] The market and its successors went through many phases including closures in 1869 and 1937.

The first futures markets in the Western hemisphere were developed in the United States, in Chicago. These markets (in grain) had started as spot markets and gradually evolved into futures trading. This evolution occurred in stages. The first stage was the starting of agreements to buy grain in the future at a predetermined price with the intention of actual delivery. (This corresponds to the concept of non-transferable specific delivery forward contracts in commodities in India.) Gradually these contracts became transferable and over a period, particularly during the American Civil War between 1860 and 1865, it became commonplace to sell and resell agreements themselves, instead of taking delivery of the physical produce. Traders found that the agreements were easier to buy and sell if they were standardised

---

3   H. H. Bakken, 'Futures Trading—Origin, Development and Economic Status', *Futures Trading Seminar*, Mimir Publishers, Wisconsin, 1966.

in terms of quality of grain, market lot and place of delivery, thus creating modern futures contracts.

The CBOT, which opened in 1848, is the world's oldest futures and options exchange.[4] The general rules framed by CBOT in 1865 became a pacesetter for many other markets. In 1870, the New York Cotton Exchange was founded. The London Metal Exchange was established in 1877.

The next big wave of expansion in derivatives trading happened after the 1970s. In the first phase of this expansion, new derivatives instruments and markets were developed in the western countries, particularly the United States and the UK. The first financial futures market was the International Monetary Market, founded in 1972 by the CME. This was followed by the London International Financial Futures Exchange in 1982. Towards the end of the twentieth century, as large countries including India and China moved away from socialism and exchange controls towards market-based economies and free movement of foreign capital, derivatives began to expand rapidly in the developing world. Today, many emerging market economies have thriving derivatives markets. China has become a major centre for commodity futures trading in recent years at the Dalian Commodity Exchange, Shanghai Futures Exchange and Zhengzhou Commodity Exchange.

There is evidence of options in wheat and other agricultural commodities during the middle ages in England. In seventeenth century Holland, there were options on tulip bulbs. Options trading in agricultural commodities and in shares came into existence in the United States from the 1860s. However, these were not standardised traded options, but one-to-one deals between traders (over-the-counter in today's parlance). The problem with such options was that there was no openness in operations, no secondary market and no method of guaranteeing that contractual obligations would be honoured by the option writers. Options trading remained peripheral and never grew as much as futures trading till the 1970s.

The first exchange-traded options market was started by CBOT on 26 April 1973. For the first time, standard maturities, standard strike prices, and standard delivery arrangements were evolved. The risk of default was virtually eliminated by introducing a clearinghouse and a margin system. Trading

---

4   In 2007, the CBOT merged with the Chicago Mercantile Exchange (CME) to form the CME Group.

was done through the open outcry method, so that prices were announced in the open, reducing scope for malpractice and allowing dissemination of price information. Initially, options on futures contracts were not permitted. These commenced only in 1982. Nowadays many options are in fact options to purchase/sell a particular futures contract rather than the underlying commodity itself.

Box 1.1: Thales' call options on olives

The Greek philosopher Thales (pronounced Thay'leez) had been ridiculed as one whose philosophy was useless. Evidence of this was his extreme poverty. However, because of his extraordinary ability to read the stars, Thales forecast that the autumn olive harvest would be unusually large. It is believed that he secretly travelled to the olive farmers and purchased the right of first refusal on their olives at a fixed price (a call option). Because this was nine months before the harvest, the farmers were willing to sell this right very inexpensively. Since he was correct, Thales was able to purchase the entire olive crop at the pre-agreed upon price. He now controlled the entire crop and those who needed olives had to buy them at his price. Apparently, he made a fortune and silenced his critics.[5]

Options trading existed in India long before the introduction of regulated and exchange traded equity options in 2000. The Marwaris traded in indigenous options (*satta*), giving the buyers the right, but not the obligation, to buy or sell a certain commodity at a specified future date and price. These could be *teji* (call) or *mandi* (put), with the premium paid by the buyer of the option known as *nazrana*.[6] Commodity options were banned after independence by the Forward Contracts (Regulation) Act, 1952.

The introduction of traded options opened the way for the evolution of more complex derivatives. (As will be shown later in the book, virtually all derivatives are based on the two building blocks of futures and options. Since traded options became commonly available only in the early 1980s, it is no surprise that complex derivatives started appearing only from then.)

---

5   This is one of three versions of this story. Source: Lecture Notes (Chapter 15), Course No. 3600 on Investments by Dr Timothy Mayes, Metropolitan State College of Denver. Available at: http://slideplayer.com/slide/6895061/, accessed on 24 December 2016.

6   Harish Damodaran, 'The Marwari Business Model I and II', *The Hindu Business Line*, 7 and 8 April 2013.

The first swap transaction took place in 1981 between the World Bank and International Business Machines (IBM). This transaction was a currency swap. Interest rate swaps also commenced in 1981. The International Swap Dealers Association (as it was then known) introduced partial standardisation of the contract terms in 1985. However, swaps do not have much of a secondary market even now and hence they are largely not readily transferable. Other derivatives like forward rate agreements (FRAs), range forwards, collars and the like evolved in the second half of the 1980s.

Derivatives played a role in causing the global financial crisis of 2008 (see Appendix 1.1 for details). Since then, volumes of derivatives trading have stagnated or fallen in western markets but have continued to grow in developing countries.

Derivatives in India

As already mentioned, some form of forward trading probably existed in India also in the pre-modern era. Unfortunately, India has not had as good a tradition of written record-keeping as the west, and therefore, hard evidence of forward trading in our history is lacking. Organised forward markets came into existence in India in the late-nineteenth and early-twentieth century starting in 1875 with cotton in Mumbai followed later by trading in jute and jute goods in Kolkata.[7] Several new markets grew over the first half of the twentieth century. Options trading also existed, as already mentioned, although not through recognised exchanges.

Chronologically, India's experience in organised forward trading is almost as long as that of the United Kingdom and certainly longer than many developed nations (not to speak of developing countries). However, the tidal wave of price controls, nationalisation and state intervention in markets which swept through all economic policymaking after independence, led to a rapid decline in the number of futures markets. Regulations under the Forward Contracts (Regulation) Act, 1952 imposed increasingly severe restrictions and banned options. Frequently, markets were closed due to the feeling that they were responsible for sudden movements in commodity prices; the presumption was that speculation on forward markets was creating or exacerbating price pressures.

Winds of change began to blow across the Indian economic landscape

---

7   M. G. Pavaskar, *Economics of Hedging*, Popular Prakashan, Mumbai, 1976.

from the 1980s and these winds gathered in strength in the 1990s and the first decade of the new millennium. India's balance of payments crisis in 1991 spurred economic reforms and the government began to unshackle many areas of economic activity from government control. After 2002, the commodity futures markets in India experienced an unprecedented boom in terms of the number of exchanges, number of commodities allowed for derivatives trading as well as the value of futures trading in commodities.[8] Prohibition of futures trading in many commodities was lifted in 2003. Whereas exchanges had previously been confined to one commodity or commodity group (for example pepper in the Indian Pepper and Spice Trade Association, Cochin, jute and jute goods in the East India, Jute and Hessian Exchange, Calcutta etc.), new multi-commodity exchanges came into existence and introduced modern methods of trading. The NSE also entered the field of derivatives.

Apprehensions about the role of futures in raising food prices became prominent again around 2007 and there was a partial reversal of the trend with the banning of futures in several essential commodities in which they had been introduced. In the year 2015–16, the aggregate turnover at all the exchanges in the domestic commodity derivatives segment increased by 9.1 per cent to ₹ 66,96,380 crore (a little under $1.0 trillion based on the spot exchange rate of the Indian rupee against the US dollar) compared to ₹ 61,35,672 crore in 2014–15.[9]

The Indian stock market had a system of forward trading of indigenous origin known as *badla*. These transactions were also a form of derivatives, and were quite sophisticated, but because the *badla* market was unregulated, it left a lot of scope for manipulation. India's capital market regulator, Securities and Exchange Board of India (SEBI) banned the practice altogether in 2001, soon after the NSE and the Bombay Stock Exchange (BSE) both commenced trading in equity derivatives. Futures on the Nifty equity index were launched in the Indian markets in June 2000 followed by options on the index in June 2001, options in individual stocks in July 2001 and futures in single stocks in November 2001. Turnover on options and futures on equities (single stocks and

---

8   N. L. Ahuja, 'Commodity Derivatives Market in India: Development, Regulation and Future Prospects', *International Research Journal of Finance and Economics*, ISSN 1450-2887, Issue 2, 2006.

9   *Securities and Exchange Board of India Annual Report 2015-16* (published on 19 August 2016 and accessed on 20 August 2016)

stock indices) boomed in the first decade of the century and surpassed the cash market turnover. In recent years, equity options turnover has grown steadily while equity futures volumes have fluctuated, partly because of favourable tax treatment for options.[10]

Causes of rapid expansion of derivatives trading

The decades after 1970 have witnessed a dramatic increase in volume, large expansion in scope and rapid globalisation in the reach of derivatives. There were several reasons for this.

The first reason was a major increase in the level of financial risks because of systemic changes in the financial markets. In the late 1960s and early 1970s, the two most important currencies of that time (the US Dollar and Pound Sterling) came out of the fixed exchange rate system and became floating currencies. Because of this, the exchange rate of these currencies became uncertain whereas it had been fixed earlier. For example, an exporter of textiles who expected to receive dollars in three months from his date of sale no longer knew how much would he actually receive in his local currency. The 1970s also saw a great degree of volatility in commodity prices, due in part to the oil price hike by the Organization of the Petroleum Exporting Countries (OPEC) and the turmoil in the currency market.

In the late 1970s, another very important change occurred. Earlier, central banks had followed a policy of relatively stable interest rates. But guided by the advice of monetarist economists like Milton Friedman, central banks began to exercise greater control over money supply and started using interest rate changes as a means for controlling it. As a result, frequent changes of interest rate –both upwards and downwards – became the order of the day. These *changes in financial markets increased uncertainties*. The greater the risk, the greater the need to manage it. Necessity being the mother of invention, the increased risk led to the growth of risk management tools – derivatives.

The second reason was a *change in economic philosophy in many countries*. In economic matters, China moved away from communism in 1980. India moved away from socialism in 1991. The Soviet Union collapsed in 1990. These and

---

10 Securities transaction tax is levied only on the premium in an option but on the whole value in a futures contract.

many other countries which had controlled economies with limited room for market forces, liberalised and moved to market-based economies. Eventually they also allowed the establishment of derivatives markets.

The third reason was the change in the international system of trade. Traditionally, international trade had been characterised in most countries by high tariffs (i.e., import duties) and non-tariff barriers (e.g., import quotas, licensing). The creation of the World Trade Organisation (WTO) in the 1990s and the liberalisation of international trade (through reductions in import duties and the ending of many kinds of import restrictions) greatly increased the volumes of exports and imports. For many years, most countries also had exchange controls (controls on conversion of domestic currency into foreign exchange) and capital controls (controls on remittance of capital to a foreign country). From the Second World War until 1979, the UK, one of the world's most developed economies, still had exchange controls and restrictions on convertibility of the pound to foreign currency. Beginning in the late 1970s, often with encouragement from the International Monetary Fund (IMF), many countries abolished exchange controls and capital controls. This resulted in a big increase in the flow of capital from one country to another, whereby funds borrowed or raised in one country would be invested in another. The *combination of international trade liberalisation and liberalisation of international capital flows* greatly increased the volumes of transactions which would need protection against exchange rate and interest rate fluctuations. This greatly increased the need for derivatives.

The fourth reason, applicable particularly in the United States, was *deregulation* (removal of regulatory restrictions) of derivatives trading towards the end of the twentieth century. Under the Commodity Futures Modernisation Act of 2000, various controls and regulations in America applicable to derivatives were either abolished or liberalised. This allowed a further increase in derivatives volumes as transactions which were not allowed earlier became legally permissible. (This deregulation was later found to be one of the causes of the global financial crisis of 2008.)

A fifth reason was the *development of new mathematical techniques* for valuing complex derivatives. The development of the Black-Scholes Option Pricing Formula in the 1970s greatly enhanced the ability of market participants to determine the price of many kinds of derivatives.

However, to do such calculations manually was tedious and this restricted the extent to which such derivatives could be introduced and traded. This difficulty ended because of the sixth change: the *development of computing power*, enabling complex mathematical calculations to be done in seconds. The computer revolution and the ability to perform such calculations instantly at a terminal enabled such derivatives to be introduced and traded actively.

Aims and organisation of the book

This book aims to describe and to explain the various derivative instruments, and how they are used and priced. As far as possible, English rather than mathematics is used to explain the concepts, functions, pricing and valuation of derivatives. There are two reasons for this. First and foremost, the approach of the book is to make derivatives more understandable and less daunting. Risk arises not only from volatility or uncertainty but also from ignorance: what is not understood is the most risky. Therefore, the book seeks to de-mystify and make the concepts accessible to a wide spectrum of readers with different backgrounds. (Advanced readers and those desirous of further research into these topics will find useful references to go beyond the discussions offered in this book.) Secondly, mathematics has often bestowed a spurious sense of precision to financial and economic models creating a false sense of security in the minds of the users of those models.

The book has 21 chapters organised into seven parts. This chapter and the next introduce the reader to derivatives and to some basic concepts which are necessary for an understanding of the rest of the book. Part II, comprising chapters 3 to 7, deals with forward and futures trading. Part III, consisting of chapters 8 and 9, deals with swaps. Part IV, consisting of chapters 10 to 14, covers options. Chapters 15 and 16, which form Part V, examine other derivatives and certain financial instruments which may or may not be derivatives in the strict sense of the term but which have some characteristics akin to derivatives. Part VI, comprising chapters 17 to 19, describe the accounting, taxation and the regulatory framework for derivatives with particular reference to India. The concluding part looks at derivatives in the context of portfolio management (chapter 20) and finally (chapter 21) at the management of risks arising from derivatives trading. For some chapters, more detailed or more advanced material, not essential for an understanding of the chapter, is placed in appendices.

Appendix 1.1

The global financial crisis of 2007–08

Derivatives were a factor in the global financial crisis of 2007–08, one of the most important economic events of recent decades. This appendix provides a brief description of the causes of the crisis and the role of derivatives.

Causes of the crisis

Between 2000 and 2006, there was a rapid growth in lending by US banks to American residents for purchasing house property. Interest rates were very low in the US at this time. When borrowing money for a house, the borrower is required to 'mortgage' the property to the bank, i.e., the bank has the legal right to take over the property if the loan and interest are not paid on time. Thus, this kind of lending is referred to as mortgage lending. All mortgage borrowers are expected to ensure that the value of their loan is less than the value of the house property. The difference between the house value and the amount of loan is the 'equity' that the owner of the house has to contribute towards the cost and to maintain.

Borrowers with good creditworthiness (i.e., those who are assessed as very likely to repay the loans with interest on time) are known as prime borrowers. Over a period, mortgage lending was extended even to 'sub-prime' borrowers, i.e., those whose creditworthiness (income and assets) was below that normally expected for bank lending. The lending was on very liberal terms with very small levels of equity contribution by the borrower. It was based on optimism that house prices would continuously rise and therefore the borrower's lack of creditworthiness or inadequacy of equity would not be a problem in recovering the loan. Sub-prime borrowers were often allowed to start with very low payments using a low 'introductory rate' initially, with the interest rate and monthly payments increasing after a year or two.

The individual loans were 'securitised' or 'packaged' by banks into 'Mortgage Backed Securities' (MBS), consisting of a group of mortgage loans. (The term 'Asset Backed Securities' is similar and refers to a wider class of assets.) These were then further grouped together into 'collateralised debt obligations' (CDOs). A CDO would have several MBS in it, with different credit ratings. The CDO would then have different tranches or slices with different credit ratings. The highest slice or tranche might have a very high (AAA) credit rating.

Based on the credit rating, the owner of the CDO securities would enter into a derivative transaction called a Credit Default Swap (CDS – described later in the book in chapter 15) which is like credit insurance. The buyer of the CDS would pay a premium to the seller. If the borrowers failed to pay their dues on the underlying loans that went into a CDO, the CDO would stop yielding cash flows to its owner. That could be deemed a default. In that case, the seller of the CDS would have to reimburse the buyer for the amount of the shortfall. That is why a CDS contract is akin to an insurance contract. The buyer of a CDS contract buys default protection from the seller. Buyers and sellers of CDS included many banks and insurance companies and the amounts involved were very large.

After 2006, housing prices in the US unexpectedly began falling. One reason was that the low introductory rate period ended and the monthly payments required from many of the sub-prime borrowers went up. When they were unable to pay these higher monthly instalments, their property was 'foreclosed' and 'repossessed' (taken over) by the banks. When the house value fell, many loans began to have negative equity, i.e., house value became less than the value of the loan. Being sub-prime borrowers, the owners were unable to make up the difference and the loans went into default. The rate of default on such loans turned out to be much higher than had been anticipated by the credit-rating agencies. As a result, many of the CDOs (groups of mortgage loans) also began to suffer default on the payments. Those who had insured against such defaults by purchasing derivatives (CDS) began to invoke the CDS and this created an unexpected liability for the banks and insurance companies who had sold the CDS. Many of them were unable to meet the liabilities.

Eventually many 'venerable' financial institutions collapsed. Bear Stearns, Northern Rock, American Insurance Group, Lehman Brothers were among those that collapsed (or were nationalised on the verge of collapse) while many others suffered catastrophic losses. The economic damage caused by the crisis was estimated at between $6,000 billion and $14,000 billion, and the latter figure is close to one full year's GDP of the United States.[11]

---

11 David Luttrel, Tyler Atkinson and Harvey Rosenblum, 'Assessing the Costs and Consequences of the 2007-09 Financial Crisis and its Aftermath', Federal Reserve Bank of Dallas, 2010.

The availability of CDS derivatives had two effects. Firstly, once holders of the security had purchased a CDS they felt very safe (since the risk had been 'insured') and therefore increased their exposure to such securities. This is called 'moral hazard' in economics. Secondly, the instrument of CDS transmitted the problem to a much wider set of institutions who sold CDS without directly being involved in the mortgage loans. Even some Indian private sector banks were affected. It made it very difficult to quantify and pinpoint the location and extent of the problem. If CDS had not been available, the banks involved may have been more cautious and fewer of them would have been involved. Thus, without CDS, the impact of bad loans would have been smaller and would have been distributed over a smaller number of institutions.

Overall, there were several causes for the crisis:

- a monetary policy that was too loose and led to very low interest rates and imprudent expansion in credit;
- misplaced faith in the benefits of unregulated free financial markets and an assumption that the market would always act in an economically optimal manner;
- too much deregulation of derivatives in the US after 2000 when many regulatory restrictions were removed; this in turn led to excessive financial 'innovation' through creation of new instruments, including derivative instruments, whose risks were not properly understood; and
- credit rating failures by the rating agencies which gave very optimistic ratings to certain derivative instruments.

Impact of the crisis

Prior to 2008, there were many who felt that derivatives markets were self-regulating and that government regulation was largely unnecessary. That has changed irrevocably. American Congressmen Chris Dodd and Barney Frank took the lead in authoring a new set of regulations in 2009 for the financial sector in America. (By virtue of the inter-dependent nature of global finance and its strong links with American finance in particular, these have had influence far beyond the USA.) The law requires greater standardisation and margin requirements for OTC derivatives and effectively pushes them towards an exchange-traded derivative model which would facilitate netting out of positions and make market volumes and exposures more transparent.

There have been moves to introduce the 'Volcker Rule', based on the idea of Paul Volcker, former Chairman of the US Federal Reserve. Volcker's basic idea was to reseparate proprietary trading and other 'non-bank' risk-taking and potentially harmful speculation from 'traditional' banking. Governments in most countries provide deposit insurance to protect bank depositors. Since the safety of deposits is guaranteed by the government, the government (and hence all citizens) bear a contingent liability for failures of the banking system. But profits are earned only by the owners of the banks, thus the risks incurred by banks create a 'negative externality'. The asymmetric nature of risks and compensations creates a 'moral hazard'. The idea behind the Volcker Rule is to make sure that the government's support is confined to commercial banking and docs not extend to investment activities undertaken by banks.

In sum, the crisis has led to a more cautious approach among regulators to derivatives as a whole especially in those countries where they had earlier been very lightly regulated.

2

Some Basic Concepts

This chapter introduces the reader to some basic concepts that will be useful when reading subsequent chapters and in gaining a deeper understanding of derivatives. It describes the main types of derivatives, the economic functions of derivative markets and some related concepts.

Types of derivatives

Derivatives are described and classified in many ways. The primary method of describing derivatives is based on the type of contract.

Types of contracts

The main contract types are:
- Forward contracts
  - Futures contracts (which are special types of forward contracts traded through an exchange and thus a sub-set of forwards)
- Swaps (in theory, these are similar to a string of forward contracts)
- Options contracts
- Complex derivatives (futures and options are the basic building blocks of complex derivatives)
  - Forward rate agreements
  - Range forwards
  - Exotic options
  - Collars
  - Swaptions

Underlying

Each of these types of contracts may have as its 'underlying' one of various kinds of assets. Thus, a futures contract can be on the share of an individual company (say, Tata Consultancy Services or TCS) or on a commodity (e.g., gold) or on a foreign currency (e.g., Japanese yen) and so on. Similarly, there can be options or swaps on various kinds of underlying assets or liabilities. Derivatives are thus often described on the basis of the type of contract and the nature of the underlying, e.g., 'pepper futures' means a futures contract with pepper as the underlying commodity, a 'currency swap' means a swap contract where the underlying is a foreign currency and so on.

Underlying assets are also grouped into classes, like commodities or financial instruments. Based on this classification, derivatives can be classified into the following.

- Financial derivatives in which the underlying is a financial instrument (individual share, a stock market index, bonds, a foreign currency, a cost of living index, a credit risk etc.).
- Commodity derivatives in which the underlying is a commodity which may include:
  a. gold, silver and platinum often collectively known as 'bullion markets';
  b. base metals like nickel, tin, lead, copper etc.;
  c. 'soft' commodities like coffee, cocoa, cotton, etc.; and
  d. other commodities.
- Weather and catastrophe derivatives in which the underlying is an index related to weather or other natural conditions like rainfall, temperature, etc.

Economic functions of derivatives markets

It goes without saying that an elaborate structure of derivatives markets would not exist without some definite function or purpose. What then, are the purposes and are they economically useful?[1]

The primary economic function and *raison d'etre* of derivatives markets is

---

1 For a full discussion of this subject, see Chapter 3 of *The Economics of Derivatives*, T. V. Somanathan and V. Anantha Nageswaran, Cambridge University Press, 2015. Academic readers interested in studying the different viewpoints can also refer to the following: J. B. Baer and O. G. Saxon, *Commodity Exchanges and Futures Trading*, Harper & Row, New York, 1948, 30–31; W. R. Natu, *Regulation of Forward Markets*, Asia Publishing House, Bombay, 1962, 16–17; H. S. Houthakker and P. J. Williamson, *Economics of Financial Markets*, Oxford University Press, New York, 1996, 255–56. For a comparative study, see T. V. Somanathan, *Commodity and Financial Futures Markets: An Economic Analysis*, Unpublished Ph D Dissertation, Calcutta University, 1993, 8–13.

the hedging function also known as the *risk-shifting* or *risk transference function*. Derivatives markets provide a vehicle by which participants can hedge, i.e., *protect themselves from adverse price movements in a commodity or financial instrument in which they face a price risk, by transferring that risk to others.* This primary function is common to all derivative instruments: futures, options, swaps and exotic derivatives, whether or not they are exchange traded.

Apart from this primary function, some kinds of derivatives may perform secondary economic functions. The secondary (or incidental) functions are the following:

- Price discovery function: Futures markets provide a mechanism by which diverse and scattered opinions of the future are coalesced into one readily discernible number which provides a 'consensus of knowledgeable thinking'. Organised spot markets perform a price discovery function too, but only in respect of the spot (i.e., current) price. Futures prices provide an expression of the consensus of today's expectations about some point in the future. By publishing and disseminating this, they also perform an *information* or *publicity function*. The process of price discovery also leads to the *inter-temporal inventory allocation function*, by which market participants are able to compare the current and future prices and decide the optimal allocation of their stocks of an asset between immediate sale and storage for future sale. Over-the-counter transactions where prices are not published do not contribute to price discovery. Options and swaps do not directly contribute to price discovery for the underlying itself.

- Information discovery: Options and swaps markets do not contribute to price discovery in the underlying itself. However, they may contribute useful information by helping to discover the prevailing market perceptions of the level of various risks. For example, the market for Credit Default Swaps helps to 'discover' the probability (according to market perceptions) that a particular borrower will default. The actual practical utility of such information is however, debatable.

- Financing function: The trading of contracts in derivatives exchanges makes it easier to raise finance against stocks of commodities, since lenders have an assurance of quality and quick liquidity. Again, this function is not unique to futures or derivatives as spot markets perform the same function. However, there is a small part of the financing function that is unique to derivatives markets. This is the fact that lenders are often more willing to finance hedged inventories than unhedged inventories, since the former are protected against risk of loss of value.

- Liquidity function: Futures markets operate on a fractional margin whereby the buyer and seller deposit only a fraction of the contract value (say 10 per cent) at the time of entering into it. This enables traders to buy and sell a much larger volume of contracts than in a spot market, and makes markets more liquid, so that large transactions can be put through with ease. Other derivatives also do not require the payment of the full value of the underlying and so perform the financing function.

Price stabilisation and destabilisation

While the functions noted above are not disputed, there is another function which is the subject of debate and controversy. Traditionally, economists believed that speculation on markets is stabilising in nature and therefore that futures trading, by facilitating speculation, performs a price stabilising function by reducing the amplitude of short term fluctuations. However, in more recent years, it has been shown that in certain circumstances and situations, futures trading can exercise a destabilising influence too. Other derivatives, which do not perform a price discovery function for the underlying, do not have a stabilising influence.

An alternative view: Futures markets as implicit loan markets

In the discussion above, hedging (to avoid price risks) was treated as the primary function of futures markets. This is the conventional consensus in the literature. Jeffrey Williams challenged this consensus and opined that futures markets are primarily implicit loan markets which enable commodities to be lent and borrowed, just as the money market enables money to be lent and borrowed. According to Williams, like money, commodities also have a 'transactions' and 'precautionary' demand. Users will pay to have access to a commodity. For example, a wheat mill may be willing to pay to have access to wheat stocks (beyond normal predictable requirements) to take care of any disruption in supply, so that idle time of costly machinery is prevented. The motive is similar to that for having a line of credit with a bank, for access to money in case of a sudden need for working capital. Thus, the commodity has a 'yield' to the access-holder. One way of having access is to buy the commodity, but since the need is temporary, another way is to borrow it.

According to Williams, hedging is essentially a repurchase agreement akin to the repurchase or 'repos' transactions in the financial markets. In a repurchase transaction, sale and pre-determined repurchase of a bill or bond is used as a device for borrowing/lending money. The difference between the sale and repurchase prices is the interest to the lender. In Williams' view, the commodity lender charges a commodity-specific interest rate as a reward for parting with its use value or yield, but he has to simultaneously borrow money and pay interest thereon. The interaction between the money interest rate, the commodity-specific interest rate and the physical storage cost determines the relationship between spot and futures prices.[3]

A detailed discussion of Williams' theory is beyond the scope of this book. The implicit loan market concept adds a new perspective, but, given the strong evidence that many users actually use the markets for hedging, it is somewhat difficult to accept it as the primary function of futures markets.

Derivatives trading: A 'zero sum' activity

Derivatives' trading is almost always a 'zero sum game' where gains of one party are equal to the losses of the counter-party. However, this does not by itself imply that derivatives trading has no economic utility.

The 'zero sum' characteristic is not confined to derivatives. When existing shares are bought and sold on the stock exchange (ignoring transaction costs and taxes), the buyer will gain exactly as much as the seller loses (notionally) if share prices go up, and vice versa if share prices go down. If A buys a share of Reliance at ₹ 800 per share from B and if after a month, the price of Reliance shares is ₹ 850, then A's ₹ 50 unrealised profit is the same as B's ₹ 50 notional loss. Seen in this context, the trade is indeed zero-sum. However, this does not imply that this type of trading has no social utility. Continuous trading helps in price discovery, and makes investors more willing to buy and to hold shares, which indeed makes a real difference to companies in raising capital from investors. Effectively, *the presence of a liquid secondary market makes*

it easier to raise resources on the primary market and thus lowers the cost of capital.
Likewise, the presence of an efficient futures market enhances the efficiency
of the spot market.

Another simple example of a zero sum but socially useful financial instrument
is group or mutual insurance. If 1,000 workers in a farming community get
together and decide to pay ₹ 1 per day and distribute all the premium proceeds
to whoever happens to die that year, it is a zero sum activity; but it is obviously
socially useful because it reallocates and spreads the risk. Similarly, derivatives too
can be useful in allocating risk from those less willing or able to bear it to those
more willing or able to bear it, and in other ways. Trading of futures, options,
swaps and other derivatives gives market participants better information on the
likely range of future prices, default probabilities, price volatility etc. Therefore,
while there may indeed be valid criticisms of derivatives markets, the fact that
they are 'zero sum' is not one of them.

The 'law' of one price

In economic theory, if markets are free and efficient then, ignoring transport and
transaction costs and tariffs, all goods will cost the same throughout the world.
This is called the 'law' of one price though, like many 'laws' in economics, it is
based on specific restrictive assumptions and may not actually be true in real life.

A more realistic formulation of this 'law' is that when transport costs,
transaction costs and tariffs are low, prices of goods are not likely to diverge
much between countries. For example, crude oil whether it is delivered in
Europe or in India does not have a large price difference. Therefore, crude oil
derivatives traded in India denominated in rupees often 'track' (i.e., are closely
correlated with) the crude oil market in other countries, adjusted for exchange
rate fluctuations.

The 'law' of one price is 'enforced' in the marketplace through arbitrage
(see next section). In the marketplace for real goods, traders, exporters and
importers buy and sell to reduce the difference between prices at different
locations. In the derivatives marketplace, financial traders do the same, with the
added contribution of removing price discrepancies over time too. Therefore,
ignoring currency movements, just one derivative for each underlying could be
theoretically enough for global use. In the case of crude oil, even if an importing
country does not have a separate derivatives contract, local speculators and

hedgers may be manage most of their price risk by just trading in the foreign contract. They might still need local derivatives to hedge their currency risk. However, if the commodity is costly to store and transport, then no global standardised derivatives contract can be used as a benchmark. Natural gas is a good example. Unlike crude oil (or agricultural products and metals), natural gas is difficult to transport and hence the landing price in an importing country can be many times higher than the price in the exporting country.

If understood properly, the 'law' of one price is a useful theoretical concept in helping market participants identify opportunities for profitable arbitrage and identify situations where 'mispricing' (i.e., pricing not reflecting market conditions accurately) occurs. However, when the assumptions do not hold, the 'law' may not work.

Hedging, speculation and arbitrage

It was noted earlier that the primary purpose of derivatives markets is to provide hedging facilities to those who wish to transfer risks. When one party transfers risks, there has to be another party to take on the risk. In some cases, two parties may have opposite risks and may be able to transfer the risk in a mutually beneficial manner – for example, when a rice mill and a paddy farmer are able to agree on a future price, both are benefitted by reduced uncertainty, but such exact equivalence of quantity, value and timing would only be a rare coincidence. Taking futures markets as an example, *a priori*, there is no reason why the volume of sales by hedgers should equal the volume of purchases by hedgers, since these groups have different reasons for hedging and respond differently to price changes. If a futures market was restricted to hedgers alone, it is quite conceivable that one or other group of hedgers – the longs or the shorts,would be unable to hedge because of the absence of counterparties to the transactions.

Risk transference: The speculator's role

It is here that the role of the speculator becomes apparent. Speculators take up the slack in the market and provide liquidity for both long and short hedging. The speculators have no specific interest in the commodity *per se*. They are risk seekers whose interest stems from the profit which they expect to make from assuming the price risk.

A liquid and active hedging market cannot exist without speculation. In a broader sense, one could say that futures markets are an extension of the principle of specialisation: speculators take onto themselves the burden of bearing risk. By specialisation in this field, they are able to carry the risks better than other market participants. For those (i.e., hedgers) who are mainly interested in the use of a commodity, price risk is a nuisance that they would normally prefer to do without. Futures trading enables them to delegate this process to the breed of speculators, leaving the hedgers to specialise in what they know best. Thus, hedging in cotton enables the textile mill to concentrate on its manufacturing activity instead of cotton price fluctuations, while hedging in foreign exchange enables the exporter to concentrate on export price and quality, instead of worrying about exchange rates.

Thus, derivatives market participants are of two main types:

- hedgers who are off-loading price risk so as to *avoid loss*; and
- speculators who are taking up price risk in order to *make profit*.

Arbitrage

It was seen earlier that the law of one price indicates that the price of a particular good or instrument should tend to be the same between different locations, unless there are transport costs, transaction costs or tariffs. Arbitrage is the term used to describe transactions that involve buying and selling a good or asset in two different markets in order to achieve a riskless profit through the difference in price between them. While hedgers and speculators are the two main types of participants in the markets, the arbitrageur is a third type of participant – one who trades only to realise profits from discrepancies in the market. Of course, in real life the arbitrageur is not a separate class of person: either a hedger or a speculator can indulge in arbitrage when the opportunity arises.

Example 2.1

On a particular day, the shares of X Ltd are selling at ₹150 in the NSE while at the same time the price in the BSE is ₹ 152. A stockbroker simultaneously buys the share in the NSE and sells it in the BSE. By doing so, he realises a profit of ₹2 without any risk. This is an arbitrage transaction.

Example 2.2

A commodity is trading at ₹ 5,000 per tonne in the spot market and at ₹ 5,200 per tonne in the futures market for delivery after one month. The interest rate is 12 percent per annum, i.e., 1 per cent per month. The storage cost (including insurance) of the commodity is 6 per cent per annum, i.e., 0.5 per cent per month. In this case, it is possible to earn a riskless arbitrage profit by simultaneously buying on the spot market and selling the one-month futures:

Buy 1 tonne on the spot market for:	*5,000*
Incur 1.5 per cent thereof as interest and storage cost:	*₹ 75*
Total cost:	*₹ 5,075*
Selling price on futures market:	*₹ 5,200*
Profit:	*₹ 125*

Note that the cost or value of every element in this transaction can be fixed at the time of entering into the transaction and is not dependent on future events.

Arbitrage plays a big role in ensuring that prices in futures markets do not diverge from the level dictated by supply and demand and in ensuring speedy correction of any pricing anomalies. In the Example 2.1, the arbitrageur bought shares in the cheaper (BSE) market. By adding to the demand in that market, he exerted an upward pressure on the price. At the same time, he sold in the costlier (NSE) market. By doing so, he added to the supply and imparted a downward push to the price there. In Example 2.2, the arbitrageur bought in the spot market and sold in the futures market; he added to demand in the spot market thus imparting upward pressure on the spot price and sold in the futures market exerting downward pressure on the futures price. This type of arbitrage will continue until the price difference is eliminated. Thus, arbitrage opportunities are temporary and self-correcting. Arbitrage is even more effective in derivatives markets (compared to spot markets) because of the higher liquidity and ease of trading.

Wider use of the term 'arbitrage'

Nowadays, the term arbitrage is also used somewhat loosely to describe any trade where positions of opposite direction are taken in the same or a similar underlying, even if the trade is not completely riskless. The so-called arbitrage is based on a statistical analysis of the past which shows that a particular ratio or numeric value has normally prevailed in the past. In practice, such arbitrage trading (statistical arbitrage) has often led to large unexpected losses. Therefore, the reader should always consider the term in its proper context and not assume that arbitrage is necessarily risk-free.

Example 2.3

The various outcomes of a single die throw can be marked as {1,2,3,4,5,6} [all equally probable], and the outcomes of a coin toss as {0,6} [corresponding to tails and heads respectively, and again both equally probable]. The average outcome of the die throw is 3.5, (i.e., 21 divided by 6) and that of the coin is 3. Consider a game where the player will receive a payment of one rupee multiplied by the result of the die throw and lose one rupee multiplied by the result of the coin toss. Thus, the player is 'long' on the die throw and 'short' on the coin toss. The combined outcome of the two actions would range from −5 (die =0, coin = 6) to +6 (die= 6, coin =0) with the probability of each of these outcomes being 1/12th each. However, if we repeated this many times, we would on average make half a rupee every turn of this 'game', i.e., 3.5 minus 3 multiplied by one rupee. A strategy of repeatedly combining these two actions would be a highly simplified example of statistical arbitrage. If players play this game long enough, they will ultimately come out ahead. If they play this game a 1,000 times, they are likely to earn for themselves ₹500. But they have a 1/144th chance of losing ₹10 in the first two rounds, even though the expected gain is only 50 paisa; in other words, the loss in the first two rounds could be ten times the expected gain. If the transaction had been 'geared' by taking debt (such that the amount payable was the outcome of the die throw/coin toss multiplied by ₹10, say), the consequences could be larger. If the game was being played by a small boy with ₹10 in his pocket it may mean that he would not be able to even play the game beyond the first two rounds even though in the long run he could earn a decent sum. Institutions and individuals with deep pockets (i.e., sufficient capital to withstand initial losses) can however, play this game with success.

In real life, most examples of statistical arbitrage involve probabilities that are based on past observation and not *a priori* probabilities as in throwing a coin or a die. This introduces a much greater level of risk. The collapse in 1998 of Long Term Capital Management, a hedge fund managed by Nobel laureates, happened because spreads on bonds and derivatives that were expected to narrow actually widened because of unexpected events (the Russian sovereign default). Since the fund was highly leveraged, it could not by its own admission remain 'solvent longer than the market could remain irrational' (to quote John Maynard Keynes). This is why strategies like statistical arbitrage are sometimes called 'picking small coins in front of a roller coaster'. The higher the leverage used by the statistical 'arbitrageur', the bigger and closer the roller coaster gets. Statistical arbitrage depends heavily on mean reversion, or the closing in of spreads that 'should' be either narrower or 'should' not exist in the first place. But, things do not always turn out the way they should' and the theories that indicate convergence are usually merely theories.

When combined with the risks from leverage, statistical arbitrage is often not low risk at all and the use of the term 'arbitrage' (though well-established among industry participants) is actually misleading. In this book, the term 'arbitrage', when used without any prefix or suffix, is generally used in its precise economic sense of a riskless transaction, and the terms 'arbitrage trading' or 'statistical arbitrage' are normally used to refer to the looser concept of a trade which is not completely risk-free but expected to be low risk based on past observation.

Hedging vs. insurance

Insurance is essentially confined to those types of risks, which are subject to some form of theoretical or empirical probability distribution. In any insurance contract, the assumption is that the probability of loss (that is, the probability of the risk coming true) to any one individual is less than the probability of no loss. Thus, the eventuality against which insurance is taken is always more remote than the prospect of no loss. Furthermore, the risks are often independent of each other. The occurrence of a fire in Kolkata does not increase the risk of a fire in Delhi. Because of this, risks can be pooled, through insurance, among many people.

For market price risks however, this is not the case. These are highly unpredictable (notwithstanding the vast industry of analysts who make a living from predicting them), and are not subject to any reliable probability distribution. Both the size, as well as the frequency of risks are too large for conventional insurance. Risk pooling also may not apply. If the market price moves in an unanticipated direction, all participants may be affected at the same time, so no pooling may be possible. Hence, the need arises for hedging as a form of risk transference. Insurance cannot, and will never be able to, perform this role.

The distinction between insurance and hedging can perhaps be better understood on an analytical plane by looking at the distinction between risk and uncertainty. Knight used the distinction between objective and subjective probabilities to distinguish between 'risk' and 'uncertainty' with risk being insurable and uncertainty being non-insurable.[2]

In terms of this analytical distinction, hedging can, therefore, be described as a method of *protection against uncertainty* (with 'uncertainty' used in its economic sense à la Knight). However, it provides a lower degree of protection than insurance since (as will be seen later) hedges are often only partially effective.

---

2   F. H. Knight, *Risk, Uncertainty and Profit*, Houghton Mifflin, Boston, 1921, 224–25.

Speculation vs. gambling

Critics of derivatives markets argue that the speculation which such markets engender is little different from gambling and should therefore be discouraged. However, there are several important differences between speculation and gambling, as Baer and Saxon[3] very clearly brought out. Firstly, speculation is based on existing risks, which are not created by the speculator. Gambling, on the other hand, usually involves the deliberate creation of risks for the purpose of laying the wager. The risks inherent to producers and consumers in commodity prices would not disappear if speculation were eliminated whereas a horse race has no 'risk' unless a person chooses to gamble. Thus, speculation is a transaction involving transference of risk while gambling is an exercise in the deliberate creation of risk. Secondly, there is a legal distinction. Many speculative contracts, and particularly futures contracts on a recognised exchange, are recognised by law as contracts in which the speculator is fully and legally bound. In fact, when a person enters into a futures contract, there is no way of determining whether he is a speculator or hedger purely by examining the contract itself. The distinction between a speculative futures contract and a hedge contract lies purely in the intention of the party concerned. On the other hand, a gambling contract may not be enforceable in law, as it does not involve giving and taking of valid consideration. Thirdly, speculation is arguably an integral part of the marketing process and has been shown to play a useful role therein. It thus has economic utility. Gambling serves no such purpose. However, many modern derivatives markets do bear resemblance to pure gambling vehicles and in practice, the distinction is not always clear. This is particularly so in those markets where there is little or no hedging activity and most participants are speculators. The increasingly frequent use of the term 'bet' by modern financial writers in the context of financial investments is a clue to the growing similarity between speculation and gambling especially in the case of exotic derivatives.

Is speculation desirable?

The short answer to this question is yes, though the longer answer is more complicated. Speculation is distinct from manipulation, which is a deliberate attempt to move the price artificially in a favourable direction, which is always

---

3   Baer and Saxon, *Commodity Exchanges and Futures Trading, op. cit.*, 58–63.

undesirable. Without speculation, as has already been pointed out, there can be no effective hedging since the volume of demand for long and short hedging will not be equal except by occasional coincidence. Secondly, speculative activity increases the liquidity of markets thereby enabling hedgers to transact large volumes of business on the market quickly, easily and without unduly affecting the market price. In a 'thin' market, a single large transaction would have an unduly high impact on the market price and might, in the process, defeat the aims of the hedger. Thus, speculation, by facilitating hedging and increasing liquidity, reduces the costs of marketing. The reduction in marketing costs accrues (eventually) to the consumer.[4] Thirdly, speculation in futures markets is expected, in conventional theory, to reduce inter-temporal price disequilibria by reducing seasonal fluctuations and several empirical studies have corroborated this.

However, there may be certain situations in which speculation can be destabilising (i.e., destabilise spot prices) and in those situations, speculation may indeed give rise to undesirable consequences. Recent economic studies have shown that the possibility of destabilisation is real in certain situations and circumstances.

---

4   T. A. Hieronymus, *The Economics of Futures Trading*, Commodity Research Bureau, New York, 1977, 146.

Part – II
Forwards and Futures

3

Futures and Forwards

As pointed out in chapter 1, futures trading, or more accurately forward trading, was the first form of derivatives trading. This chapter reviews the basic concepts of futures trading – its functions, the mechanism by which risk is transferred, the role of speculation and related issues. At the outset, it is necessary to understand clearly what futures trading means.

Definitions

A forward contract is an agreement between two parties to buy or sell, as the case may be, a commodity (or financial instrument or currency or any other underlying) on a pre-determined future date at a price agreed when the contract is entered into.

The key elements are that:

- the date on which the underlying asset will be bought/sold is determined in advance; and

- the price to be paid/received at that future date is determined at present.

Example 3.1

In the month of August, a rice mill agrees to buy 2.35 tonnes of rice of IR-8 variety from X, a farmer, in the following February at a price of ₹ 38,000 per tonne. This is a forward contract. Note that the farmer will receive (and the mill will pay) ₹ 38,000 x 2.35 = ₹ 89,300 in February irrespective of whether the market price in February is ₹ 40,000 per tonne or ₹ 36,000 per tonne. According to its terms, this contract may or may not be transferable by the mill or the farmer to any other person and accordingly may be called a 'transferable' or a 'non-transferable' forward contract.

A *futures contract* is a contract to buy or sell, a standard quantity of a standardised or pre-determined grade(s) of a certain commodity at a pre-determined location(s), on a pre-determined future date at a pre-agreed price. If this definition is studied carefully, the differences between a futures contract and a forward contract become apparent:

a. There is no reference to an agreement 'between two parties' – this is because futures contracts are almost always entered into through an intermediary (the exchange or its clearing house) that acts as the buyer to each seller and seller to each buyer. This is illustrated below:

Figure 3.1: Forward

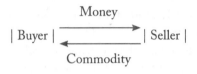

Figure 3.2: Futures

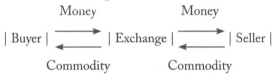

The absence of a one-to-one relationship between the buyer and seller also means that these contracts are freely transferable.

b. There is a standard quantity for contracts, which is fixed by the exchange. (For example, in the international gold futures markets, transactions are in lots of 100 oz. each.)

c. There is a pre-determined or standardised grade or, grades of the commodity, specified by the exchange, which can be delivered/taken delivery of. Where several varieties are deliverable, one variety is specified as the 'deliverable grade' or 'basis variety' or standard variety;[1] if any other variety is delivered, a premium or discount is charged/offered.

d. The giving or taking of delivery is at a location specified by the exchange.

Example 3.2

In the same case as example 3.1, if the transaction takes place through a commodities exchange, the mill will buy 2 tonnes of month of February rice at the prevailing futures price of ₹ 38,000. The farmer will simultaneously sell 2 tonnes of February rice at a price

---

1 The term 'basis variety' has been in common use in Indian commodity markets to describe the standard variety of a commodity futures contract. This should not be confused with the term 'basis' which denotes the price difference between spot and futures at any given time.

of ₹ 38,000. This is a futures contract. Note that it is not possible to transact 2.35 tonnes or specify precisely the variety of rice to be delivered as these are based on standardised lot sizes and standardised deliverable varieties. The farmer will receive from the exchange, and the merchant will pay to the exchange, ₹ 38,000 per tonne in February irrespective of whether the market price in March is higher or lower.

Essentially, therefore a futures contract is a standardised forward contract. In a futures contract, all matters except price are pre-determined, making the contract freely transferable between different participants, as they know exactly what is being traded. In a forward contract, all these have to be specified in each contract, i.e., which variety or grade, what quantity, where delivery is to be given/ taken, since there is no standardisation. Thus, every futures contract is a forward contract; not every forward contract is a futures contract. In the remainder of this chapter, the terms forward and futures will be used interchangeably.

Seasonality in commodity markets

Commodities are different from purely financial assets in some critical ways. It costs money to store and safeguard commodities when compared to financial instruments like bonds or shares which are either pieces of paper or mere book entries in a ledger. Production (supply) and consumption (demand) may be seasonal.

Consider the case of a farmer – an agricultural entrepreneur, taking risk in the true sense – who grows wheat. Wheat in India is largely a *rabi* crop, i.e., it grows primarily in the winter. Some wheat is also produced outside the *rabi* season. Thus, the crop is grown predominantly in one season but consumed throughout the year. During the time when the crop is not being harvested, it needs to be stored. Storage has direct costs (rents, pest spraying etc.) and indirect costs (deterioration, loss due to pests) amongst others. In addition, when someone buys wheat, funds are locked up in the purchase of wheat and the funds have an opportunity cost in the form of the interest that could have been earned on them. In such a case, where the crop is highly seasonal, the price for the future prices of wheat will be a zigzag pattern whereby costs keep on rising till the winter harvest season comes and then prices fall. Next year, the same pattern will repeat. The underlying secular price trend could be up, down or flat or ambiguous but that does not detract from the above point.

Here is a forward pricing graph drawn from the United States where wheat is grown twice a year – once in winter, once in spring followed by a six month or so gap for next year. It displays the expected zigzag pattern.

Figure 3.3: Hard red winter wheat futures' seasonality

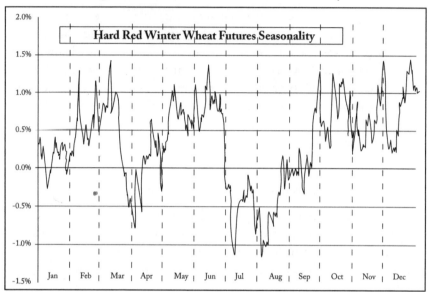

Source: Equityclock.com. Y-axis shows change in price.

Example 3.3

Wheat is selling for . 25 per kilo (that is,. 2,500 per Indian quintal, which is equivalent to 100 kgs). Assume that the cost of storing for one month is 50 paise per kg. The interest rate is 1 per cent per month. What is the cost of storage of 10 quintals of wheat for four months? (Ignore wastage losses and convenience benefits).

Solution:

Cost of 10 Indian quintals = 1000 kg =	*₹ 25,000 initial cost.*
Interest cost per month = 1 per cent x ₹ 2500/ quintal x 10 quintals = ₹ 250	
Storage cost per month = ₹ 0.5/kg x 1000 kg =	*₹ 500*
Total additional cost = ₹ 750 per month x 4 months =	*₹ 3,000.*

If wheat could be grown every four months (three times a year) and otherwise the price remains absolutely stable, the future cost of wheat would be a linear zigzag from ₹ 15,000 to ₹ 18,000 with the frequency being three times per year.

The extent of this zigzag pattern would depend on the extent of the storage cost *vis-à-vis* the cost of the commodity as well as on the seasonality of production. Seasonality implies that production arrives in periodic bursts after harvests. In the case of wheat, the storage costs are significant. In the hypothetical case in Example 3.3, the storage costs were larger than the interest cost. This is typical of grains and other agricultural commodities which are bulky and subject to deterioration through pests etc.

Gold's storage cost is a much lower fraction of its price than in the case of wheat.[2] It is also mined continuously and there is a large stock of gold relative to the annual 'flow' from mining (since gold is not 'consumed' or eaten away but retained in ornament or bullion form).

These characteristics (continuous production like gold vs. discontinuous production like wheat, low relative cost of storage like gold vs. high relative cost of storage like wheat, large stock vs. small flow in the case of gold, large annual flow vs. relatively small stock in the case of wheat) help to explain the different pricing patterns of different kinds of commodity and financial markets. This will be explored further in chapter 4.

Hedging: The mechanism of risk transference

In the previous chapter, it was seen that hedging is the primary function of derivatives markets. In the case of futures markets, how exactly is risk transferred through hedging?

In general, a person wishing to avoid upward price risk would BUY futures contracts, thereby defining for himself the price at which he will eventually purchase. A person wishing to avoid downward price risk would SELL futures contracts. This is best understood by examples.

Example 3.4

In the month of May, a textile mill anticipates a requirement of 5,000 bales of cotton in the month of October. The prevailing price of cotton is ₹23,000 per bale. Based on this price, the company has entered into other financial arrangements, including for the eventual marketing of its output. It is important to the mill that, at the time the cotton is actually purchased, the price is not substantially higher than this. It therefore buys 5,000 bales of cotton on the cotton

---

2   Nevertheless, there are economies of scale when it comes to security and insurance of collective gold deposits which may explain partially the popularity of Gold ETFs.

futures market, where it is currently quoted at ₹23,900. Note that the futures price is not identical to the spot price. The difference between them (₹ 900) is called the 'spread' or 'basis'.

In the month of October, it turns out that cotton prices have risen sharply with the current spot price being ₹ 30,000. The corresponding futures price for October cotton is found to be ₹ 29,850. (Note that the spread is now a negative amount of ₹ 150.)

At this point, the mill has two options:

(a) It can sell its futures contract on the market at the ruling rate, and buy its requirement separately from the spot market.

In this case, the financial implications will be as follows:

October cotton bought at:	₹ 23,900
October cotton sold at:	₹ 29,850
Gain on the transaction at:	₹ 5,950
Current spot price of cotton:	₹ 30,000
LESS profit on futures per candy:	₹ 5,950
Nett cost per candy:	₹ 24,050

Thus, the futures transactions have ensured the minimisation of upward price risk to ₹ 1,050 per candy even though the price went up by ₹ 7,000. The net price does not work out exactly to ₹ 23,000 because of changes in 'spread'. The spread has changed from +900 to –150, which is ₹ 1,050.

(b) The mill could take delivery of cotton directly from the futures market. In this case, the price paid by it would be. ₹ 23,900, as per its original futures contract. However, delivery in a futures market may consist of any one out of several specified varieties of cotton. This may not suit the mill as it may not be the exact variety which the mill needs. As such, this practice is not common, and most hedgers do not take delivery but instead 'close out' the contract as outlined in (a) above.

In either case, the price paid by the mill is close to the level it wished to pay when entering into the hedge.

Example 3.5

A soya bean farmer anticipates a bumper crop amounting to 200 quintals, which he expects to harvest in the month of October. Currently (in the month of May) soya bean is selling at ₹ 3,750 a quintal. This price is acceptable to the farmer and will give him a sufficient return. However, he is apprehensive of a fall in price by the time the crop is ready. He, therefore, sells 200 quintals on the soya bean futures market at the current rate of ₹ 3,700. Note that the spread or basis is ₹ 50.

In the month of October, it turns out that soya bean prices have in fact risen, instead of the expected fall. The current spot price is ₹ 4,000 a quintal. The ruling rate on the futures market is ₹ 3,975. Note that the spread is now minus ₹ 25 .

As with the case of the textile mill, the farmer also has two options:

a. He can buy back 200 quintals of October soya bean on the futures market at the present futures price of ₹ 3,975. He can then deliver his actual crop of soya bean in the spot market at the ruling rate of ₹ 4,000. In this case, the financial consequences are as follows:

October soyabean sold at:	*₹ 3,700*
October soyabean bought at:	*₹ 3,975*
Loss on transaction per quintal:	*₹ 275*
Price actually obtained on spot market:	*₹ 4,000*
LESS loss on futures market per quintal:	*₹ 275*
Net price obtained is:	*₹ 3,725*

This is very close to the spot price prevailing at the time of the transaction but not exactly equal because of changes in spread. He has realised a price of ₹ 3,725 against the target of ₹ 3,750. The difference reflects the change in spread from −50 to −25.

b. Alternatively, he can deliver in the futures market at ₹ 3,700 a quintal.

It may be seen that, in either alternative, as a result of hedging the actual net price obtained by the farmer is almost the same as that which he had budgeted for. No doubt, in this particular example the farmer would have been better off by not hedging. But the price of avoiding unfavourable price risk is the forgoing of favourable price risk. After all, one cannot eat the cake and have it too!

Thus, hedging through futures involves:

● purchase of futures by those hedging against upward price risk; and

● sales of futures by those hedging against downward risk.

The multi-purpose concept of hedging

Having identified hedging as the main function of a futures market, it is worth looking at the different types of hedging. Hedging, in its broadest sense, is the act of protecting oneself against loss. In the more specific context of futures trading, hedging was (and to a large extent still is) regarded as the use of futures transactions to avoid or reduce price risks in the spot market. Originally, hedging was thought to be of only one kind (known as routine or naive hedging), whereby the trader always hedged all his transactions purely with the intention of cutting out all price risks, in the manner of examples above. However, Holbrook Working[3] (a pioneer in the field of economic research

---

3   H. Working, 'Hedging Reconsidered', *Journal of Farm Economics*, Vol. XXXV, November, 1953.

on futures trading) challenged this view and propounded the multi-purpose concept of hedging which has now received universal acceptance. He showed that hedging was used for many other purposes:

a.   Earning a carrying charge for a stockist (*carrying charge hedging*): According to Working, stockists watch the price spread between the spot and futures prices; and when the spread is such as to cover their carrying costs, they buy ready stocks. Thus, whereas traditional theory had it that hedges are used to protect against loss on stocks held, Working felt the decision is 'not primarily whether to hedge or not, but whether to store or not'.[4]

b.   *Operational hedging*, meaning the use of futures markets as a substitute for cash or forward transactions because futures markets are more 'liquid' and have a lower difference between 'bid' and 'asked' prices. This is because the futures market is often so liquid that large transactions can speedily be effected with very small impact on ruling prices. A transaction of similar size on the spot market cannot be put through without causing a significant ripple. Later, the required purchases or sales are gradually effected on the spot market, with hedge positions being correspondingly reduced over time. Thus, in such cases, hedges are used because they are operationally convenient, not because they are risk-reducing.

c.   *Selective or discretionary hedging* whereby traders do not always (i.e., routinely) hedge themselves but only do so on selective occasions when they anticipate an adverse price movement. Thus, hedgers do not seek to avoid price risks, but rather adverse price risks, meaning in effect that they may hedge only when adverse price risk is expected. Even at such times owing to their uncertainties about expectations, they may hedge only partially.

d.   *Anticipatory hedging* which is resorted to in anticipation of subsequent sales or purchases; thus a farmer might hedge by selling futures in anticipation of his crop, while a processor might hedge by buying futures in anticipation of subsequent raw material needs.

Based on his multi-purpose hedging concept, Working defined hedging as 'the use of futures contracts as a temporary substitute for a merchandising contract'.

---

4   H. Working, 'New Concepts Concerning Futures Markets and Prices', *American Economic Review*, Vol. LII, No. 3, June 1962, 438.

While Working was undeniably correct in dispelling the previous notion of hedging as a mechanical process, one is inclined to agree with R. Pavaskar[5] that Working played down the risk aversion aspect rather too strongly. Even the other forms of hedging, essentially flow from the basic fact that, hedging is of a risk-avoiding nature. But for the fact that hedging is risk reducing, none of the other forms of hedging can take place. Carrying cost hedging is undertaken because stockists are confident of earning carrying costs, in other words they avoid the risk of not earning their costs. While it may be true that positive price spreads may encourage stockists to increase their stocks, those who are in the merchandising business cannot really avoid stocking altogether even if the basis is unfavourable. To this extent, merchandisers must carry out traditional hedging. Operational hedging is undertaken for convenience, but it is only possible because the futures market moves in tandem with the spot market, thereby obviating the price risk involved in not immediately buying up/selling on the spot market. Similarly, anticipatory hedges essentially aim at avoiding business uncertainties (if not price risks). As M. G. Pavaskar puts it, the risk-reduction aspect of hedging is therefore the major plank which supports the grand edifice of Working's multi-purpose concept of hedging.[6]

The significance of this conclusion is that whatever the motivation behind hedging, the risk-reducing concept can be used to measure the actual hedging efficiency of markets. However, it redounds to the credit of Working that he integrated the economist's traditional and naive risk avoidance concept with the complexities of real life commercial activity. Furthermore, the multi-purpose concept of hedging is also helpful in a more realistic interpretation of empirical results.

Hedging by governments

Hedging is not necessarily confined to the private sector. Derivatives can be used by governments to stabilise the prices of essential food imports or a country's export earnings or to protect farmers. Some countries are already making extensive use of futures and options for this purpose. For instance, Mexico has used options as part of a scheme to protect cotton growers: the

---

5   R. Pavaskar, *Efficiency of Futures Trading*, Popular Prakashan, Bombay, 1977, 22.

6   M. G. Pavaskar, *Economics of Hedging*, Popular Prakashan, Bombay, 1976.

Mexican government offers a guaranteed minimum price to cotton growers; a government agency then purchases options in the international markets, thereby offloading the risk.[7] Ghana has used futures to hedge against falling cocoa prices (Ghana is a major cocoa exporter). Futures and options can be (and are) used by governments to hedge against short-term rises in import prices (e.g., the price of crude oil). In 2011, Mexico used corn futures to protect domestic consumers from rising corn prices. The use of derivatives by governments in developing countries is likely to increase and is being promoted by the World Bank as a measure of economic stabilisation.

Gearing or leverage[8]

The precise manner of speculation on futures markets is very similar to speculation through spot markets (like the cash segment of the stock market). However, there is one important difference: this is what is known as the gearing factor. A person who buys or sells futures contracts does not make full payment of the value thereof. Instead, he pays what is known as a 'deposit' or 'margin money', which is usually around 10 per cent of the contract value. This means that a person can 'gear up' his capital ten times, so that his profit or loss, as a proportion of his capital, is ten times magnified. This is illustrated by the example below.

Example 3.6

A speculator on the gold futures market anticipates a price increase from the current futures price of $1,450. The market lot being 100 oz., he buys 100 oz. of gold at $1,450 for a value of $145,000. But the speculator is only required to pay out a margin or deposit of $14,500. Now assume that a 10 per cent increase occurs in the price of gold, to $1595. The value of 100 oz. at $1,595 is $159,500. Subtracting original contract value, the profit on the transaction is

$159,500 - $145,000 = $14,500.

As far as the speculator is concerned, he has achieved a profit of $14,500 on a capital of $14,500. In short, he has achieved a 100 per cent profit through a 10 per cent price rise.

Thus, the gearing factor multiplies the effect of price fluctuations. This is one of the reasons for the attractiveness of the futures markets to speculators.

---

7   P. Varangis, T. Akiyama and D. Mitchell, *Managing Commodity Booms and Busts*, World Bank, 1995.

8   Gearing is the British English term; in American parlance gearing is known as 'leverage'.

While it is possible to achieve similar gearing in the stock market through the mechanism of margin trading (i.e., borrowing against shares), the act of borrowing involves a separate loan with attendant transaction costs; the futures market allows the gearing automatically without having to seek a loan or have an evaluation of creditworthiness. Also, even when margin trading is possible, the extent of gearing often does not match that of futures.

Of course, gearing also enhances losses and it is for this reason that regulation of speculative trading volume is necessary. Otherwise, it is conceivable that speculators may be unable to meet their obligations during a period of losses.

Short selling in futures markets

In the spot market, a person can only sell something which he has. Thus, if one wants to sell wheat today, one must first own wheat or at least borrow some wheat from someone else before one can sell it. However, in the futures market, it is possible to sell something without having it in the first place. Since delivery is only required after an interval of time, it is quite feasible for one to sell wheat on the futures market without possessing any wheat at the time of the sale. This is known as short selling. Because of this, it is possible to speculate on a fall in price with as much ease as it is to speculate on a rise in price. This greatly enhances the attraction of futures markets for speculation and leads to greater liquidity.

Trading mechanism of futures

Futures used to be traded in pits, but they are now mostly traded on electronic exchanges. Thus, there has been a change from floor-based trading based on shouting and gesticulations to a calmer yet faster environment of human beings on machines, and often algorithms doing high-frequency trading all by themselves.

A client who has opened a futures position incurs profits or losses on a daily, indeed during trading hours, second-by-second, basis but he does not need to hold his long or short contract until maturity. He can 'square it up', or offset it, by selling or buying another contract. Hence, if a speculator has bought a June Nifty futures contract in March, she can at any time close out the transaction by simply selling one June Nifty futures contract. She will pay or receive the net price difference between the two transactions.

There are two kinds of settlements that can be done for many financial derivatives – 'delivery' and 'cash'. Delivery settlement means actually giving or taking the underlying, while cash settlement means settling in cash (i.e., squaring up) based on the difference of prices between the initial price (during the initiation of the contract) and the maturity date's price of the underlying.

An important point worth noting is that 'margin' in the stock (cash) market is different from 'margin' in the futures market. In the former, it represents a loan to an investor to buy shares. In the latter, it represents a safety margin and not a loan. It is the amount kept aside with the exchange just in case the market moves faster than additional margin collection and the relevant party defaults.

Margin requirements in futures markets are of multiple types. There is an initial margin requirement and there is a maintenance margin requirement, with the maintenance margin being lower than or equal to the initial requirement.

Box 3.1: The National Spot Exchange Limited case

In India, as elsewhere, when somebody buys an exchange-traded futures contract, the trader or investor has to post a margin. For options, there are also premium margins, and for the clearing members – often the big brokerages – there is an additional 'assignment margin'. These margin requirements are there to ensure the safety of the two parties transacting through the exchange. Generally, the system works well. But if the there are problems with the *exchange itself*, the system may fail and this can have widespread adverse consequences. The National Spot Exchange Limited (NSEL) in India (not to be confused with the National Stock Exchange, NSE) is a commodities exchange that was forced by regulators to suspend trading as it allegedly committed irregularities. Amongst other things, regulators alleged that it did not have the physical underlying commodities in its warehouses, on which it was liable to ensure delivery to people who bought forward contracts on them. It defaulted on payment liabilities amounting to over ₹ 5,000 crores. While the matter is still the subject of court cases and some of the facts are in dispute, regulators alleged that NSEL created contracts which were effectively loans against commodities but did so without the borrowers depositing the underlying commodities as they were supposed to. NSEL has denied the allegations. The wider point is that counter-party risk in futures and exchange-traded options is absent only if the exchange functions properly.

Measurement of hedging volume *vis-a-vis* speculative volume

It is of much interest to regulators and economic analysts to be able to distinguish between those transactions carried out for hedging and those carried out for speculation. The regulatory authorities usually have some kind of statistical data on hedging volume in order to give (or take away) exemptions from margin requirements. However, it is quite conceivable in practice that a transaction which is classified for regulatory purposes as a hedge may be entered into with a speculative motive. From an analytical point of view therefore, such data is unreliable though, where available, it is better than nothing.

M. G. Pavaskar[9] propounded the view that the volume of actual deliveries against a futures contract can be taken as a rough indication of short hedging volume. However, as Baer and Saxon[10] pointed out, there is little need for a short hedger to give delivery and most hedging transactions are in fact concluded by means of the 'closing out' process. It is possible for a speculator to give or take delivery as part of his speculative transaction. For an economic analyst, therefore, there is considerable difficulty in making reliable quantitative distinctions between hedging volume and speculative volume. This is perhaps understandable because the distinction between hedging and speculation lies purely in the intention behind the transaction and intentions are not public knowledge. In many futures markets, especially nowadays, the speculative volume is known to exceed the hedging volume greatly.

Long vs. short and long hedging vs. short hedging

The use of the terms 'short' and 'long' in derivatives markets is a source of much confusion to the uninitiated. The difference between short and long does not, as might appear at first sight, have anything to do with the length or duration of a transaction as it does not correspond to 'short term vs. long term'. In market jargon, 'going short' means selling and 'going long' means buying. Correspondingly, in a general sense, 'being short' means having a net sold position, or a commitment to deliver, while 'being long' means having a net bought position or an actual holding of the commodity or financial instrument or other underlying asset. The terms 'long' and 'short' apply to both spot and futures markets, and have a wide connotation.

---

9   M. G. Pavaskar, *Economics of Hedging, op.cit.*

10 Baer and Saxon, *Commodity Exchanges and Futures Trading, op.cit.*, 54.

A person who holds stocks of a commodity is obviously regarded as 'being long' in the spot market; but it is not necessary to actually hold stocks. A farmer who expects to harvest a crop is also regarded as 'being long' in the commodity (on the spot market). A person who has made a forward sale is (obviously) regarded as 'being short' (on the spot market); but a person who needs a commodity (or financial instrument) at some future date and does not have it, is also regarded as 'being short' (on the spot market). Therefore, in an analytical sense, 'being long' means having (or expecting to have) stocks of the asset in question, while 'being short' means having (or expecting to have) negative stocks (meaning a need for stocks). The terms are sometimes used as nouns for traders – i.e., a 'long' is a person holding a long position and a 'short' is a person holding a short position.

A person who is long on the spot market benefits from price increases and loses from price decreases. To protect himself from a fall in price, such a person would hedge by selling in the futures market, i.e., by going short in futures. Thus, such a person is known as a *short hedger since he hedges by going short in futures.*

A person who is short on the spot market benefits from a decrease in price, and loses from an increase in price. To protect himself against rise in price, such a person would hedge by *buying* in the futures market, i.e., by going long in futures. Thus, such a person is known as a *long hedger since he hedges by going long in futures.* The following table summarises the distinction:

Table 3.1: Short hedger vs. long hedger

	Short hedger	**Long hedger**
Position in spot market	Long	Short
Protection needed against	Price fall	Price rise
Position in futures market	Short	Long

4

Futures Trading: Pricing and Hedging

This chapter covers more advanced aspects of the economics of futures trading. It has two sections. The first deals with the relationship between spot and futures prices while the second discusses the relationship between the 'basis' or price spread and hedging effectiveness. The discussion will be based primarily on futures in commodities, but the discussion is also applicable to futures in financial instruments etc., with minor modifications which will be discussed in subsequent chapters.

The relationship between spot and futures prices

Intuitively, it is not difficult to see that spot and futures prices must be inter-related. After all they are prices of the same asset, albeit at different points in time, which means that the basic factors affecting supply and demand are the same. Also, the option of delivery (meaning that a futures contract can be closed by means of actually giving or taking delivery of the physical commodity or financial instrument) means that on the maturity date spot and futures prices must be in close proximity. This implies that the difference between the two prices must narrow over time and eventually be whittled down to nil or thereabouts. This leaves the question of how the difference is determined. There are several theories which attempt to explain the relationship between spot and futures prices. The essence of these is set out below. In the following discussion, readers should note that:

- when the futures price is higher than the spot price, the futures price is said to be at a 'contango'; and

- when the futures price is lower than the spot price it is said to be at a 'backwardation'.

The expectations approach

This school of thought, owing its origins to such luminaries as J. M. Keynes, J. R. Hicks and N. Kaldor, sees the futures price as the market expectation of the price at the future date. Thus, the October gold futures price in June is what the market in June expects or forecasts will be the gold price in October. Any major deviation of the futures price from the expected price is likely to be corrected by speculative activity.

Example 4.1

On 3 June, the S&P 500 share index futures for October maturity is trading at 1,450 (say). It is generally expected that the level of the index in October will be 1,550. Thus, the futures price is below the expected price. Speculators will now see a profit opportunity. They can buy up futures contracts in the expectation of a profit. The speculative purchases will increase the demand in the futures market and push the price upwards. This tendency will continue until the futures price is close to the expected price. (Because of brokerage and other transaction costs, exact equality may not necessarily arise.)

Example 4.2

On 20 April, the price of silver for July delivery in the futures market is $40/oz. The general expectation is that the price of silver in July will only be $30/oz. Speculators will now see a profit opportunity in short-selling silver futures, since they can sell at 40 dollars and hope to square up the contracts in July by buying back at 30 dollars. The speculative sales will increase the supply of silver in the futures market and push the price downwards. This tendency will continue until the futures price is close to the expected price.

It is obvious that the expectations approach has substance. However, it must be remembered that the speculative transactions described in the examples above are risky transactions, not arbitrage. The transactions are based on expectations which may or may not turn out to be correct. Since speculators, like other humans, are generally risk averse, it is quite possible that deviations from the expected price (over and above deviations due to transactions costs) may persist. It is only when the gap between futures and expectations is large, that speculative interest can be expected in large volume.

The theory of normal backwardation

It has been observed in many futures markets, that the volume of short hedging exceeds the volume of long hedging (see Table 3.1 for details of what is short vs. long hedging). This net short hedging pressure has to be taken up by long speculators. Keynes postulated that, in order to induce long speculators to take up the net short hedging volume, the hedgers had to pay a risk premium to the speculators.[1] Thus, according to Keynes, the futures price would generally be less than the expected price, by the amount of risk premium.

i.e., $F = E - r$

where, F = futures price for a future date

E = expected price at that date

r = risk premium

Keynes thus felt that futures price would be related to expected price but would normally be at a backwardation (i.e., discount) to expected prices.[2] A lot of empirical research has been conducted over the years to test whether futures prices do indeed exhibit a normal backwardation. Several studies have confirmed its existence while some others did not find any evidence of it. However, in thin markets where speculative volume is low, the normal backwardation does exist and plays a role in attracting sufficient speculation to balance the excess hedging pressure.[3]

Reasons for excess short hedging volume

The theory of normal backwardation is based on the existence of an excess of short hedging. Is there any underlying reason why short hedging tends to predominate in many different futures markets? The first attempt to provide a theoretical rationale for this phenomenon was by Hicks who attributed it to technological reasons.[4] He pointed out that entrepreneurs generally had a freer hand in acquiring new inputs (which are necessary for production processes), than in the disposal of outputs. Once the process of production is commenced it cannot be reversed and the entrepreneur has to necessarily arrange to sell the output, whereas he can always refrain from acquiring an input in the event of unfavourable price changes. Therefore, Hicks felt there would be a greater

---

1   J. M. Keynes, *A Treatise on Money*, Vol. II, Macmillan, London, 1930.

2   Normally, the term backwardation is used to refer to a situation where the spot price exceeds the futures price; in this case it is used to denote that the expected price exceeds the futures price. This may be a little confusing but since this was the terminology used by Keynes himself, it has been retained here.

3   R. W. Gray, 'The Characteristic Bias in Some Thin Futures Markets', in A E Peck (ed.), *Selected Writings on Futures Markets*, Vol II, Chicago Board of Trade, Chicago, 1977.

4   J. R. Hicks, *Value and Capital*, 2nd ed., Oxford University Press, 1964, 137.

need and urgency to hedge planned sales than to hedge planned purchases, thereby leading to an excess of short hedging. However, this argument was criticised by Houthakker.[5] The most important criticism is the fact that futures market participants include a large proportion of merchants. For merchants, the commodity does not go through any production process and the technological considerations are clearly irrelevant. The Hicks argument is thus an incomplete explanation at best.

The second important reason for the oft-observed excess of short hedging lies in the seasonality of agricultural production on the one hand and the non-seasonality of consumption on the other.[6] Because of this, the processors and exporters (long hedgers) only need to hedge a small quantity at a time (say, requirements for the next two months), whereas the merchants and stockists (short hedgers) need to hedge the whole stock that they are carrying. In the immediate post-harvest period, this may cover a year's production.

Excess of long hedging

The observation of an excess of short hedging volume, and its explanation, evolved primarily from studies of futures markets in agricultural commodities. The combination of seasonality and technological factors explains the phenomenon in these markets. In recent years, a number of futures markets in non-agricultural commodities have become active. It has also been observed that some of these markets do not have an excess of short hedging.[7] In markets where there is generally an excess of long hedging (which is conceivable though, in practice, not common) the futures price would exhibit a 'normal contango' instead of a normal backwardation, so that the long hedgers would pay a risk premium to short speculators. In such cases, the relationship between expected prices and futures prices would be as follows:

$F = E + r$

5   H. S. Houthakker, 'Normal Backwardation', in *Value, Capital and Growth—Papers in Honour of Sir John Hicks*, edited by J. N. Wolfe, Edinburgh University Press, Edinburgh, 1968.

6   B. A. Goss and B. S. Yamey, *The Economics of Readings Selected, Edited and Introduced* (2nd ed.), Macmillan, London, 1978, 27.

7   J. L. Stein, *The Economics of Futures Markets*, Basil Blackwell, Oxford, 1986, 12–14. He also shows that the predominance of short hedging has declined even in agricultural markets, 55.

The carrying cost approach

Holbrook Working, whose contribution to the economics of futures trading is as significant as Keynes' contribution to macro-economics, postulated that futures prices essentially reflect the carrying cost of commodities, rather than an expected price at a future date. According to Working, expectations affecting futures price would usually also affect spot price equally and thus not affect the difference between them. Instead, according to him, the inter-relationship between spot and futures prices reflect the carrying cost, i.e., the amount to be paid to store a commodity from the present time to the futures maturity date.[8]

Carrying costs are of several types. Firstly, there are costs of warehousing, insurance, etc. Secondly, there are costs due to deterioration of a commodity over time; these may be high in the case of crops like potatoes, low in the case of food grains and non-precious metals, and nil for precious metals. Thirdly, there is interest on capital locked up in the stocks. The first two are applicable only to commodities, not to financial instruments, but the interest cost applies to all assets. For a given time period, these costs are normally constant per unit of the asset held.

Apart from the carrying cost of holding stocks, however, there could be a 'convenience yield' from holding stocks. Take the case of a wheat miller-cum-bread manufacturer. However good his purchasing arrangements, there can be disruptions because of (say) bad weather holding up lorries, or strikes, or innumerable other reasons. If he runs out of stock of wheat, his costly machinery and labour have to remain idle, causing a loss, apart from the adverse effects on customer goodwill. These losses can be avoided by retaining a minimum level of stocks. Alternatively, assume that he receives a special urgent order for bread. If his stocks do not cover this extra requirement, he will have to turn down the order and forgo the profits involved. Thus, *up to a certain level, stock holding has a yield, this yield being the savings in lost profits that could occur in the event of a stock-out, plus the profits of unanticipated demand.*[9] Beyond this minimum level (the level required to avoid stock-outs), there is no convenience yield. The yield can be regarded as a negative carrying cost. (In the case of financial instruments,

---

8   H. Working, 'The Theory of the Price of Storage', *American Economic Review*, Vol. 31, December 1949.

9   M. J. Brennan, 'The Supply of Storage', in B.A. Goss and B.S. Yamey, *op. cit.*

there may be a real yield – going beyond mere convenience – by holding the financial instrument through interest or dividends.)

The net marginal carrying cost for any given quantity would thus be:

$C_t = c_t - y_t$

where C = net carrying cost for that quantity

c = gross carrying cost for that quantity

y = convenience yield of that quantity

t = time period of storage

When the stock level in a particular commodity is low, the marginal convenience yield is higher because the chance of a stock-out is greater. As stocks rise, the chance of a stock-out recedes and the convenience yield diminishes gradually to zero. The marginal gross carrying cost remains constant over a large range of stock levels, but may increase at very high stock levels; this is because, for instance, godown space may be exhausted and godown keepers may demand a higher charge.[10] The net carrying cost can thus be portrayed as in Figure 4.1.

Figure 4.1: Carrying costs of a commodity at different storage levels

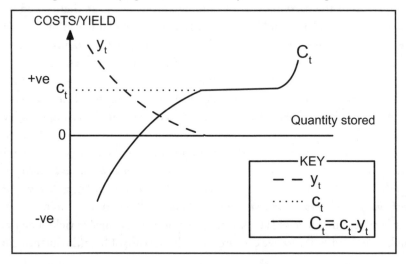

---

10 Brennan (see Reference) also postulates that at higher stock levels, the perceived risk of loss due to any unexpected price fall in the commodity is greater, and this further adds to carrying costs.

This curve is usually called the supply of storage curve (as per Working's original terminology). According to Working, merchandisers look at the spread between spot and futures and decide their quantity of storage accordingly. This can be viewed in another way – the spread is determined by the stocks available. When stocks are low, spreads are negative. When stocks are high, the spread is equal to the full carrying cost.[11]

If the prevailing price spread is below the carrying cost (including yield), it does not pay to store; instead it is optimal to sell the stock immediately. Such sales will tend to depress the spot price, thereby widening the spread until it matches the carrying cost. If the prevailing price spread is above the net carrying cost, merchandisers will buy spot stocks, sell futures and thus earn a profit. This will tend to increase spot prices and reduce futures prices, thereby narrowing the spread. Thus, according to the carrying cost approach, the futures price will approximate to the ready (spot) price plus the carrying cost:

i.e.,   *F is approximately equal to S + C*

where F = Futures price

S = Spot (i.e., ready) price

C = Carrying cost to the date of maturity of the contract.

The next section explores this *approximate* relationship so as to go to a more precise mathematical statement of the relationship.

Asymmetry in positive and negative spreads

At first sight, it would appear that the futures price cannot go above or below the carrying cost because of the mechanism referred to above. A closer examination shows that there is in fact an asymmetry.

Example 4.3

In May, the price of August pepper is ₹ 18,000 per quintal (say), while the spot price is ₹17,200. The carrying cost per quintal for three months is ₹ 200. Any market participant, whether a pepper merchant or a speculator now has the incentive to immediately:

—buy spot and store it

—sell futures and deliver it in August

---

11 For a comprehensive explanation of how spreads are determined by the interaction of the supply of storage and the demand for storage, see Brennan, ibid.

By doing so, the profit is:

₹ (18,000 — 17,200 — 200) = ₹ 600.

Example 4.3 shows an arbitrage opportunity; the profit is a guaranteed riskless profit. Thus, traders can be expected to act immediately and on a large scale. The process of buying spot and selling futures will tend to raise spot prices and reduce futures prices until the spread equals the carrying cost.

Example 4.4

In May, the price of August pepper is ₹16,600. All other facts are as in example 4.3. Here, profits can be made by:

— selling spot and delivering it

— buying futures

The resulting profit would be ₹17,200 – 16,600 = ₹600

However, to carry out the strategy in Example 4.4, it is necessary to deliver physical stocks now. Only those already holding physical stocks or those who can borrow stocks can employ the strategy. The general speculator is excluded. Thus, *the extent to which such trades can be put through is limited by the extent of available stocks.* Besides, much of the existing stock may be committed to specific production or merchandising activities and may not be available for use in this type of transaction. Therefore, it is likely that the extent of arbitrage will not be adequate to increase the spread to the level of carrying costs.

Looking at the two examples together, an asymmetry is apparent. Arbitrage potential is unlimited in situations where spreads exceed carrying costs; arbitrage will thus go on until the spread is swiftly reduced to the level of carrying costs. On the other hand, in situations where spreads fall short of carrying costs, the potential for arbitrage is limited (especially in the case of commodities), and spreads may remain below the level of carrying costs indefinitely. *Therefore, while the spread cannot exceed the carrying cost, it can fall short of it.*[12] This asymmetry in turn leads to a difference in the expected returns to long and short hedging.

When this is taken into account, the approximate mathematical relationship mentioned earlier viz. '*F* is approximately equal to *S+C*' can be defined more precisely as follows:

12 For the earliest clear identification and explanation of this asymmetry, see Gerda Blau (Miss), 'Some Aspects of the Theory of Futures Trading', *Review of Economic Studies*, Vol. 12, 1944–45, 11.

In the absence of a convenience yield:

$F \leq S+C$,

i.e., the futures price will not exceed the spot price plus the carrying cost, where carrying cost is calculated net of any convenience yield.

If the convenience yield is taken into account separately, then the price relationship can be stated as:

$F \leq S+C-Y$

Where, F = Futures price

S = Spot price

C = Carrying cost till maturity of the contract

Y = convenience Yield until maturity of the contract.

An integrated approach

The various theories presented above may well have left the reader confused. On the one hand, it appears that futures prices are based on expectations or forecasts, but on the other hand, they seem to depend purely on stock levels and carrying costs. A number of empirical studies have attempted to verify the correctness of these theories and have resulted in greater clarity on their applicability. This section attempts to integrate the various strands of theory into one coherent whole.

One of the key criteria which determines the futures price behaviour is the continuous or discontinuous nature of stock-holding in a particular asset.[13] A continuous storage good is one in which stocks are held throughout the year, even though production may be discontinuous (i.e., seasonal). Food grains are a good example; they are easily storable for long periods and stocks are held year-round. Several agricultural crops, like potatoes and other vegetables, are examples of discontinuous storage goods which are not stored year-round. There is often a gap between exhaustion of one crop and harvest of the next. Another type of good is one with continuous (i.e., non-seasonal) production – for example, metals and crude oil. The continuous production goods are generally also continuous storage goods but there are some exceptions: in the USA, there are

---

13 W. G. Tomek and R. W. Gray, 'Temporal Relationships among Prices in Commodity Futures Markets: Their Allocative and Stabilising Roles', in A. E. Peck (ed.), *op. cit.*

futures markets for pork bellies and eggs which are clearly perishable and thus not storable, but which can be produced continuously. (No doubt modern cold storage techniques have made these capable of storage for a considerable period in developed countries where power supply is reliable.) These characteristics of various assets are summarised below in Table 4.1.

Table 4.1: Production and storage characteristics of various assets

Production	Storage	
	Continuous	**Discontinuous (difficult to store)**
Continuous (non-seasonal)	Financial instruments, oil, metals, jute goods, industrial goods	Eggs, meat, dairy products, thermal electric power
Discontinuous (seasonal)	Food grains, jute, cotton, tea, non-perishable agricultural commodities	Potatoes, several fruits, vegetables and perishable agricultural commodities, hydro-electric, wind and solar power

Armed with this classification, one can summarise as follows:

a. Futures prices in goods which are continuous storage goods, broadly follow the carrying charge approach.

b. Financial instruments are not perishable and can be stored indefinitely without damage. They can be 'produced' (i.e., issued) at any time. They generally follow the carrying charge approach (with the change that there is a real yield rather than a convenience yield). Usually, expectations play little or no role and the futures pricing relationship becomes an equation rather than an inequality, i.e., $F=S+C-Y$ with Y denoting the actual yield in the form of interest or dividends. C becomes the interest cost forgone in holding the asset, plus some costs such as (say) fees to maintain a dematerialised account.

c. Commodities where production is continuous but storage is discontinuous may follow either approach, based on the degree to which the good can be stored and the available production capacity *vis-à-vis* current demand. If the goods can be stored for some time and the industry has surplus capacity to meet increases in demand, then they follow the carrying charge approach. An extreme case is electricity which is very difficult to store. In situations where there is little spare generation capacity *vis-à-vis* current demand, electricity futures prices are almost entirely expectations-based.

d. Futures prices in goods where production and storage are both discontinuous (Table 4.1, the shaded portion) tend to follow the expectations approach for months beyond the period for which existing stocks last. (For months relating to existing stocks, they behave like continuous storage markets.)

e. Even in continuous storage or production markets, expectations do play a role. It was seen that while there is a maximum limit for the spread, determined by the carrying cost, there is no minimum. Fluctuations within the maximum are often related to expectations. Prices for distant months which involve new harvests, do involve a substantial element of expectations, but such expectations also influence the spot price simultaneously. This is because the stocks become a link mediating between the current crop and future harvests.

f. Expectations may predominate even in continuous storage or production markets, for periods demarcated from the present by some future event which is expected to change the market situation.[14]

Example 4.5

In the month of February, there is a port strike in Chile and a railway wagon shortage in land-locked Zambia, both of which are leading copper producers. This disrupts the flow of copper supplies to world markets. Stocks are adequate to meet normal consumption requirements for about three months. The prices of copper on the London Metal Exchange (in dollars per tonne) are as follows:

Spot	*12,000*
March	*12,100*
April	*12,175*
July	*11,980*
Sept.	*11,750*

The prices for the near months reflect the fact that there is an on-going port strike/railway disruption in producing countries; thus, prices of these months would be formed on the basis of existing stocks only. The contango for near months reflects carrying costs; since stocks are

---

14 B. A. Goss and B. S. Yamey, *op. cit.*, 16.

adequate, the convenience yield is negligible. Prices for distant months are based on the expectation that the disruption will not continue for that long and hence a large quantity, including the backlog for the months with transport disruption, will reach the market by then. Because of this, prices for distant months are at a backwardation, reflecting the expected change in circumstances.

Another example of an external event in the context of financial futures markets, could be an expected election with, say, a proposal for major public borrowing through issue of government securities, which will take effect after a particular date if one of the parties wins, or an expected budget proposal affecting future periods only. These circumstances, depending on the exact nature of the expected changes, may well influence futures prices differently from spot prices.

Normal backwardation tends to exist in those markets which are relatively thin, where speculators have to be induced to come in. In other markets, it may or may not exist depending on the extent of *suo motu* speculative interest. A simple way of summarising the relationship is that:

- The carrying cost approach provides a limit or upper bound to the futures price. Thus, $F \leq S + C - Y$, i.e., the futures price cannot exceed the sum of the spot price and carrying cost (net of any convenience yield).

- However, in some cases, expectations may cause the price to fall below the upper limit.

- The relative influence of carrying costs vs. expectations varies. At one extreme is electricity futures where storage is very difficult and sometimes impossible and production of some kinds of electricity is discontinuous – this market is dominated by expectations. At another extreme are futures in financial instruments where carrying cost (net of yield) is the predominant factor with very rare exceptions. Most other markets fall somewhere in between.

Basis (price spread) and hedging regurns

The returns to hedging depend on the size and change in the gap between spot prices and futures prices. The difference between these two prices is generally called the 'basis'. The term 'price spread' is also used by economists (though in the financial markets this term usually has a different connotation connected with options) and this book uses both terms. Basis is usually defined as spot price minus futures price, and that is the definition adopted in this book. (However, readers should note that it is sometimes defined as futures price minus spot price; in such contexts, the pricing relationships and definitions given below will have to be suitably changed.)

When the futures price is greater than the spot price, the basis is negative. As mentioned at the beginning of this chapter, the term 'contango' is also used to describe such a relationship, i.e., 'the futures price is at a contango'. The extent of the negative basis is the extent of the contango. For instance, if the spot price of castor seed is ₹ 4,000 per quintal and the November futures price is ₹ 4,200, the basis is

₹ (4,000 – 4,200) = ₹ minus 200 per quintal.

In this situation, November castor is at a contango of ₹ 200 *vis-à-vis* spot.

When the futures prices is lower than the spot price, the basis is positive. As noted earlier, the term 'backwardation' is also used to describe such a relationship, i.e., 'the futures price is at a backwardation'. The extent of the positive basis is the extent of the backwardation. On the other hand, if the spot price of soya bean is ₹ 4,000 per quintal while the December futures price is ₹ 3,600, then the basis is:

4,000 – 3,600= ₹ 400 per quintal.

In this case, December soyabean is at a backwardation of ₹ 400.

The correspondence between these terms is summarised in Table 4.2

Table 4.2: Futures vs. spot price relationship

Futures price vis-à-vis spot price	Basis	Description of relationship
Futures price is higher than spot price	Negative	Contango
Futures price is lower than spot price	Positive	Backwardation

To make it easier to understand how basis affects hedging returns, assume initially that there are no carrying costs. A short hedger buys in the spot (ready) market and sells simultaneously in the futures market at the start of the hedging period (time *t*). At the end of the hedging period (time *t)*, he sells in the spot market and buys in the futures market. In each market, his profit or loss is the difference between the sale price and purchase price.

Gain/loss in spot market   = Sale price – Purchase price

$$= S_t - S_0$$

Gain/loss in futures market   = Sale price – Purchase price

$$= F_0 - F_t$$

Total gain/loss
$$= (F_0 - F_t) + (S_t - S_0)$$
$$= F_0 - S_0 - F_t + S_t$$
$$= (F_0 - S_0) - (F_t - S_t)$$
$$= (S_t - F_t) - (S_0 - F_0) \qquad (4.1)$$

But, by definition, the basis (spread) at any given time is the difference between the spot and futures prices.

Basis at time 0 = $S_0 - F_0$

Basis at time t = $S_t - F_t$

Thus, equation (4.1) shows that the return to short hedging is the difference between the closing basis and the opening basis.

In the case of a long hedger, the initial sale is on the ready market, say in the form of a non-transferable forward contract. Assuming there are no carrying costs, his price is likely to be same as the spot price. Thus, at time 0, he sells in the spot market and buys (to 'place' the hedge) in the futures market. At time t (end of the hedge period) he buys in the spot market (so as to deliver against his obligation) and sells in the futures market (to 'lift' the hedge). In each market, his gain or loss is the difference between the sale price and the purchase price.

Gain/loss in spot market   = Sale price – Purchase price

$$= S_0 - S_t$$

Gain/loss in futures market = Sale price – Purchase price

$$= F_t - F_0$$

Total gain/loss
$$= (F_t - F_0) + (S_0 - S_t)$$
$$= F_t - S_t - F_0 + S_0$$
$$= (F_t - S_t) - (F_0 - S_0)$$
$$= (S_0 - F_0) - (S_t - F_t) \qquad (4.2)$$

Thus, from equation (4.2), it is seen that the return to long hedging is the difference between the opening basis and the closing basis. It should be noted that equation (4.2) is the exact negative or obverse of equation (4.1).

Though equations (4.1) and (4.2) are incomplete in as much as they ignore carrying costs, they illustrate the basic point that hedging returns depend on spread changes. Indeed, for this reason, some authors have gone so far as to say that hedging is merely speculation on the basis or price spread. This is, however, a somewhat misleading characterisation. It is true that hedging on a futures market substitutes basis risk (i.e., risk of spread change) for price risk, but this substitution usually results in a large reduction in the degree of risk for the following reasons:

a. For hedges where the underlying held in the spot market is identical to a deliverable variety or grade in the futures market and where the hedge is held to the maturity of the futures contract and delivered against it, there is no 'basis risk', i.e., risk of unexpected change in the basis or price spread. The change in basis is entirely predictable and hence not a 'risk'.

b. In other cases, i.e., where the underlying held in the spot market is not identical to a deliverable variety or where the contract is not held until the maturity of the contract or where actual delivery is not given/taken, some basis risk remains.

c. Because the basis is smaller than the price itself, it is intuitively apparent (and empirically proven[15]) that basis changes are generally smaller in magnitude than price changes.

d. Because closing spreads normally tend to zero, the basis normally changes in a predictable way over the life of a futures contract, whereas prices fluctuate either way.

Convergence of spot and futures prices

The basis on a given date reflects the carrying costs or expected prices, as was seen earlier. However, on the maturity date, the spot and futures price would have to be equal, since they refer to the same commodity or asset, at the same point of time. If there was any difference, arbitrageurs could make riskless profits, and this arbitrage will ensure equality. Thus, the closing price spread or basis of a futures contract is expected to be zero. This means that the basis—positive or negative, shrinks over the life of a contract; thus the spot and futures price converge over time, though both may fluctuate heavily (see Figures 4.2 to 4.4).

---

15 See for instance the studies by T. F. Graf and B. S. Yamey, cited by B. A. Goss in *The Theory of Futures Trading*, Routledge & Kegan–Paul, London, 1972, 32–33. The same result has been confirmed by several empirical investigations both in India and abroad.

Figure 4.2: Futures price at a backwardation

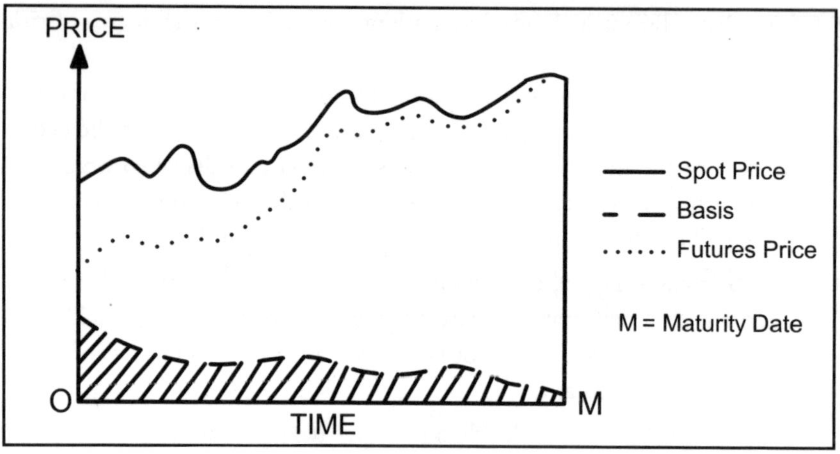

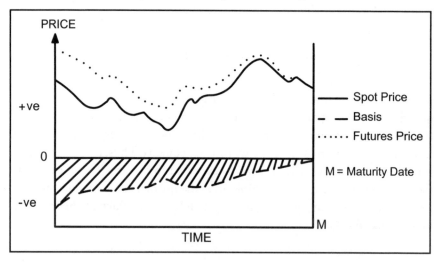

(The figure shows a typical profile of a backwardation, where the backwardation diminishes over time, though not necessarily uniformly.)

Figure 4.3: Futures price at a contango

(The figure shows a typical profile of a contango, where the contango diminishes over time, though not necessarily uniformly)

Figure 4.4: Backwardation turning to contango

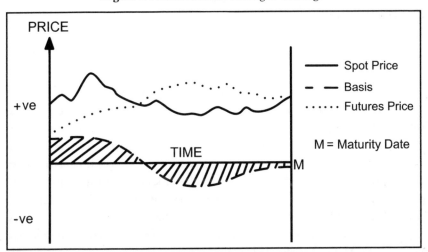

(The figure shows an irregular spread pattern typical of a market which has received an exogenous shock in between, e.g., imposition of export controls during a period of shortage which suddenly makes domestic supply more abundant. Nevertheless, the basis diminishes to nil at maturity. Such irregular spread patterns can lead to perverse or risk-enhancing hedging returns for hedges lifted prior to maturity.)

Closing spreads may exist, however, where the spot market variety is different from the deliverable variety in the futures market. In a futures market, there is usually a 'deliverable variety' or 'contract grade';[16] other specified varieties can also be delivered but a premium or discount known as tendering difference is charged to reflect the quality difference. Such spreads are generally stable and predictable, and thus do not materially affect hedgers since they can be planned for. They do not vitiate the inherent principle that:

- on the maturity date, the spot and futures price of the same variety must be equal; and

- spot and futures prices converge over the life of a contract.

---

16 This may sometimes be called the 'basis grade' which should not be confused with the meaning of 'basis' as a price spread.

Hedging bias

Several early empirical studies showed that short hedgers earned lower returns than long hedgers. Such a result would be consistent with the theory of normal backwardation which postulated that futures prices had a downward bias. There is, however, a much more basic factor at work.

It was seen earlier, that there is an asymmetry between positive and negative spreads. Positive spreads (negative basis) have an upper limit, but there is no lower limit for negative spreads (positive basis). It was also seen that spreads tend to narrow over time. The existence of an asymmetry together with an inherent tendency for spreads to narrow, leads to a corresponding asymmetry in outcomes for short and long hedging. The link between the asymmetry in spreads and the effects thereof on hedging returns was initially identified by Houthakker, but he did not build the convergence tendency into this theory. A clear enunciation of what can be called the theory of inherent hedging bias, was made by M. G. Pavaskar.[17] He showed that futures markets are inherently biased against short hedgers, and that the bias is based on the asymmetry of the spreads. Subsequent research by Somanathan confirmed the inherent bias, but showed that the extent of the bias was less than originally propounded by Pavaskar. This resulted in the modified theory of inherent bias.[18] Based on the modified theory of inherent bias, the extent of *a priori* hedging bias in futures markets is summarised in Table 4.2.

Table 4.3: Hedging returns for long and short hedgers

Long hedgers	Short hedgers
Over the long-term, on the average:	Over the long-term, on the average:
(a) Spot market losses will be fully, or more than fully, compensated for by the futures market.	(a) Spot market losses will be partially, or at best fully, compensated for by the futures market.
(b) Spot market gains will be partially, or at worst fully, offset by the futures market.	(b) Spot market gains will be fully, or more than fully, offset by the futures market.

---

17 M. G. Pavaskar, *Economics of Hedging*, Asia Publishing House, Bombay, 1976, 16–18.

18 T. V. Somanathan, *Commodity and Financial Futures Markets: An Economic Analysis*, Unpublished Ph D Dissertation, Calcutta University, Calcutta, 1993.

Table 4.2 covers only the long-term scenario. A more comprehensive description of all possible scenarios of hedges in the deliverable variety on any futures market[19] is as follows:[20]

Individual hedges

a.   Net return on long hedging cannot be negative if the hedge is held until maturity.

b.   Net return on short hedging cannot be positive if the hedge is held until maturity.

c.   Both long and short hedging may have positive or negative (or nil) net return, if hedges are lifted prior to maturity; the outcome depends on the nature of price-spread movements in each individual case.

d.   Net return on long hedging cannot be negative when price spread decreases uniformly over time.

e.   Net return on short hedging cannot be positive when price spread decreases uniformly over time.

Long term[21]

f.   In the long-term, return on long hedging cannot be negative.

g.   In the long-term, return on short hedging cannot be positive.

h.   In the long-term, long hedgers:

- will be fully compensated or over-compensated by the futures market for adverse spot market price risks; and
- will have favourable risks partially or, at worst, fully offset by the futures market.

i.   In the long-term, short hedgers:

- will be partially or, at best, fully compensated by the futures market for adverse spot market price risks; and

---

19 T. V. Somanathan, *ibid.*

20 This analysis holds for any market where carrying costs are positive.

21 The expression 'long-term' in this context signifies, at any given time, an average or aggregate computed over a period longer than the remaining duration of all currently traded futures contracts.

- will have favourable spot market price risks fully or more than fully offset by the futures market.

At first sight, the reader may well ask 'why should anyone engage in short hedging when he knows his returns are (generally) going to be negative?' To understand this, one should be clear that the 'return on hedging' referred to is the net return from his cash market and futures market transactions put together and after considering carrying costs. A negative return means the futures market did not fully compensate for the spot risks, but some compensation is better than none if one is seeking to reduce risk.

Appendix 4.1 presents a series of case studies which illustrate hedging in commodity markets and also illustrate the operation of the factors described above.

Liquidity and depth

In the context of markets, liquidity is the ability for a buyer or seller to carry out the purchase or sale that they intend to engage in, very quickly or instantaneously. A liquid market is one where a counterparty (i.e., seller to the buyer, buyer to the seller) is readily available. An illiquid market is one where a person wishing to trade does not find a counterparty at the prevailing market price immediately or readily. Depth is a related concept – a deep market is one which is not only liquid but has high trading volumes so that even large transactions can be done quickly. An exchange may allow trading in several different maturities for one particular underlying. However, not all of them may be liquid.

Roll over and attendant risks

When hedging through a futures contract, the maturity date of the futures contract may not exactly match the needs of the hedger. Also, though the period for which the hedge is needed is, say, seven months, the futures contracts which are liquid and easy to trade may be of only three months maturity. In these and similar situations, a hedger may have to first enter into a hedge in one futures contract and then close that hedge while simultaneously entering a new hedge in a contract with longer maturity. The process of rollover may however involve certain transaction costs (brokerage fees and taxes, for instance) and in addition, there may be a change in the basis when rolling over. Hedgers have to weigh these factors when deciding on which futures contract to choose.

Cross-hedging

Often a futures market is used for cross-hedging, i.e., hedging one good or instrument by trading in another related but different good or instrument. For instance, one can hedge platinum prices through trading in gold futures, since the prices of platinum and gold are closely (though not fully) correlated. A holding of corporate debentures may be hedged using the gilt futures market. A holding of one company's shares may be hedged by using a futures contract on a broad stock market index or on another company's shares. Such cross-hedges are often necessary because a liquid futures contract corresponding exactly to the risk being hedged may not exist. (A liquid market is one where buyers and sellers are readily available for large volumes of trades.) However, cross hedges face the risk that the previously observed correlation between the two markets may not actually hold in the future.

Equivalency or hedge ratio

When a futures market in one underlying is used to hedge a different (albeit, correlated) underlying, there is always some residual risk. A cross hedge may not exactly offset the spot market risk. Nevertheless, the expectation is that the cross hedge,while not eliminating the risk,will reduce it.

The futures contract may fluctuate more or less than the spot exposure being hedged. Therefore, it becomes necessary to either increase or decrease the quantity of futures hedged vis-à-vis the quantity involved in the spot market, in order to achieve as close a hedge as possible. The number of futures contracts needed to hedge a single lot of the item being hedged is called the equivalency or hedge ratio. A commonly used method of calculating the ideal or 'optimal hedge ratio' is based on the assumption that the volatility of the hedged asset should be as low as possible (a perfect hedge would mean no volatility). To do this it is necessary to know the extent to which the futures contract is correlated with the spot (the correlation coefficient) and the respective volatilities (tendencies to fluctuate) of the two assets. In simple terms, the equivalency or hedge ratio can in most cases be derived from the following formula:

$$h = \frac{\text{SD of changes in the cash market price of the asset being hedged} \quad x \quad r}{\text{SD of changes in the futures price}}$$

Where,

h = optimal hedge ratio

SD = standard deviation for a given period

r = correlation coefficient between the SD of the changes in spot price of commodity and SD of the change in futures price

The hedge or equivalency ratio calculated in this manner is called the 'minimum variance hedge ratio' since it tries to achieve the minimum variance in the value of the hedged asset (i.e., spot plus futures combined). However, the data required to use this generic formula may often not be available. It should also be noted that, even when available, the information on correlation and standard deviation based on past trends may not accurately reflect what may happen in the future. Thus, such calculations are not fool-proof in ensuring an appropriate cross hedge.

Basis risk in cross hedging

The concept of basis risk was introduced earlier in this chapter – it is the risk that the price spread (basis) may change in an unexpected way. When comparing the spot price of a commodity with the futures price of the same commodity, the normal pattern or expectation is that the basis will diminish over time to nil. If the closing basis is not zero, it would be because the varieties delivered against the contract may be different from the variety used for calculating the spot price.

Basis risk is a bigger issue when cross-hedging. It should be noted that when cross-hedging, the basis is: Spot price of the item being hedged – Future/forward price of the contract used for hedging.

Thus, it is the spot price of one thing minus the futures price of another thing (e.g., spot price of palladium vs. futures price of gold or spot price of Reliance Petroleum vs. futures price of Reliance Industries or the spot price of petrol versus the futures price of crude oil). In such a case, the basis exists permanently and it does not become zero on the date of maturity of the futures contract. The basis in this case has two parts – a part related to carrying costs or expectations in the futures contract itself and a part related to the price difference between the underlying in the futures and the underlying being held in the cash market.

Appendix 4.1

Case studies in hedging through commodity futures

N.B.

1. All the case studies are on the turmeric futures market. In order to enable the reader to connect and compare the different scenarios, it is preferable that all the cases deal with the same market. A commodity has been used because examples involving financial futures have added complications, e.g., dividend yields, interest payments etc. which would obscure the essential features that the cases are intended to illustrate.

2. The case studies are hypothetical as also the prices and figures of carrying cost used therein and should not be construed as an indication of the prevailing level of prices or costs.

Series I

A: Hedges Held to Maturity

Case Study 1: $F_0 - R_0 < C_m$ *

On 1 May, turmeric prices at Sangli are as follows:

	₹ per quintal
Spot	9,250
Futures (July)	9,400

Storage costs of one quintal from 1 May up to delivery date (15 July) are estimated at ₹ 250 (i.e., ₹ 100 per month). On 15 July, both spot and futures are trading at ₹ 9,100. Mr. Long enters into the following transactions:

1 May: Sell small lots aggregating to one quintal to various retailers at a fixed price, of ₹ 9,500 per quintal for actual delivery in July.

1 May: Buy one quintal July futures at ₹ 9,400

15 July: Buy one quintal spot at ₹ 9,100

15 July: Sell one quintal July futures at ₹ 9,100

The financial outcome of this sequence of transactions is summarised in the following table:

---

* C_m denotes carrying cost to maturity. Fo/Ro and Fn/Rn denote futures and ready prices at time 0 and time n, respectively.

Exhibit 1(a)
Mr Long: Return from Holding Hedged Commitment

Transaction	Spot market		Future market	
	Date	Price (₹)	Date	Price (₹)
Sell	1/5	9,500	15/7	9,100
Buy	15/7	9,100	1/5	9,400
Gain/(Loss)		400		(300)
Net return (₹)				100

During the same period, Mr. Short carried out the following transactions:*

1 May: Buy one quintal spot at ₹ 9,250**

1 May: Sell one quintal July futures at ₹ 9,400

15 July: Buy one quintal July futures at ₹ 9,100

15 July: Sell one quintal spot at ₹ 9,100

---

* In practice, forward sales/purchase by long/short hedgers might be made in small instalments at different points of time, with the aggregate being hedged on a particular day. Also, it is not necessary that there is an actual spot market 'sale' or 'purchase' behind every long or short hedge; hedging may be undertaken merely to 'lock in' a particular price, based on which other economic transactions are undertaken. For instance, a farmer would hedge (as a short hedger) without 'buying' on the spot market--- his hedge would be against his anticipated crop of the commodity: the hedge would be placed to ensure that his income from the crop does not fall below that indicated by the current market price. In order to avoid obfuscating the basic theoretical issues, such complications have been ignored in the Case Studies, in which each long/short hedge is placed against an actual spot market sale/purchase.

** In real life the market lot is 50 quintals. One quintal is used here purely to simplify the illustration.

Exhibit 1(b)
Mr. Short: Return from Holding Hedged Stocks

Transaction	Spot market		Future market	
	Date	Price (₹)	Date	Price (₹)
Sell	15/7	9,100	1/5	9,400
Buy	1/5	9,250	15/7	9,100
		(150)		300
Pay Storage Cost	15/7	(250)		
Gain (Loss)		(400)		300
Net Return (₹)			(100)	

A comparison of Exhibits 1(a) and 1(b) shows that Mr. Long obtained a positive return of ₹ 100 while Mr. Short lost ₹ 100. To put it differently, the futures market did not fully offset Mr. Long's spot market gain; correspondingly it did not fully compensate Mr. Short for his spot market loss.

Case Study 2: $F_0 - R_0 = C_m$

On 1 June, turmeric prices at Sangli are quoted as follows:

	₹ per quintal
Spot	9,600
Futures (July)	9,750

Storage cost of one quintal from 1 June till 15 July (maturity date) is estimated at ₹ 150. On 15 July, as already described earlier, the price is ₹ 9,100.

Mr. Long has the following transactions:

1 June: Sell one quintal for actual delivery in July at ₹ 9,750

1 June: Buy one quintal July futures at ₹ 9,750

15 July: Sell one quintal July futures at ₹ 9,100

15 July: Buy one quintal spot at ₹ 9,100

Exhibit 2(a)
Mr. Long: Return from Holding Hedged Commitment

Transaction	Spot market		Future market	
	Date	Price (₹)	Date	Price (₹)
Sell	1/6	9,750	15/7	9,100
Buy	15/7	9,100	1/6	9,750
Gain (Loss)		650		(650)
Net Return (₹)			NIL	

Mr. Short's is transactions are as follows:

    1 June: Buy one quintal spot ₹ 9,600

    1 June: Sell one quintal July futures at ₹ 9,750

    15 July: Buy one quintal July futures at ₹ 9,100

    15 July: Sell one quintal spot at ₹ 9,100

Exhibit 2(b)
Mr. Short: Return from Holding Hedged Stocks

Transaction	Spot market		Future market	
	Date	Price (₹)	Date	Price (₹)
Sell	15/7	9,100	1/6	9,750
Buy	1/6	9,600	15/7	9,100
		(500)		650
Pay storage cost	15/7	(150)		
Gain/(Loss)		(650)		650
Net return (₹)			Nil	

Thus, where the price spread exactly equals the carrying cost to maturity, long and short hedgers obtain nil return, or in other words, the futures market exactly offsets the gains/losses in the cash market.

B: Hedges Lifted Prior to Maturity
Case Study 3

On 15 June, turmeric prices at Sangli are as below:

	₹ per quintal
Spot	9,700
Futures (September)	9,791

Storage cost is estimated at ₹ 100 per mensem. On 15 August, prices are as follows:

	₹ per Quintal
Spot	9,200
Futures (September)	9,260

Mr. Long undertakes the following transactions:

15 June: Sell one quintal for actual August delivery at ₹ 9,700
15 June: Buy one quintal September futures at ₹ 9,791
15 August: Sell one quintal September futures at ₹ 9,260
15 August: Buy one quintal spot at ₹ 9,200

Exhibit 3(a)
Mr. Long: Return from Holding Hedged Commitment

Transaction	Spot market		Future market	
	Date	Price (₹)	Date	Price (₹)
Sell	15/6	9,700	15/8	9,260
Buy	15/8	9,200	15/6	9,791
Gain (Loss)		500		(531)
Net Return (₹)			(31)	

Mr. Short's transactions are as follows:
15 June: Buy one quintal spot at ₹ 9,500
15 June: Sell one quintal September futures at ₹ 9,791.

15 August: Buy one quintal September futures at ₹ 9,260
15 August: Sell one quintal spot at ₹ 9,200

Exhibit 3(b)
Mr. Short: Return from Holding Hedged Stocks

Transaction	Spot market		Future market	
	Date	Price (₹)	Date	Price (₹)
Sell	15/8	9,200	15/6	9,791
Buy	15/6	9,500	15/8	9,260
		(300)		531
Pay Storage Cost	15/8	(200)		
Gain/(Loss)		(500)		531
Net Return (₹)			31	

In the above transaction, Mr. Short was over-compensated by the futures market for his spot market loss; Mr. Long lost more on the futures market than he gained on the spot. It should be noted that this Case Study brings out clearly the fact that a short hedger can earn a positive return. This result has come about without violating the condition at any time:

$$F_n - R_n \leq C_m$$

as 7,790 - 7,500 < 300 (storage cost for three months 15/6 to 15/9) and 7,260 - 7,200 < 100 (storage cost for one month from 15/8 - 15/9)

Case Study 4
On 30 June, turmeric prices at Sangli are as below:

	₹ per Quintal
Spot	9,600
Futures (September - matures on 15/9)	9,830

Carrying cost is estimated at ₹ 100 per mensem. On 30 August, prices are as follows:

	₹ per quintal
Spot	9,250
Futures (September)	9,300

Mr. Long's transactions are as follows:

30 June: Sell one quintal for actual August delivery at (fixed price) ₹ 9,800

30 June: Buy one quintal futures at ₹ 9,830

30 August: Sell one quintal futures at ₹ 9,300

30 August: Buy one quintal spot at ₹ 9,250

Exhibit 4(a)

Mr. Long: Return from Holding Hedged Commitment

Transaction	Spot market		Future market	
	Date	Price (₹)	Date	Price (₹)
Sell	30/6	9,800	30/8	9,300
Buy	30/8	9,250	30/6	9,830
Gain/(Loss)		550		(530)
Net return (₹)		20		

Mr. Short's dealings are as follows:

30 June: Buy one quintal spot at ₹ 9,600

30 June: Sell one quintal September futures at ₹ 9,830

30 August: Buy one quintal September futures at ₹ 9,300

30 Augus: Sell one quintal spot at ₹ 9,250

Exhibit 4(b)
Mr. Short: Return from Holding Hedged Stocks

Transaction	Spot Market		Future Market	
	Date	Price (₹)	Date	Price (₹)
Sell	30/8	9,250	30/6	9,830
Buy	30/6	9,600	30/8	9,300
		(350)		530
Pay storage cost	30/8	(200)		
Gain/(Loss)		(550)		530
Net Return (₹)			(20)	

This case study ends up with a result opposite to that in case study 3, the long hedger gains while the short hedger losses.

C. Uniform Decline in Price Spreads

(Note: The term 'uniform decline in price spread' is used to mean that the spread exhibited by the futures market declines by equal instalments in equal internals of time, in such a way that the spread on the maturity date is nil. For instance, three months before maturity date, spot and futures turmeric might be trading at ₹ 8,000 and ₹ 8,150 respectively. For uniform decline, every month the spread should diminish by ₹ 50. Thus when there are two months left to maturity the spread would be ₹ 100, when one-and-a-half months are left it would be ₹ 75 and so on).

Case Study 5

Assume all details as in Case Study 3 supra, except that, on 15 August prices are as follows:

Spot	₹ 9,200
Futures	₹ 9,297

The price spread between spot and futures has declined to ₹ 97 when a month remains. In the two months which have elapsed, the spread has decreased by ₹ 194, which gives a rate of decline of ₹ 97 per month.)

Exhibit 5(a)
Mr. Long: Return from Holding Hedged Commitment

Transaction	Spot Market		Future Market	
	Date	Price (₹)	Date	Price (₹)
Sell	15/6	9,700	15/8	9,297
Buy	15/8	9,200	15/6	9,791
		500		(494)
Net Return (₹)			6	

Exhibit 5(b)
Mr. Short: Return from Holding Hedged Stocks

Transaction	Spot Market		Future Market	
	Date	Price (₹)	Date	Price (₹)
Sell	15/8	9,200	15/6	9,791
Buy	15/6	9,500	15/8	9,297
		(300)		494
Pay Storage Cost	15/8	(200)		
Gain/(Loss)		(500)		494
Nett Return (₹)		(6)		

Despite the fact that the spread at the time of placing the hedges was identical to that in case study 3, it is found that in this instance Mr. Long makes a small gain while Mr. Short makes a small loss. The difference between this case and Case Study 3 is that the price spread decreased uniformly over time.

Series II

Case Study 6

Assume all the facts and transactions as in Case Study 3; in that instance Mr. Short earned a positive return, while Mr. Long had a corresponding negative return. That transaction (referred to as the 1st Hedge) was immediately followed by another set of hedge transactions (2nd Hedge), which were completed only on the maturity date, 15 September. Prices were as follows:

		₹ per quintal
15 August:	Spot	9,200
	Futures (September)	9,260
	[As in Case Study 3]	
15 September:	Spot	9,100
	Futures	9,100

The transactions undertaken on the 2nd hedge were as follows:

Mr. Long

15 August: Sell one quintal for actual September delivery at fixed rate of ₹ 9,300

15 August: Buy one quintal September futures at ₹ 9,260

15 September: Sell one quintal September futures at ₹ 9,100

15 September: Buy one quintal spot at ₹ 9,100

Exhibit 6(a)
Mr. Long: Return from Holding Hedged Commitment (2nd Hedge)

Transaction	Spot Market		Future Market	
	Date	Price (₹)	Dat	Price (₹)
Sell	15/8	9,300	15/9	9,100
Buy	15/9	9,100	15/8	9,260
Gain/(Loss)		200		(160)
Net. Return (₹)			40	

Mr. Short

15 August: Buy one quintal spot at ₹ 9,200

15 August: Sell one quintal September futures at ₹ 9,260

15 September: Buy one quintal September futures at ₹ 9,100

15 September: Sell one quintal spot at ₹ 9,100

Exhibit 6(b)
Mr. Short: Return from Holding Hedged Stocks
(2nd Hedge)

Transaction	Spot Market		Future Market	
	Date	Price (₹)	Date	Price (₹)
Sell	15/9	9,100	15/8	9,260
Buy	15/8	9,200	15/9	9,100
		(100)		160
Pay Carrying Cost	15/9	(100)		
Gain/(Loss)		(200)		160
Net Return (₹)			(40)	

It can be seen that the 2nd hedge has yielded a gain of ₹ 40 to Mr. Long with a ₹ 40 loss to Mr. Short. Considering the results of the 1st and 2nd hedges together:

		₹
Mr. Long:	1st Hedge - Loss	(31)
	2nd Hedge - Gain	40
	Net Gain	**9**
Mr. Short: 1st Hedge - Gain		31
	2nd Hedge - Loss	(40)
	Net Loss	(9)

In spite of the 1st hedge having yielded positive return to short hedgers, this has been wiped out by the 2nd hedge which was held to maturity. The 1st hedge had a negative spot market price risk of:

$$R_t - R_0 - C = ₹ (9,200 - 9,500 - 200) = ₹ 500 (-ve)$$

This represented a gain to short hedgers and a loss to long hedgers. The futures market compensated for this by a price change of:

$$F_0 - F_0 = ₹ (9,260 - 9,791) = ₹ 531 (-ve)$$

In short, the futures market over-compensated for the spot market price risk. On this occasion, this benefitted Mr. Short at the expense of Mr. Long.

The 2nd hedge also had a downward (negative) price risk of:

This was compensated for by the futures market by a price movement of
₹ (9,100 - 9,260) = ₹ 160 (-ve)

On this occasion the futures market under-compensated for the spot market price risk, thereby benefitting Mr. Long to the detriment of Mr. Short.

Considering the two hedges together:

Combined (downward) spot market price risk

$$= ₹ (9,100 - 9,500 - 300) = - ₹ 700$$

Futures market price change

$$= ₹ (9,100 - 9,791) = - ₹ 691$$

Percentage compensation

$$= -691/-700 = 98.7 \text{ per cent}$$

This case study illustrates the fact that, over the long-term, downward price risks will be compensated for by 100 per cent or less, but not more.

Case Study 7

On 15 January, turmeric prices were as follows:

	₹ per quintal
Spot	8,100
Futures (March)	8,290

Storage costs of turmeric are ₹ 100 per mensem per quintal. On 15 February and 15 March (delivery date), prices are as follows:

	₹ per quintal
15 February: Spot	8,300
Futures (March)	8,250
15 March: Spot	8,500
Futures (March)	8,500

Mr. Long's transactions are as follows:

1st Hedge:
15 January: Sell one quintal for actual February delivery at ₹ 8,200
15 January: Buy one quintal March futures at ₹ 8,290

2nd Hedge:
15 February: Sell one quintal for actual March delivery at ₹ 8,400
15 February: Buy one quintal March futures at ₹ 8,250

15 March: Sell one quintal March futures at ₹ 8,500
15 March: Buy one quintal spot ₹ 8,500

Exhibit 7(a)
Mr. Long: Return from Holding Hedged Commitments

Transaction	Spot Market		Future Market	
	Date	Price (₹)	Date	Price (₹)
1st Hedge				
Sell	15/1	8,200	15/2	8,250
Buy	15/2	8,300	15/1	8,290
Gain/(Loss)		(100)		(40)
2nd Hedge				
Sell	15/2	8,400	15/3	8,500
Buy	15/3	8,500	15/2	8,250
Gain/(Loss)		(100)		250
Net Returns:				
1st Hedge	₹ (140)			
2nd Hedge	₹ 150			
Total	₹ 10			

Mr. Short's transactions were as follows:

1st Hedge

15 January: Buy one quintal spot at ₹ 8,100
15 January: Sell one quintal March at ₹ 8,290
15 February: Buy one quintal March at ₹ 8,250
15 February: Sell one quintal spot at ₹ 8,300

2nd Hedge

15 February: Buy one quintal spot at ₹ 8,300
15 February: Sell one quintal March at ₹ 8,250
15 March: Buy one quintal March at ₹ 8,500
15 March: Sell one quintal spot at ₹ 8,500

Exhibit 7(b)
Mr. Short: Return from Holding Hedged Stocks

Transaction	Spot Market		Future Market	
	Date	Price (₹)	Date	Price (₹)
1st Hedge				
Sell	15/2	8,300	15/1	8,290
Buy	15/1	8,100	15/2	8,250
		200		40
Pay Carrying Cost	15/2	(100)		
Gain/(Loss)		100		40
2nd Hedge				
Sell	15/3	8,500	15/2	8,250
Buy	15/2	8,300	15/3	8,500
		200		(250)
Pay Carrying Cost	15/2	(100)		
Gain / (Loss)		100		(250)
Net Returns (₹)	1st Hedge	140		
	2nd Hedge	(150)		
	Total	(10)		

This case study is an example of positive (upward) price risk. Although the 1st hedge gave positive return to Mr. Short, this was wiped out by the 2nd hedge. Mr. Long lost in the 1st hedge but more than recouped his loss in the 2nd hedge. The 1st hedge had a spot market price risk of

$$R_1 - R_0 - C = ₹\,(8{,}300 - 8{,}100 - 100) = ₹\,100\ (+ve)$$

However, the futures market exihbited a negative price change:

$$F_1 - F_0 = ₹\,(8{,}250 - 8{,}290) = ₹\,(40)\ (-ve)$$

Thus, short hedgers had their spot market gains increased by the futures market, while losses of long hedgers were exacerbated the futures market.

The 2nd hedge had a spot market risk of

$$₹\,(8{,}500 - 8{,}300 - 100) = ₹\,100\ (+ve)$$

This represented a gain to short hedgers and a loss to long hedgers. The futures market offset this by a price change of

$$₹ (8,500 - 8,250) = ₹ 250 (+ve)$$

Considering the two hedges together:
Combined (upward) spot market price risk

$$= ₹ (8,500 - 8,100 - 200) = ₹ 200 (+ve)$$

Futures market price change

$$= ₹ (8,500 - 8,290) = ₹ 210 (+ve)$$

Percentage compensation = (210/200) = 105 per cent

This case study illustrates the fact that upward price risks (adjusted for carrying costs) will, over the long-term, be compensated for by 100 per cent or more, but not less.

5

Interest Rate Futures

As discussed in the introduction, interest rates have become quite volatile in the modern era. Changes may occur either because of policy action by the central bank or because of changes in the money market triggered by macro-economic changes in the domestic market, or even because of fluctuations in the foreign exchange market. Whatever the cause, institutions and individuals who borrow or lend significant sums, especially those who borrow or lend at floating interest rates, are exposed to risks arising from fluctuations in interest rates. Interest rate futures are an instrument allowing hedging and speculation in these risks. Interest rate futures are a sub-set of interest rate derivatives.

Interest rate futures or debt instrument futures

Strictly, interest rate futures are not futures contracts on interest rates *per se*, but rather futures contracts on *underlying interest-bearing debt instruments* like corporate, government and other bonds or short term deposits with a pre-specified face value and coupon (i.e., interest rate). When the maturity value of a bond or deposit is known, the implicit rate of interest (yield) can be calculated.

The underlying can be either a short term debt instrument (like a bank deposit) or a long term debt instrument (like a bond or debenture). Therefore, a futures contract on a debt instrument is *ipso facto* a futures contract on interest rates, but the relationship is inverse. This is different from stock or commodity futures: when one talks about these terms, one knows that one is substantially and directly dealing with the price movement in the stock and/or commodity itself, and not some implicit number therein.

The price in its own domestic market of a sovereign (i.e., central or federal) government security denominated in local currency varies exclusively and inversely on the basis of interest rates because credit and liquidity risks are nil. The coupon rate of interest on a bond reflects the rate of interest prevailing at the time the bond was initially issued, but interest rates change over time.

Example 5.1

In 2014, the prevailing market interest rate on long dated gilt-edged securities in a country is 10 per cent. The government issues a new 'gilt-edged' (i.e,. government-backed) security (known variously as gilts, government securities, government bonds or treasury bonds) with a coupon rate of 10 per cent. By 2016, the market interest rate for long-dated gilts is 14 per cent. New issues of gilts bear a coupon rate of 14 per cent. An investor in the gilt-edged securities market can now choose either to buy the new bond (producing a return of 14 per cent) or to buy the old bond. Naturally, he will not buy the old (10 per cent) bond at its issue price when he can get 14 percent on the latest issue. If however the price falls to a level such that the yield is 14 per cent, he will be willing to buy it. If this level is x, then

$$\frac{10}{x} = \frac{14}{100}$$

$$x = \frac{10 \times 100}{14}$$

= ₹71.42 per ₹100 of nominal or par value

For every ₹100 of nominal value, the holder gets interest of ₹10 (since this is a ten per cent coupon security). But since he only pays ₹71.42, his yield is

10/71.42 = 14 per cent

Thus, the price of a ₹100 bond will fall to ₹71.42.

Now assume that in 2018, the rate of interest falls to 9 per cent. Persons holding the old (10 per cent) bond, acquired at par, can get a higher return than on fresh issues. Sellers of the bond know that the market rate is 9 per cent and will thus be unwilling to sell the bond at any yield in excess of 9 per cent. The new price of the gilt will be y such that

$$\frac{10}{y} = \frac{9}{100}$$

y = (10 x 100)/ 9 = ₹111.11 per ₹100 nominal

The buyer of ₹100 nominal gets ₹10 as annual interest but has paid ₹111.11. His effective yield is thus

10/111.11 = 9 per cent

(The simple relationship illustrated here applies only to perpetual securities; for redeemable securities, the formula is more complicated but the principle is the same.)

Hence, the relationship between the price of a bond and the prevailing interest rate is inverse: when market interest rates rise, bond prices fall; when market interest rates fall, bond prices rise. These price changes occur so that the yield on an already-issued security is the same as that on a new one issued at the current rate. Therefore, bond futures are effectively an inverse form of interest rate futures.

Interest rate futures are used for hedging by banks, financial institutions, pension funds and others whose assets or liabilities can be affected by changes in interest rates. In the interest rate futures markets, short hedgers are those seeking protection against rising interest rates while long hedgers are those seeking protection against falling interest rates. The method of quotation is structured so that a short hedger sells futures and benefits from a fall in price (rise in interest rate) in his futures transaction while a long hedger buys futures and benefits from a rise in price (fall in interest rates) in his futures transaction. This mirrors the situation in any other futures market.

The first interest rate futures were traded in October 1975 on the CBOT. Since then, the market has exploded. Another exchange that developed such derivatives along with the CBOT was the CME. CBOT specialises more towards the longer maturity (i.e., bonds maturing in the distant future) whereas the CME is more specialised in shorter maturity ones, such as Eurodollars (see below).

Interest rate futures are now actively traded in several developed country markets. American treasuries, Japanese bonds, German Euro-denominated sovereign bonds and other government notes have liquid derivatives' markets.

Another very active interest rate futures market is the market in Eurodollars. Eurodollars are typically short-term dollar debt (bank deposits) held outside the US. (The term 'Eurodollars' also has nothing to do with the Euro vs. dollar currency exchange rate; the Euro currency came into existence many years after the Eurodollar market.) The banks which hold such deposits could be foreign banks, or foreign branches of US banks. London dominates the Eurodollar market, and this market is generally based on the LIBOR or the London Inter-bank Offered Rate. It is the interest rate at which banks lend funds to other banks and much corporate debt is quoted on a 'LIBOR plus' basis, that is this rate plus a spread depending on the relevant party's credit and other risks.

The underlying for the most popular Eurodollar futures contract, and indeed the most popular futures' contract in the USA across categories is the $1 million, non-transferable three month Eurodollar futures contract traded on the CME. Such contracts trade are also traded actively in other countries, the Singapore Monetary Exchange being an example.

The Eurodollar contract, when it started trading in 1981, was the first derivatives' contract to use a notional basis and cash settlement instead of a 'delivery' settlement on expiry. For commodity derivatives, the underlying is a physical commodity but for financial derivatives, the underlying represents financial promises, often very liquid themselves. Hence the derivative contract on such promises can be settled in cash without causing any major spot-future discrepancy.

A characteristic feature of short-term interest rate futures is their manner of quotation. They are quoted by *deducting the yield per annum* from 100. The yield would be the one applicable to the contract term for that particular currency – for instance the rate applicable to the three month Eurodollar contract will be the three month US dollar LIBOR, while for a 30-day dollar contract, the one month US dollar LIBOR would apply.

Example 5.2

The Eurodollar futures contract for June is quoted at 96.00 while that for September is quoted at 96.50. This means the yield on a three-month deposit made in June is expected by the market to be

100 – 96.00 = 4.00 per cent per annum (interest received for three months would be 1 per cent)

The yield on a three-month deposit made in September is expected to be

100 – 96.50 = 3.50 per cent per annum (interest received for three months would be 0.875 per cent)

This also implies that the market is expecting interest rates to fall between June and September.

Interest Rate Futures (IRFs) in India

In India, interest rate futures were introduced in June 2003 but for a long time there was little liquidity in the market. These futures are traded on the NSE. The instruments listed are:

- 91-day (short term) treasury bills, and
- 10-year (long term) government bond or 'gilt'.

Treasury bills are zero-coupon short term securities, i.e., no interest payment is made but the bill is purchased at a price less than 100 and the difference between the purchase price and the maturity value of 100 is the implicit interest.

IRFs on NSE 'are standardised contracts based on six year, ten year and thirteen year Government of India Security' (NBF or NSE Bond Future II) and ninety one day Government of India Treasury Bill (91DTB)'.[1] These futures contracts on NSE are cash-settled.

---

1   https://nseindia.com/products/content/derivatives/irf/irf.htm.

The Reserve Bank of India is planning to introduce money market futures based on the overnight call money rate. This is partially because Interest Rate Futures (IRF) turnover is around 1 per cent of the equity derivatives volume and around 10 per cent of currency futures volume.[2]

Pre-2014 system: Notional basis

It was noted earlier in the discussion on exchange-traded futures that there may be more than one deliverable variety in a futures market and that if a variety other than the basis grade is delivered, price adjustments would be made. This is of particular relevance to interest rate futures. Until 2014, one 'lot' of the long term gilt security (abbreviated as 10YGS7, signifying Ten Year Government Security 7 per cent) was equivalent to a notional government bond of ₹ 2 lakh maturity value.

Participants may hold or need to hedge various government securities of different maturities and coupon interest rates, whereas the futures market will have only one of them as the basis variety. The basis variety in this case was, until 2014, notional and there may have been no security with exactly a 10-year maturity and exactly a 7 per cent coupon rate. These necessitated pricing adjustments which are called 'conversion factors'. Therefore, while futures trading took place on the basis of the notional variety, settlement of contracts is based on adjustments to take account of the actual securities involved.

In the case of the 10YGS7 contract, the conversion factor 'would be equal to the price of the deliverable security (per rupee of principal) on the first calendar day of the delivery month, to yield 7 per cent with semiannual compounding'.[3] As an illustration, Table 5.1 gives the conversion factors for certain government securities maturing in 2021 and 2022 as of September 2012.

Table 5.1: Deliverable basket and conversion factor for September 2012 contract

Sr. No.	ISIN nomenclature	Date of maturity	Conversion factor
1	IN0020110022 7.80% 2021	11-Apr-2021	1.0506
2	IN0020060318 7.94%2021	24-May-2021	1.0595

---

2 http://www.thehindubusinessline.com/money-and-banking/interest-rate-futures-lose-steam-in-2016/article8490493.ece.

3 NSE website.

Sr. No.	ISIN nomenclature	Date of maturity	Conversion factor
3	IN0020010040 10.25% 2021	30-May-2021	1.2056
4	IN0020110030 8.79% 2021	8-Nov-2021	1.1180
5	IN0020060037 8.20 % 2022	15-Feb-2022	1.0805
6	IN0020020072 8.35% 2022	14-May-2022	1.0925
8	IN0020039031 5.87%2022	28-Aug-2022	0.9210

Source: NSE website (exact data points not available as refreshes on a real time basis).

This table helped buyers and sellers to determine the amount to be paid for the actual security delivered against the contract. The quantity (principal amount) of bonds delivered would be the same as the principal amount of the futures contract: if one lot of 10YGS7 had been sold, the seller would have to deliver a government security with ₹ 2 lakh nominal value (since ₹ 2 lakh is the lot size of the contract) but the price paid would be based on the conversion factor. If a security has a conversion rate of 1.2, it means that one unit of the security is equivalent to 1.2 units of the notional security and hence the price payable will be 1.2 times the price of the notional security on the settlement date. For the futures contract maturing in September 2012, the notional futures contract was based on a 10 year notional government bond expiring in September 2022 with a 7 per cent semi annual coupon. The trade could actually be settled by giving equivalent quantity of April 2021 Government of India bonds having a 7.8 per cent coupon rate. Since a bond with higher coupon is being delivered the actual amount of cash received by the seller will be the settlement price of the futures contract multiplied by 1.0506 (see line 1 of the table). If the seller delivered the August 2022 Government of India bonds having a 5.87 per cent coupon rate, then the amount received by the seller would be the settlement price of the contract multiplied by 0.921 (see line 8 of the table), and so on.

Post-2014 system: Cash settlement based on a single security

One of the reasons why interest rate futures on the NSE had not been liquid is because they were settled by actual delivery (of only Government of India bonds, with the appropriate conversion factor). While various commodity hedgers and speculators can often get their hands on various standardised commodities to keep the market liquid, it is more difficult in the case of Indian government bonds because most of them are owned by public sector banks. In 2013, the Reserve Bank made a fresh attempt to popularise them, and in January 2014 a new instrument was launched. From 2014 onwards, contracts are based on an identified actual Government of India security with approximately ten years to maturity (rather than a notional security) with a contract size of ₹ 2 lakhs and settled only by cash with no actual deliveries. The long term bond futures market has become more liquid. The market does not allow delivery, so conversion factors etc. are no longer applicable. (However, the US Treasury bond market uses a notional basis with conversion factors.)

A second reason for interest rate futures not becoming active in India is that the bond market itself is inactive. A third factor is that in India short term and long term interest rates tend to move together, reducing the need for hedging of mismatches between assets and liabilities. Analysis by Shah showed that from 1997 to 2009, the simple correlation coefficient of the 90 day rate and the ten year rate was around 0.75 in the USA but around 0.95 in India.[4]

Understanding the underlying

Interest rate futures have developed their own conventions and terminology over time. Given the relative recency and limited liquidity of the Indian IRFs, examples from the US interest rate futures markets will primarily be used to illustrate certain concepts relating to interest rate futures.

Duration

The duration of a bond (or a bond portfolio) does not literally mean the remaining time or average time to maturity, as it may seem from the colloquial meaning of the word (though it is a fact that, for a given coupon and other factors being equal, securities with a longer period left to maturity have a longer 'duration'). More precisely, duration is a measurement of how long, in years, it takes for the price of a bond to be repaid by the cash flows (interest and principal) coming from the bond. For a normal or 'vanilla' bond (where there are periodic

---

4   'How useful are the new interest rate futures?' Available at: http://ajayshahblog.blogspot. sg/2009/09/how-useful-are-new-interest-rate.html, 7 September 2009.

interest payments followed by a final repayment of principal), the duration will be less than the time remaining for maturity—this is because a part of the price paid for the bond is being received each year. For a zero-coupon bond, i.e., one issued at a price lower than the amount payable at maturity but with no periodic interest payment, the duration is equal to its time to maturity. For this reason, bond duration (also called the 'Macaulay duration') is expressed in time or number of years.

Duration is a measure of the *sensitivity of the price of a security to a change in interest rates* – the higher the duration, the more the price of the security will change for a given change in interest rates; a bond with a duration of seven years will fluctuate more when interest rates change than a bond with a duration of two years. When using duration for the purpose of measuring sensitivity, another definition, known as 'modified duration', is often used. Modified duration is discussed later in this chapter.

Day count fraction conventions

Bond coupons are payable at specified intervals of time, say every six months. But a calendar year has an odd number of days. Similarly, different months have different numbers of days – 28 or 29 in February, 30 in June, 31 in March etc. The question that arises is how to reckon the amount of interest due for fractional periods. The contract could be based on assuming that a 'year' consists of 360 days with each month having 30 days. Alternatively, it could be measured by the exact number of days. It is important that parties to a transaction know the convention in advance. To avoid ambiguity about the amount of interest and timing of payment, conventions have evolved for counting the time period, known as 'day count fraction conventions' or simply 'day count conventions'. (This is sometimes abbreviated to 'DCF', not to be confused with Discounted Cash Flow.) The convention used for a particular contract will determine the exact period of time to which the interest rate applies, and the period of time used to calculate accrued interest (when the instrument is bought or sold between coupon dates).

In the US Treasury bond market – the world's most liquid market – the interest due is calculated by using actual numbers of days for both months and years. On the other hand, in the corporate and municipal bond markets, durations are rounded up to 30 days for a month and 360 days for a year. For example, under the latter convention there are 30 days in February 2013, but only 28 days by the former convention and thus the amount payable as coupon in February will vary between the two markets. The US money market (short-term private debt) market has a mixed convention known as Actual/360. Under this convention, the numerator is always the actual number of days like in the treasury market, but the denominator is based on a 360-day convention. For this reason, under this convention, a 10 per cent bond will earn slightly more than 10 per cent in a single year – since the interest payable will be 365/360 x 10 per cent. These three conventions are referred to simply as Actual/Actual (use actual number of days divided by 365 or 366 in a leap year), 30/360 and Actual/360, and there are more variants. The LIBOR (discussed earlier) is also quoted on an Actual/360 basis, except for GBP or British Pound which is quoted on an Actual/365 basis.

India generally follows the actual (i.e., actual number of days in each month and 365/366 days per year) basis. For example, a bond of ₹ 1,000 maturing in 180 days paying an annual coupon of 7 per cent will accrue/deliver:

(180/365) x (0.70 x 1000) = ₹ 34.52

If a 360 day convention had been used, it would have accrued/delivered ₹ 35:

(180/360) x (0.70 x 1000) = ₹ 35.

Short-term instruments are often traded not by quoting their market prices, but by their 'discount rates'. For example, if the face value is $1000 and the 'price' of a 182-day Treasury bill is 10, this implies that the *annualised* rate of interest is 10 per cent of the face value of 1000 USD, i.e., $100. For Treasury bonds and notes, the US still follows the anachronistic system of reporting prices in thirty-secondths i.e., fractions with thirty-two as denominator.

Accrued interest

When bonds are bought or sold between the dates of two interest payments, this needs to be properly reflected in the pricing to reflect the interest which has accrued on the date of purchase. For treasury securities in America, the formula used is:

Cash price or 'dirty price' = quoted price or 'clean price' + accrued interest amount since last payment date.

Conversion factor and cheapest-to-deliver (CTD) concept

As in the case of the pre-2014 long term bond futures market in India, the US futures markets are usually based on a notional underlying allowing actual delivery of bonds of the same basic type (i.e., treasury bond for treasury bond, corporate bond for corporate bond etc.) with somewhat different expiry dates and coupon rates. (Under the rules of the futures contract, very different coupon rates and expiry dates may not be acceptable because they may not serve the needs of the long position holder.) When a short position holder delivers a bond against the futures contract, he receives:

Most recent settlement price × Conversion factor + Accrued interest

The conversion factors for delivery are set in advance and actual movements in the cash market for various bonds may not exactly match the prices given by these conversion formulae. This means that those who are 'short' in the futures contract (i.e., have to deliver the bond at the time of expiry) should be watchful to *deliver the one that costs the least to them.* Example 5.3 illustrates this. (This concept is not applicable to IRFs on India's NSE since 2014 since the contract does not allow actual delivery and allows only cash settlement.)

Example 5.3

A fund holding a large and diversified portfolio of bonds was short US treasury futures because it expected interest rates to rise (when interest rates rise, generally bonds fall in value – other things being equal). Instead of squaring up its position, the fund decided to hold its position until expiry. Now, it must deliver some bonds to the exchange. The most recent settlement price is 95–16 or 95.50 (since the price is quoted in 1/32nds, 95–16 means 95 and 16/32 i.e., 95.50). Four bonds are eligible for use for settlement in lieu of the notional underlying:

Bond 1: Quoted price of 101.25 and conversion factor of 1.047

Bond 2: Quoted price of 153.75 and conversion factor of 1.602

Bond 3: Quoted price of 159.50 and conversion factor of 1.654

Bond 4: Quoted price of 125.00 and conversion factor of 1.301

Taking Bond 1, its market value (based on the quoted price) is 101.25. If it is delivered against the contract, the amount received will be the settlement price adjusted for the conversion factor, i.e.

95.5 x 1.047 = 99.9885.

This is less than the market value of the bond. By delivering this bond, the fund will incur a loss of 101.25 – 99.9885 = 1.2615 per bond due to the pricing difference between the bond (cash) market and the formula used in the futures market (this is a kind of 'basis' issue). Similarly, the market value and delivery value of the other bonds can be computed, producing the following list of the net loss (or cost) from delivering different bonds:

1. 101.25-(95.5 x 1.047) = $ 1.262
2. 153.75-(95.5 x 1.602)= $ 0.759
3. 159.50-(95.5 x 1.654)= $ 1.543
4. 125.00-(95.5 x 1.301)= $ 0.755

Therefore, the cheapest-to-deliver or 'CTD' bond in this case is Bond 4.

Pricing of interest rate futures

The same relationship used to determine the futures or forward price in other markets can be used for IRFs too. The standard futures or forward pricing formula as shown in chapter 4 was:

$F \leq S + C - Y$

In the case of debt instruments, there are no storage costs and no convenience yields. However, there is a carrying cost reflecting the opportunity cost of the funds deployed and a real yield reflecting the interest rate on the bond involved. The carrying cost and the yield can be simply calculated by multiplying the relevant interest rate for the relevant period of time by the amount involved (i.e., the spot price). Financial instruments are not subject to discontinuities in production or storage (see Table 4.1). Therefore, they generally reflect the carrying cost approach to futures pricing and the formula becomes an equation rather than an inequality:

$$F = S+C-Y$$

i.e., $F = S + (C-Y)$

i.e., $F = S + S(c_t-y_t)$

i.e., $F = S (1+ c_t-y_t)$

Where S = spot price of the bond

c = interest rate on funds borrowed (opportunity cost) for the time t (not per annum)[5]

y = interest rate on the bond for the time t (not per annum)[6]

t = time period involved

---

5   If the applicable rate of interest is 12 per cent per annum and the period under consideration is three months, then for this purpose i_t will be 3 per cent.

6   If the applicable rate of interest is 6 per cent per annum and the period under consideration is three months, then for this purpose y_t will be 1.5 per cent.

Typically, the yield on bonds exceeds the short term opportunity cost of capital so
$y_t > c_t$ and $Y > C$.

Let the net amount of the yield on the bond (after subtracting cost of funds) be

$Y - C = I$

and let $y_t - c_t = i_t$.

Then, substituting I for $C-Y$ and i_t for c_t-y_t, the formula becomes

$F = S-I$

i.e., $F = S(1-i_t)$

where,

F = futures price

S = spot price of the bond

I = amount of interest (absolute amount) earned for the period after deducting cost of funds

$i_t = y_t - c_t$ = percentage yield on the bond nett of cost of funds for the time period t (not per annum).[7]

This formula ignores the compounding factor. If continuous compounding is used it can be shown mathematically that the formula becomes:

$F = (S-I)e^{rt}$

Where,

$r = c$ = risk free rate of interest *per annum* (generally taken as the Treasury bill rate)

t = time period measured in number of years involved (e.g., three months =0.25)

e is a mathematical constant (like π) known as Euler's number or the exponential constant (approximately equal to 2.7182818282).

The risk free interest rate means the interest rate which does not reflect any premium for the possible credit risk (i.e., risk of the borrower not repaying). Hence, the rate of interest paid by the government on its Treasury Bills is generally taken as the risk-free rate.

---

7   If the cost of borrowing is 12 per cent per annum and the yield on the bond is 6 per cent per annum and the period under consideration is three months, then i_t will be 1.5 per cent (i.e. 12 per cent minus 6 per cent but for a period of three months or 0.25 years).

Example 5.4 Bond futures

In March, a company finds it has a temporary surplus cash of ₹ 10 lakhs, which it will require for other uses by September. It wishes to invest the amount in gilt-edged stock because of the attractive interest yield but is apprehensive about a possible rise in market interest rates which may reduce the bond price. It therefore buys ₹10 lakhs nominal of 9 per cent Government of India bonds, whose current spot market rate is ₹ 92 per ₹100 of nominal bonds. (This happens to be the bond used as the basis for the futures contract too.) It hedges the transaction on the futures market and the results are as follows:

Date	Action	
	Spot market	**Futures market**
1 March	*Buy ₹ 10 lakhs nominal at 92 per cent* *Pay ₹920,000*	*Sell ₹10 lakhs nominal of September futures at 93 per cent.* *Pay ₹93,000 as margin (deposit)*
31 August	*Sell ₹10 lakhs nominal at 89 per cent* *Receive ₹890,000.*	*Buy ₹10 lakhs nominal of September futures at 89 per cent* *Receive ₹(930,000 − 890,000) = ₹40,000 as profit plus ₹93,000 margin refund.*

As shown above, interest rates did indeed increase by August, resulting in a fall in gilt prices from 92 to 89. The financial institution has received coupon interest for the half year of ₹45,000, but if it had not hedged itself, it would have lost ₹30,000 through fall in bond values. However, because it had hedged itself, its spot market loss of ₹30,000 is compensated for by a gain of ₹40,000 on the futures trade. (The slight excess gain reflects the change in futures-spot spread.)

Eurodollar futures

As mentioned, one of the most heavily traded IRF contract in the world is the three-month or ninety-day Eurodollars futures contract, traded on the CME. The standardised notional underlying is 1 million US Dollars. Deliveries are available for March, June, September and December,for many years into the future.

A one-basis point move in the relevant Eurodollar interest rate means a move (up or down) in the interest rate of 0.01 percentage points. On 1 million dollars, this corresponds to 1/10,000th multiplied by 1 million or 100 dollars.

Since the contract is of three months (or one-fourth of a year), each basis point increase in the interest rate causes a loss of \$ 25 per long Eurodollar contract (and one basis point decrease creates a profit of the same absolute amount).

Generally, the Eurodollar interest rates are very close to the LIBOR as both represent average rates at which prominent banks loan each other funds.

Example 5.5: Short term interest rate (long hedge)

On 15 April, an Indian IT company clinches a lucrative software contract and is expecting a large receipt in October for about \$10 million and would need to invest it for a three month period from then. It is apprehensive that the interest rate on deposits may fall between April and October and hedges by 'locking in' a rate of interest for the October to January period. The October Eurodollar futures are quoting at 97.500. Based on the method of price quotation of Eurodollars, this means that the rate of interest implied is

100-97.5 = 2.5 per cent.

The investor hedges by buying 10 contracts, the lot size being \$ 1million.

On October 15th the three-month Eurodollar rate is 2.1 per cent. The final settlement in the contract is thus at a price of 97.90. In the Eurodollar contract, the prices are quoted in terms of annual interest rate but the contract is for a three month deposit. Therefore a movement of 0.01 per cent or in interest rates or 1 basis point (e.g., from 97.99 to 97.98) implies a change (per contract) of

0.01per cent x ¼ x 1,000,000 = \$25

The Eurodollar future has appreciated from 97.5 to 97.9, i.e., by 40 basis points or 0.40 per cent. As the company has bought 10 contracts (worth \$10 million), the resulting gain is:

40 basis points x \$25 per basis point x 10 contracts = \$10,000

It now invests the sum of \$10 million for 3 months at the ruling interest rate of 2.1 per cent per annum for three months and earns:

\$10,000,000 x 2.1 per cent x 3/12 = \$52,500.

The total return, adding the gain on the futures contract is:

\$52,500 + 10,000 = \$62,500.

This return amounts to:

62,500/10,000,000 = 0.625 per cent for three months,

i.e., 0.625 per cent x 4 = 2.5 per cent for a full year.

Thus, the company was able to successfully fix the return at the 2.5 per cent level prevailing when the hedge was undertaken, even though interest rates fell later to 2.1 per cent.

The transactions are summarised in the following table:

Date	Action	
	Spot market	**Futures market**
15 April	Acquire 'deferred asset' (i.e. cash due in future) of $10m	Buy 10 contracts of October Eurodollar futures worth $10m @ 97.5 Pay margin of $10m x 97.5 per cent x 10 per cent =$97,500
15 October	Receive cash and deposit it at 2.1 per cent per annum for three months	Sell 10 contracts of October Eurodollar futures worth $10m @97.9. Receive refund of $97,500 _plus_ profit of (97.9-97.5) per cent x 3/12 x $10m= $(97,500+ 10,000) = $107,500.
15 January	Receive back $10m. Receive interest thereon of 2.1 per cent x 3/12 x $10m= $52,500.	

Example 5.6: Short–term interest rate (short hedge)

In July, an Indian company secures an order which will require borrowing of ₹50 crores for working capital for three months from September. The company's short term borrowing rate is 1 per cent above the Treasury Bill rate. It is apprehensive that interest rates will rise before then and hedges the risk in the 91 day T Bill market (assumed to be active). Interest rates (Treasury Bill yields) turn out to be as follows:

July 1   8.50 per cent

September 1   8.25 per cent

Date	Action	
	Spot market	**Futures market**
1 July	Acquire 'deferred liability' (i.e., payment due in future) of ₹50 cr.	Sell 2,500 contracts of 91 day T Bills at 91.50 Pay margin of 91.5 per cent x ₹50 cr. x 10 per cent = ₹457.5 lakhs

Date	Action	
	Spot market	*Futures market*
1 September	Borrow ₹50 cr. @ T-Bill rate plus 1 per cent i.e., 9.25 per cent	Buy back 2,500 contracts of 91 day T Bill at 91.75 Receive margin refund of ₹ 457.5 lakhs less loss of (91.75-91.50) per cent x 3/12 x ₹ 50 cr.= ₹ (457.5-3.125) lakhs. = ₹ 454.375 lakhs
1 December	Repay ₹50 cr. along with interest thereon of 9.25 per cent x 3/12 x ₹ 50 cr.= ₹ 115.625 lakhs	

Total cost of borrowing: ₹ lakhs

Interest paid: 115.625

Loss on futures: 3.125

                                          118.750

Effective rate of interest for 3 months = 118.75/ 5000 × 100 = 2.375 per cent

Annualised rate of interest = 2.375 × $\dfrac{12}{3}$ = 9.5 per cent

The company ends up paying 9.5per cent (i.e., 8.5per cent + 1per cent margin over T Bills)-the rate which it wanted to ensure. (Its expectation that rates of interest would rise was belied and it would have been better off by not hedging, in this particular instance,but that is with hindsight!)

Adjusting hedges to fit futures contract specifications

As pointed out above, interest rate futures contracts are often either notional (against which many securities can be delivered) or can only be settled in cash against a specified bond or instrument. In such cases, a hedger seeking to hedge a particular asset or liability has to adjust his hedge carefully so that the outcomes on the futures contract match those on the spot market. Even where the underlying is an exact match, there can be slight mismatches in other parameters: example, a month may have 28 days or 31 days whereas the contract may be for 30 days. (The examples above deliberately circumvented these issues by choosing appropriate instruments, dates and hedge sizes.) A complete discussion of all the techniques involved in ensuring near perfect hedging outcomes is beyond the scope of this book as it involves a number of complexities. In this section, an outline is given of the main points to be borne in mind in real-life hedging situations.

Hedge period vs. market months

Often a hedge may be required for a period beyond the last available maturity. Alternatively, the last maturity may be illiquid and hence the hedge may be placed in a nearer month. In such cases a roll-over transaction may be required, which usually involves a transaction cost and may also involve a small basis risk (i.e., risk of change in spread) as a result of roll-over.

Size of exposure vs market lot

The exposure to be hedged often differs from a whole number of market lots. For instance, a company may want to hedge an exposure of $ 2.3 million in Eurodollar futures. The market lot is $1 million. The hedger will have to choose the nearest whole number of contracts—in this case two. However, this leaves some exposure unhedged (or creates a new exposure in case the number is rounded upwards). The larger the size of the risk to be hedged, the easier it is to get an almost exact correspondence of the hedge quantity. If a $ 20.3 million exposure is hedged using 20 futures contracts with aggregate value of $ 20 million, the unhedged residue is just 1.5 per cent of the exposure whereas it was 13 per cent in the $ 2 million case.

Equivalency or hedge ratio

Because of differences between the instrument being hedged and the basis grade of a financial futures contract, weighted hedges may have to be used in many cases. As discussed in chapter 4, the cash-futures equivalency ratio (also called the hedge ratio) is a parameter which reflects the nominal value of futures contracts needed to hedge a given nominal value of spot market exposure. In general, for any financial futures transaction, the number of futures contracts to be bought/sold can be calculated as follows:

$$\frac{\text{Nominal value to be hedged x equivalency ratio}}{\text{Nominal value of one futures contract (market lot)}}$$

Example 5.7

Hedger wants to hedge £376,000 in the long gilt market. The contract size on the London International Financial Futures Exchange for long gilts is £50,000. The equivalency ratio has already been determined as 1.3. How many futures contracts should he trade?

Solution: (376,000 x 1.3) / 50,000= 9.776

Since partial contracts cannot be traded, the hedger should trade 10 contracts in this case.

In the example, an equivalency ratio was already given. In practice, determining it for interest rate futures is quite complicated, much more so than for other types of financial futures. Some of the main factors affecting this are given below.

Term of the hedge

When hedging a financial instrument which has a term different from the futures contract, it is necessary to weight the hedge pro rata. For instance, if a 30-day contract is being used to hedge an exposure over the month of December which has 31 days, the equivalency ratio will be 31/30, other things being equal.

Example 5.8

A hedger wants to hedge $ 5 million in a 90-day Eurodollar contract having a contract size of $ 100,000, to take care of an exposure from June 1 to August 31: How many contracts should he trade?

Solution:

The equivalency ratio has to be determined first. The period runs for 92 days as against the contract period of 90 days. The ratio is therefore 92/90.

No. of contracts needed = $(5,000,000/100,000) x (92/90) = 51.11

So he has to trade 51 contracts not 50.

Conversion factor

As already discussed, where the basis (i.e., deliverable) grade for a contract is notional, conversion factors are supplied by the exchange (equivalent to tendering differences in a commodity exchange) if settlement by delivery is allowed. Because of differences between the instrument being hedged and the basis grade of the futures contract, weighted hedges may have to be used in many cases. For instance, if the conversion factor for a particular gilt is 0.75, then this should be taken as the equivalency factor for calculating the number of contracts to be traded, so that the size of the futures trade matches the size of the spot market risk. Even in a cash–settled market, when hedging a security in the same class but with different maturity and coupon, the hedger must be careful to weight his hedge by a suitable conversion factor.

Price sensitivity

In the previous paragraph, the need to weight the hedge by the conversion factor was referred to. The use of conversion factors ensures that the overall size of the hedge is appropriate. Though this is better than an unweighted hedge, it is still not sufficient to ensure close correspondence between spot and futures price risks, because of the sensitivity factor. The extent to which the price of a long-term security changes for a given change in interest rate, is affected by several factors. Among these factors are the maturity period (or tenor) of the security as well as the coupon rate. (Even intuitively, it is easy to see that a 1 per cent change in interest rate effective for a period of one year is less significant than a 1 per cent change which will be effective for a period of 20 years.) Without getting into the complexities of bond pricing, one can say that:

a.   Other things being equal, the longer the maturity, the greater the sensitivity of the price for a given change in interest rate (e.g., a 30-year 9 per cent bond is more sensitive than a 10-year 9 per cent bond).

b.   Other things being equal, the smaller the coupon, the greater the sensitivity of the price for a given change in interest rate (e.g., a 2 per cent 10-year bond is more sensitive than a 9 per cent 10-year bond).

c.   Other things being equal, the smaller the yield[8] the greater the sensitivity of the price for a given change in interest (a bond yielding 5 per cent will be more sensitive than a bond yielding 7 per cent).

Because of this, when hedging through the gilt or bond futures markets, it is necessary to adjust for the differences in price sensitivity between:

---

8   Yield is based on the current market price whereas coupon is based on the issue or nominal price.

- the asset or liability to be hedged; and
- the notional basis instrument in the futures market (e.g. the 6 per cent coupon 15-20 year T Bond in CME) or the actual bond which forms the basis grade (as in the case of the 10 year Government of India securities futures).

Otherwise, the price change in the spot market will be under- or over-compensated in the futures market. The adjustment is done by means of adjustments for duration (or basis point value) and convexity (all of which are specific, mathematically defined, terms).

Duration has already been discussed earlier. Duration is a number reflecting the weighted average maturity period in years of a bond after adjusting for coupon rates, frequency of interest and principal payment etc., all of which affect the proportionate change in price for a given change in yield. While duration (also known as Macaulay duration) is measured in years and is an indirect measure of sensitivity, 'modified duration' is a direct measure of price sensitivity to interest rates. It is simply: Percentage change in bond price/Percentage change in interest rates.

Modified duration is in many contexts simply referred to as 'duration', and this can be confusing. Readers should note that if the term 'duration' is used, they should check the context and the unit of measurement (years vs. a ratio) to understand which concept of duration is being referred to. However, the duration and the modified duration are usually close to each other numerically, and in a very approximate and rough sense, the two terms can be used interchangeably; thus a bond with a sensitivity (modified duration) of seven (i.e., .07 per cent price change per .01 per cent change in interest rates) can be taken as having a duration of approximately seven years.

While the modified duration gives the proportionate change in price for a given change in interest rates, another related term known as the basis point value is the absolute change in price (in £, $ or ₹) per basis point change in yield and is similar to the duration except that it is calculated as an absolute amount. It is absolute value of change in bond price per 0.01 per cent change in interest rates (i.e., per basis point).

It should be noted that the modified duration and basis point value for the same bond are *different at different yield levels*. Thus, the price change caused by a drop in yield from 10 per cent to 9 per cent will be different from the price change caused by a drop in yield from 5 per cent to 4 per cent.

Example 5.9

The UK has some 'perpetual' government securities which are not redeemable and just continue to pay interest indefinitely. One such is the 3.5 per cent War Loan. This security is simple to price as there is no maturity value or maturity date and hence provides a simplified illustration of how the modified duration changes at different levels of interest rate.

Assume the current interest rate is 10 per cent. For the War Loan to yield 10 per cent, its price must be
   3.5/.1 = 35

Now assume the interest rate changes to 9 per cent. The price will change to
   3.5/0.09 = 38.89

A 1 per cent change in interest rates produced a change in price of
   (38.89-35)/35 = 11.11 per cent, i.e., modified duration = 11.11

When the interest rate is 5 per cent, the price of the War Loan will be:
   3.5/0.05 = 70

If it changes from 5 per cent to 4 per cent, the price will become:
   3.5/0.04 = 87.5

The change is:
   (87.5-75)/75 = 16.66 per cent, i.e., modified duration = 16.67.

So the modified duration has increased.

The convexity is a measure of *how the duration/basis point value itself changes at different prices.* Using the three concepts together it is possible to work out how a given price change will affect a particular bond. However, for small changes in interest rates, the convexity can be ignored for practical purposes and calculations can be done using just the duration.

Another aspect of price sensitivity is the correlation between different kinds of interest rates. At any given time, interest rates for different periods of time (short term to long term) may be different. This relationship when expressed graphically is called the 'yield curve'. Normally, long term rates are higher than short term rates. When interest rates change, they may sometimes display a similar change in all interest rates; in that case the yield curve shifts upwards or downwards in a parallel movement. However, it is also possible that the yield curve may change in shape. For example, a 1 per cent change in short term interest rates may be accompanied by only a 0.2 per cent change in the 10 year interest rate, and the change for maturities below 10 years may lie somewhere between the two. Thus, this aspect (changes to the yield curve) will also have to be factored in. Similarly, when using futures as a cross hedge – e.g., using gilt-edge government security futures to hedge a holding of corporate bonds –

the correlation may be partial. A 1 per cent change in the 10 year government bond yield may produce, say, a 1.1 per cent change in corporate bond yields. Unlike the duration, basis point value and convexity, correlations between one instrument and another cannot be determined by mathematical calculation. One can only make predictions based on past behaviour and statistical analysis which of course are subject to error. Such cross hedges are therefore not always effective.

The manner of making these adjustments is beyond the scope of this book. In crude or approximate terms however, it is possible to calculate an appropriate hedge ratio without considering convexity, yield curve changes or correlations between different interest rates.

Simplified calculation of the hedge ratio

Take the cases of an investor with a large fixed interest bond portfolio. Rising interest rates would reduce the value of the portfolio (because bond prices will fall). The risk can be hedged by 'shorting' (i.e., selling) bond futures. (A person who has taken on a floating-rate mortgage loan will also lose when interest rates rise and can, similarly, hedge by shorting bond futures.) Since some contracts for the distant future may not have enough liquidity, a good hedge may involve shorting the most liquid and easily available interest rate futures, adjusting for the effective duration of the bond portfolio.

Assume that interest rate changes equally for different maturities, i.e., the shape of the yield curve is unchanged. The long bond portfolio will change in value and the extent of the change will be approximately:

Portfolio value x portfolio modified duration x change in yield (interest rate)

$$= V_p \times D_p \times \Delta Y \ldots (1)$$

Where,

V_p = value of the portfolio (strictly speaking, this should be the value at the maturity of the hedge, but as an approximation the current value can be taken)

D_p = modified duration of the portfolio at the maturity of the hedge

ΔY = change in yield

The change in the value of the futures contract used as hedge will be approximately (per contract):

Contract price x modified duration of futures contract x change in yield

$= V_f \times D_f \times \Delta Y \ldots\ldots (2)$

Where,

V_f = value (contract price) of the futures contract

D_f = modified duration of the futures contract at the maturity of the contract

ΔY = change in yield

Here, D_f is the duration of the underlying assets underlying this contract at the maturity of this contract.

The number of contracts N needed to carry out the hedge would hedge would be:

$$N = \frac{V_p \times D_p \times \Delta Y}{V_f \times D_f \times \Delta Y}$$

Cancelling ΔY,

$$N = \frac{V_p \times D_p}{V_f \times D_f}$$

This ratio is known as the duration-based hedge ratio or the price sensitivity hedge ratio. It may have to be rounded up or down to get the actual number of futures contracts traded.

Example 5.10

A fixed income portfolio manager has been successful over the first nine months of the financial year, and she wants to lock in her profits. It is 1 January and the financial year for her firm ends on 31 March. She expects volatility and an increase in interest rates in the coming months. She controls a $100 million portfolio invested in non-US sovereign bonds. Three months from now, her portfolio duration will be five years.

She is considering using the March T-bond futures contract to hedge the portfolio. The current price of the March contract is 97-01(i.e., 97 and 1/32) or 97.03125. Since the face value of the futures contract is $100,000, the contract price is $97,031.25. The yield on this is 8 per cent, and the duration will be around 10 years at the end of March, i.e., after three months. How should she hedge the portfolio using T-bond futures?

Solution:

She has a long position in bonds and therefore needs to hedge by going short in the treasury futures. The duration is five years, which can be assumed to be a modified duration of five also. The number of contracts that she should sell should be:

$$N = \frac{V_p \times D_p}{V_f \times D_f}$$

Or,

$$N = \frac{100\ million \times 5}{97031.25 \times 10} = 515.3$$

Therefore, she should sell 515 contracts. In this way, her interest rate risk is likely to be almost fully immunised. Note however that:

- *if the interest rate on non-US sovereign bonds changes at a different rate from the interest rate on US treasury bonds, or*

- *if the five year interest rate changes by a different amount from the 10 year interest rate,*

then her hedge may not neutralise her risk and she may have a net profit or loss resulting from the hedge.

Asset-liability management (ALM) by financial institutions like banks

Banks generally lend for long durations, but take deposits for much shorter durations. That means the average duration of their liabilities is smaller than that of their assets. A sudden and sharp rise in interest rates would reduce the value of both assets and liabilities but the value of a bank's liabilities would fall less steeply than the value of assets. This would diminish the bank's equity. Hence, banks generally need to hedge against interest rate changes, and more specifically interest rate increases. (No doubt, if they hedge against rising interest rates, they are effectively forgoing the benefit from falling interest rates.)

This can be done through various ways – using interest rate futures or forwards to hedge generally involves a strategy known as duration matching. Such hedging of an entire portfolio is often called macro-hedging (as against the hedging of single bond which is micro-hedging). Investment funds and treasury departments of companies also use the process, and often call it 'portfolio immunisation'.

An important thing to remember is that:

- no macro-hedging strategy for a portfolio as a whole with many different instruments; and

- no micro-hedging strategy involving cross-hedges, i.e., hedging an instrument very different from the basis grade, is *perfect or risk-free.*

'Duration matching' only protects against parallel shifts in interest rates, not against non-parallel shifts which alter the shape of the yield curve. Changes in the shape of the yield curve may be anticipated using statistical correlations but these may turn out to be inaccurate.

6

Currency Futures

Any company or individual with dealings in foreign exchange, whether through imports or exports or through inward or outward investments, lending or borrowing, faces some degree of exchange rate risk. Currency forwards or futures are forward or futures contracts with a foreign currency as the underlying. Thus, a contract for the purchase of US dollars denominated in Indian rupees is effectively a contract on the Indian rupee – US dollar exchange rate (referred to as INR: USD). Currency forwards or futures can therefore also be referred to as exchange rate forwards or futures. The basic pricing and trading structure of currency futures and forwards is not different from examples of equity or commodity futures that were seen in previous chapters, but this chapter will explore some of the special features of currency forwards and futures in greater detail. In the foreign exchange markets, a three letter convention is commonly used to refer to currencies – INR for Indian Rupees, USD for US Dollars, GBP for Great Britain Pounds, JPY for Japanese Yen etc.

Typically, hedging needs of smaller firms and for short durations are served better by standardised exchange-traded futures, whereas larger firms with specialised needs and more long-term hedging requirements often go to the forward (OTC) market. Forward contracts are typically entered into through banks, either directly or through a foreign subsidiary. Many India-based multi-nationals, for example, access INR-USD OTC forwards of various kinds in the Singapore market.

Example 6.1

In March, P Ltd., an importer of paper and pulp machinery has a contractual requirement to pay USD 100 million in September, and any pre- or post-payment is not advantageous from an interest rate or liquidity point of view. The rupee revenue from selling these imported machines in the domestic (Indian) market is more or less predictable but P Ltd. still bears the currency risk due to the amount payable being denominated in a foreign currency. The current exchange rate is INR 60 per USD and the forward rate for September is also INR 60 per USD. (Interest rate on rupees and dollars is assumed to be zero in this example – thus there is neither a carrying cost nor a yield.)

One possibility is to buy September USD futures for 100 million through an exchange, but this may not be practicable for such a large sum given the illiquidity on the exchanges. More realistically, a forward contract would be executed through a bank.

Assume the margin required by the bank is 10 per cent, and so P Ltd. has to pay

10 per cent × 60 × 100 million = ₹60 crores

as initial margin.

Between the date of the contract and the maturity date, there will be mark-to-market (MTM) margins imposed by the bank as the market exchange rate fluctuates.

If the rupee appreciates, P Ltd. will have to pay additional margins to cover the mark-to-market losses and keep the level of margin at 10 per cent or the agreed proportion to the prevailing market value.

In the month of June, the exchange rate rises suddenly to INR 58 per USD. The loss on the contract is now

(58-60) × INR 100 million = 200 million INR = 20 crore INR.

The net margin available with the bank has diminished when this loss is taken into account. The margin available with the bank is now

(Initial margin − MTM losses) = 60 - 20 crore INR = 40 crore INR.

The bank makes a margin call and requires P Ltd. to deposit a further ₹ 20 crore.

By the time the contract matures in September, the rupee has fallen sharply and is ruling at INR 62 per USD. Since P Ltd's currency forward contract is entered into at a price of INR 60 per USD, P Ltd has to 'deliver' 600 crore rupees in exchange for receiving 100 million dollars. So far it has already paid:

₹ 60 crore in March (initial margin) + ₹ 20 crore in June (margin call)= ₹ 80 crore.

Therefore it now has to deliver the balance, i.e., ₹ (600-80) crore = ₹ 520 crore.

Had this been a futures contract, an alternative would be to 'square off' the transaction. In this case, P Ltd would sell 100 million USD at 62 and thus offset its earlier purchase. It would receive the nett amount of (62-60) x 100 million = 200 million INR or ₹ 20 crore as its profit on the currency hedge. This would offset the extra cost it would incur when making the payment to the US. Had P Ltd. remained unhedged, it would have ended up paying ₹ 620 crore to meet its liability. By hedging, it was able to fix its liability at ₹ 600 crores.

Currency prepaid forwards

As seen in Example 6.1, forwards or futures are settled at the time of expiry either:

- by delivering the agreed amount of local currency (at the rate fixed in the forward or futures contract) or

- by squaring off the contract by selling the same quantity and paying (or receiving) the difference between the exchange rate on the settlement date and the exchange rate at which the contract was entered into.

However, it is also possible to make the main payment now rather than later. Such instruments and/or contracts are called, not surprisingly, currency pre-paid forwards. Suppose in Example 6.1, the interest rate in rupees is 10 per cent per annum; for six months the rate applicable is 5 per cent (ignoring compounding). Assume that the forward rate (i.e., exchange rate on the forward market) is INR 60 per USD. The amount to be pre-paid in such an instrument after adjusting for the time value of money would be (₹ 600 crore/1.05)= ₹ 571 crore.

Pricing of currency futures: Covered interest arbitrage

In chapter 4, it was noted that the relationship between spot and forward prices is given by the following formula:

$$F \leq S + C - Y$$

In the case of currency futures, there are no storage costs and no convenience yields. However, there is a carrying cost reflecting the interest rates on the currency being sold and a real yield reflecting the interest rate on the currency being bought (this will be explained below). The carrying cost and the yield can be simply calculated by multiplying the interest rate by the amount involved (i.e., the spot price). Both of these are proportional to the spot rate and there are no lump sum costs like warehouse rents which might occur for commodities. Therefore, the carrying cost and yield can be calculated as percentages of the spot rate. Foreign exchange is not subject to discontinuities in production or storage. Thus, the expectations approach to pricing is generally irrelevant. Therefore, foreign exchange futures, like other financial futures, generally reflect the carrying cost approach to futures pricing and the formula becomes an equation rather than an inequality:

$$F = S + C - Y$$

i.e., $$F = S + (C-Y)$$

i.e., $$F = S + S (c_t - y_t)$$

i.e., $$F = S(1 + c_t - y_t)$$

where, F = forward exchange rate

S = spot exchange rate

C = carrying cost for the period t (absolute amount)

Y = yield for the period t (absolute amount)

c_t = risk free interest rate on currency being sold (usually domestic currency) for the time t

y_t = risk free interest rate on currency being bought (usually foreign currency) for the time t

This formula ignores the compounding factor. If continuous compounding is used it can be shown mathematically that the formula becomes:

$$F = (S-I)e^{rt} \quad [or] \; F = Se^{c-y}$$

Where,

I = Y − C (this term may be positive or negative depending on the relative interest rates in the two currencies)

r = risk free rate of interest per annum (generally taken as the Treasury bill rate) on currency being sold

t = time period measured in number of years involved (e.g., three months =0.25)

e is the mathematical term (similar to π) known as Euler's number or the exponential constant (approximately equal to 2.7182818282 or 2.718).

c = r = risk free interest rate per annum in the currency being sold (usually domestic currency)

y = risk free interest rate per annum in the currency being bought (usually foreign currency)

t = time period involved in years

Though the continuous compounding formulae call for the use of the risk free interest rate, if data is not available, or even otherwise, a suitable approximation (such as the LIBOR in that currency) can be used without seriously affecting the calculations.

What this formula indicates is that a forward currency exchange rate is a result primarily of the *difference in interest rates between the two relevant currencies*. If one ignores transaction costs and any risk of default, this is all that the forward exchange rate comes down to. It follows that:

a.   Currencies having lower interest rates have their future or forward prices at a premium (contango) compared to the spot exchange rate. The interest rate on the dollar is generally lower than on the rupee. Therefore, the forward exchange rate of the dollar (denominated in rupees) will be higher than the spot rate. For example, if the USD is at 55 INR today, the one year forward rate is likely to be around 60.5 INR if the USD interest rate is 10 per cent lower than the INR interest rate. In terms of the formula,

$F = S + C - Y$, i.e., $F = S + S (c_t - y_t)$

i.e., $F = 55 + 55 (10$per cent$) = 60.5$

b.   Currencies with higher interest rates will have a forward rate which is lower than the spot rate. In the INR case if there was a forward market for a currency which has a higher interest rate than India, the forward exchange rate in INR would be lower than the current exchange rate, i.e., the forward rate would be at a discount (backwardation) *vis-à-vis* the spot exchange rate. (In exchange rate theory, this is known as 'covered interest rate parity'.)

Synthetic forward contract

One can also indirectly or 'synthetically' create a *de facto* currency future instrument by lending in one currency and borrowing in another.

Example 6.2:

X wants to have 100,000 USD three months from now, while fixing the cost in rupees today. He can borrow the appropriate amount of rupees now and buy the dollars. The INR–USD rate is 50, the interest rate in rupees is 8 per cent per annum, and the interest rate in dollars is 2 per cent per annum. Ignore transaction costs and fees. How should this be done?

Solution

X needs 100,000 USD in three months. The annual interest rate in dollars is 2 per cent, so for three months it is 0.5 per cent. This means that

100,000 / 1.005 = 99,502 USD

needs to be bought right now. This will earn interest and become $100,000 in three months.

To get 99502 USD, he needs to borrow:

   99502 × 50 (current exchange rate) = 49,75,100 INR

With a rupee interest rate of 8 per cent per annum, for three months he will have to pay 2 per cent (a quarter of 8 per cent). The total amount he will have to pay including interest is:

49,75,100 × 102 per cent = ₹ 50,74,602.

This is sufficient to hedge the liability. Effectively, by paying ₹50.75 lakhs (approximately) he has obtained $100,000 three months from now. He has effectively got a fixed forward exchange rate without entering into any derivative or forward contract. The net three month forward exchange rate in the example works out to 50.75 which is nothing but,

$$F = S + S(c_t - y_t) = 50 + (2 \text{ per cent} - 0.5 \text{ per cent})50 = 50.75.$$

Note that Example 6.2 did not involve any derivative transaction. This is called 'covered interest arbitrage'. This mechanism, by providing an arbitrage mechanism, ensures that the forward price will always adhere to the equation set out earlier: in the event of any deviation, market participants can borrow rupees and buy spot dollars (as in Example 6.2) and then sell the dollar forwards and make a riskless profit. For instance, if the forward exchange rate for a three month period is 51 instead of 50.75, one can buy dollars on the spot, incur interest in rupees (with a total cost of 50.75 as per Example 6.2) and then sell dollars in the forward market and collect ₹ 51, earning a riskless profit of ₹ 0.25. This involves buying spot and selling forward – it will raise the spot exchange rate and reduce the forward rate until the forward rate becomes equal to the rate indicated by covered interest arbitrage.

The above calculations ignored compounding. For a more accurate calculation, one should use continuous compounding. The fixed-rupee cost that needs to be repaid after the required duration is:

$$Q \times S e^{(c-y)t}$$

Where,

Q is the amount in the foreign currency needed after t (in years) time [foreign currency being the one against whose variations a hedge is required]

c = (risk free) domestic currency interest rate per annum

y = (risk free) foreign currency interest rate per annum

S = spot exchange rate (number of domestic currency units needed to buy one foreign currency unit right now)

t = number of years after which the foreign currency is needed

e = Euler's number

In Example 6.2, this would be $100,000 \times 50 \times 2.718^{(.08-.02)\,0.25} = 50,75,565$ which is about ₹ 963 more than the 'non-compounding' calculation above (an error of less than 2 in 10,000 parts).

Carry trade

The term 'carry trade' simply means to borrow in a low-interest rate currency and invest in either short term deposits in a currency with a higher interest rate or other high yield assets in that currency. The idea is to borrow at a lower rate and lend at a higher rate. The risk is that the exchange rate may change. The hope behind the carry trade is that the borrowed currency will not appreciate or only appreciate slightly in such a way that the appreciation is less than the extra interest earned. In the carry trade, there can sometimes be both an interest rate gain and a currency gain if the borrowed currency depreciates in value.

According to the 'rational expectations' and 'efficient markets' hypotheses of economic theory, the market should theoretically never allow a free lunch; therefore any gains from carry trade over time are likely to be wiped out because of the inherent currency risk. The real world does not necessarily conform to these hypotheses. Currencies have been known to remain under- or over-valued relative to expected levels for long periods of time. Hence the patient, long-term and careful speculator or investor may well be successful in the carry trade. (Note however that the word used is 'may' rather than 'will' and it is equally possible for the carry trade to end in losses.)

As an example, many emerging market Asian government bonds may not be as risky as indicated by various US-centric credit rating agencies, whose rating changes often turn out to be lagging not leading indicators. If one takes this view, then he could borrow by shorting yen or dollar and investing in a diversified portfolio of Asian bonds, among other assets, hoping to profit from the unfairly high risk premia attached. Of course, there is no guarantee that such trades will be successful.

Empirical evidence has shown that returns from carry-trades show negative skew and kurtosis. In other words, carry trade strategies are profitable on the whole but are interspersed with huge losses from time to time. So, carry trades may eventually amount to picking pennies in front of a road roller.

7

Futures on Equities

This chapter deals with the special features of futures markets in equity shares, including equity indices (also known as stock futures and stock index futures). The general principles applicable to futures markets are also applicable to futures in equity markets. The *raison d'etre* of equity futures is to enable the hedging of equity positions.

A special and rather unusual feature of the equity or 'stock futures' market in India is that it is increasingly seen not as a supplement to the cash market but as a substitute. The relatively higher volume of trading on the futures markets in India *vis-à-vis* the cash stock market appears to be explained by two main factors.

The first factor is that India's futures market is one of the few that has active futures trading in *individual shares* (single stock futures) rather than in broad stock market indices. This is partly the legacy of the old Indian *badla* system that was an indigenous form of forward trading in individual shares that ended in the late 1990s and was replaced by equity futures. Because there are futures markets in individual shares, the Indian equity futures markets allow speculation on specific companies without basis risk. When only index futures are available, an investor in the stock market cannot really use futures to back his view on an individual company. The Indian market allows speculation on individual shares through futures.

The second factor is margin or leverage. The *cost, extent,* and *ease* of leverage is higher through futures:

- India's credit markets are not as well developed as in, say, the United States. Getting a loan in order to trade on equities is not easy or quick. The 'automatic borrowing' in the futures market (through the fractional margin system) makes things much easier; there is no formal credit agreement nor the attendant transaction costs and time.

- When a speculator borrows from a broker to buy stock and takes a long position with, say, a '2x' (two times) leverage, the broker lends money for half the position to the investor and charges him interest. In the case of stock futures, when a position is opened, only a fraction of the underlying amount (generally, one-fifth or so) is blocked as margin in the client's account. No interest is charged for the remaining four-fifths. Therefore, leverage through futures is cheaper.

- It is generally difficult to get more than two times leverage using actual cash stocks, i.e., the investor has to deposit 50 per cent of the cost in advance. On the other hand, the initial margin on futures is typically 20 per cent though it could be lower in some cases. The difference in leverage between stock futures and stock 'spot' can be significant: five times in futures vs. two times in cash. These figures are approximately the same in markets as diverse as India and the US, although high net worth clients can through 'portfolio margining' in the US, access more leverage for direct purchase of stocks. Thus, a short term investor can buy more than twice as many shares with a given amount of money on the futures market than on the spot market.

It should never be forgotten that leverage is a double-edged sword. It amplifies gains and losses too. Higher leverage is not always a benefit.

A third factor is the ease with which equities can be short-sold in the futures market – i.e., one can speculate on an expected decline in prices whereas in the cash market, this is difficult to do.

Portfolio theory

The portfolio theory is derived from the Capital Asset Pricing Model (CAPM) and is widely used for portfolio selection in stock markets. A full discussion of portfolio theory is beyond the scope of this book.

Essentially, portfolio theory takes the view that each asset (say a share of ITC Ltd.) has two components of risk attached to its returns, risk being defined as variability of returns.

One is *alpha* or *non-systematic risk* specific to a share (ITC in this case), which is not correlated to general stock market prices. Events such as new patents, efficiency improvements, boardroom tussles, managerial changes or takeover bids in a company, which do affect the share price, are examples of non-systematic risk affecting the company alone, without affecting the market as a whole. This risk can be avoided by diversifying into other assets.

However, there is a second element, known as *beta* or *systematic risk*, which is dependent on the general stock market. Whenever the Indian stock market rises or falls, there is an effect on ITC, the extent of the effect depending on the size of the beta. The beta factor is the sensitivity of the price of a particular share or portfolio of shares to movements in the market index. When the market rises or falls, the particular share or portfolio will also rise or fall, but the extent to which it rises or falls may be less or more than the market as a whole. This proportion is determined by the beta factor. Beta risk cannot be diversified away and hence investors need to be compensated by higher return. The CAPM therefore postulates that there is a trade-off between systematic risk and return. (Empirical evidence for this has been rather weak, however.)

The return that investors would expect in order to hold the shares of ITC would be the return that would fully compensate them for the risks incurred. Investors can earn a risk-free return by investing in government Treasury Bills. If they must be persuaded to hold ITC shares instead, they would expect a proportionately higher return to compensate for the beta (systematic) risk involved in ITC shares. On the basis of the CAPM, for ITC stock, the expected percentage return per year in Indian rupees would be:

$$R_f + \beta \, (R_m - R_f)$$

Where,

R_f = risk-free interest rate in rupees

β = beta of ITC

R_m = return on the market-as-a-whole

The R_m would be for the whole world's market (percentage return in rupees) if there was full capital account convertibility etc., in India and the rest of the world. For practical purposes now, the 'market-as-a-whole' can be assumed to be just the Indian market.

The actual choice of portfolio by any one individual depends on his degree of risk aversion. A person who wants low risk will buy low beta assets giving a steady return, but his average return over a period will be lower. Another person may go in for a portfolio with a higher average beta risk and reap higher returns over a period, but in any given year, his returns may fluctuate more widely. There could be big losses too along the way.

Portfolio theory as applied to hedging through futures

The *portfolio theory of hedging* uses the portfolio theory described above as a method of analysing hedging behaviour in futures markets. The portfolio theory of hedging views hedged stocks and un-hedged stocks as two different 'assets' with different betas that can be combined into a portfolio. A fully hedged portfolio is deemed to have lower risk (i.e., lower beta) and lower return. For a hedge involving the basis grade or variety of any commodity for a period co-terminous with the maturity date of a futures contract, there is no risk in hedging: the return from hedging is known exactly in advance (ignoring counter-party risks). Thus, the variance and risk is nil and hedged stocks are a riskless asset. (Single stock futures are an example as they have virtually no basis risk because that very stock is the basis grade; a stock position hedged against the corresponding stock's futures contract is virtually riskless.) In the case of hedging through varieties other than the basis grade, some risk may remain. When a single stock or collection of stocks is hedged against a broad stock market index, some basis risk exists but it is less than for an unhedged position. An unhedged portfolio has the highest risk and return. A partially hedged portfolio would lie in between a fully hedged portfolio and an unhedged portfolio. According to the portfolio theory of hedging, a dealer chooses an 'optimal' hedge ratio based on his degree of aversion to risk.

The portfolio theory is used extensively in investment analysis in the cash market and is generally accepted as a very useful theory for that purpose. However, its utility for analysing hedging through futures markets is debatable, though several researchers used it as a basis for empirical research on futures markets. As Stein,[1] Gray[2] and Williams[3] have pointed out; the conceptual basis for using portfolio theory in assessing hedging behaviour is weak. Firstly, Williams shows that with a small change in the starting point of the portfolio analysis as applied to hedging, the theory breaks down. Secondly, as Stein brings out, the applicability of the theory depends on the existence of a systematic risk in futures prices accompanied by a risk-return trade-off. But several studies have shown that futures prices do not show any such systematic relationship with the general market portfolio, nor is there a risk return trade-off. Even if

---

1   J. L. Stein, *op. cit.*, 18—22.

2   R. W. Gray, 'Commentary', *Review of Research in Futures Markets,* Vol. 3, 80–81.

3   Jeffrey Williams, *The Economic Function of Futures Markets,* Cambridge University Press.

systematic relationship exists in some markets, this is clearly not a theory that can be applied to the general spectrum of futures trading. Thirdly, from an empirical point of view, a major problem in applying the theory to actual hedging behaviour is the need to know the hedger's risk aversion profile. Some researchers have circumvented this problem in various ways, but the fact remains that this is a major difficulty. Indeed, the authors of this book are inclined to agree with Stein, Williams *et al*, that portfolio theory is not an appropriate approach for the analysis of hedging behaviour in futures markets. It has nevertheless been included in this book for the sake of completeness.

Pricing of equity futures

It was seen in chapter 4 that the relationship between futures and spot prices is based on the interplay of two sets of forces – expectations about the future price and the carrying cost of the asset from the present time to the future date. This leads to the following general relationship for any futures market:

$$F \leq S + C - Y$$

Where, F = futures price

S = spot price

C = carrying cost for the period t

Y = yield for the period t

Being a financial futures contract where there are no production or consumption discontinuities like harvests or weather related events, expectations are not likely to play a role in determining the futures price and the price will be very close the carrying cost approach. For a financial instrument (unlike commodities) there are negligible exogenous carrying costs (like warehouse rents) which are not directly proportional to the value of the asset. The main or only cost is interest on capital locked up and that is a percentage of the spot price; the carrying cost can be derived directly from the spot price by applying a rate of interest. The yield is a real yield (from dividends) rather than a 'convenience yield' as in the case of commodities. When all of these are taken into account, the relationship becomes as follows:

$$F = S + C - Y$$

i.e., $F = S + (C - Y)$

i.e., $F = S + S(c_t - y_t)$

i.e., $F = S(1 + c_t - y_t)$

Where, S = spot price

C = carrying cost for the period t (absolute amount)

Y = yield for the period t (absolute amount)

c_t = (risk free) interest rate on funds borrowed (opportunity cost) for the time t

y_t = yield rate on the underlying asset for the time t

t = time period involved

The formula above takes only simple interest into account. If it is assumed that the carrying cost and the yield are compounded continuously, then it can be shown mathematically that the formula becomes:

$$F = Se^{(c-y)t}$$

Where,

$c = r$ = risk free rate of interest per annum

y = dividend yield per annum on the underlying asset

e is a mathematical constant (similar to π) known as Euler's number or the exponential constant (approximately equal to 2.7182818282). As mentioned earlier, approximations to the risk free rate can also be used without major inaccuracy.

Uses of equity futures

Equity futures are of two categories – futures in individual stocks (single stock futures) and futures on a stock market index (stock index futures). Both can be used for speculation as well as for hedging.

Speculation through equity futures

A speculator who expects a particular share to increase in value can buy the futures contract of that share (if it has a futures contract). A speculator who expects a particular share to fall in value can engage in short selling of that share on the futures market. If the speculator's prediction is correct, he will make a profit. If he is wrong, he will make a loss.

On the other hand, if a speculator feels that the stock market as a whole will appreciate but does not specifically want to invest in a particular company, she can buy stock index futures. If she feels the stock market as a whole will fall, she can short sell the stock index futures.

The main advantage to speculating through futures is the higher degree of gearing, as discussed at the beginning of this chapter.

Hedging through equity futures

Those who have positions in individual shares and wish to hedge them (i.e., lock in to a particular price) without actually liquidating their cash market position can do so by selling single stock futures. This is very similar to hedging in commodities. The only real difference is that shares may yield dividends and this may have to be considered in pricing.

Those having large *portfolios* of individual stocks can approximately hedge by selling stock index futures of those stock indices that largely overlap with their current stock holdings. The exact number of stock index futures to be sold depends on several factors.

The first aspect is the composition of the portfolio (how many different shares of how much value) and the beta of those individual stock holdings with respect to the market. For this purpose, the 'market' can be taken as the premier broad-based stock index. Beta is simply a correlation term. For example, a stock with beta of 1.2 means that when the broad market goes up or down by 1 per cent, then the stock is on average likely to correspondingly go up or down by 1.2 per cent.

The beta of the stock index itself is also relevant when dealing with a narrower index. For example, a sectoral index is narrower in coverage and its beta cannot be taken as one *vis-à-vis* the broad market. When using such an index to hedge, it is necessary to calculate the beta not only of the individual shares and/or portfolio being hedged, but also of the particular stock index used for hedging. The index used for hedging is calculated by statistically regressing its values against the broad market index. For example, to hedge a portfolio of IT stocks by selling CNX IT index futures in India, it is necessary to have the beta of the individual stocks with respect to the NSE, and also the beta of the CNX-IT index *vis-à-vis* the NSE.

When hedging a portfolio, the hedger needs to decide on the target level of volatility (i.e., beta). It should be remembered that a fully hedged portfolio will protect against downside risk, but also prevent any gains from upside risk. A fully hedged stock portfolio (if the hedge is perfectly matched etc.) would have a beta of zero (just like a fully hedged bond portfolio would have a duration of zero, assuming parallel shifts in interest rates across maturities). It would mean that if the stock market moves up or down, the portfolio's value would remain unchanged. A fully hedged portfolio may be appear pointless in theory (since the same result could be achieved by liquidating the portfolio and holding cash) but it may sometimes be necessary for practical reasons relating to taxation, financial reporting etc. It is also a theoretical extreme which helps in understanding the concept. The actual target of portfolio beta values will be based on risk aversion and other factors like tax implications, accounting year-ends etc. Depending on the target beta, the hedger will decide the share of the portfolio to be hedged, ranging from 100per cent to nil.

Optimal hedge ratio

In chapter 4, a general approach to calculating equivalency in any futures market was given, based on the correlation coefficient between the asset being hedged and the futures contract and the standard deviations of the two assets. The formula for the optimal hedge ratio (also known as the minimum variance hedge ratio) given there was,

$$h = \frac{\text{SD of changes in the cash market price of the asset being hedged}}{\text{SD of changes in the futures price}} \times r$$

Where,

h = optimal hedge ratio

SD = standard deviation for a given period

r = correlation coefficient between the SD of the changes in spot price of commodity and SD of the change in futures price

In the case of hedging of a particular share using the futures contract of the stock market index, it can be shown mathematically that the optimal hedge ratio is in fact the same as the beta of the share,

i.e., $h = \beta$

Therefore, the optimal hedge ratio of a single stock for the purposes of hedging using the broad market index is the beta itself.

This ratio must then be adjusted for the size of the portfolio itself. The number of contracts to be traded to achieve the hedge will then be as follows:

$N = h \times P / V.$

Since, $h = \beta$,

$N = \beta \times P / V$

Or,

N = (β × P) / (F × Q)

Where,

N is the number of future contracts to be bought/sold for hedging,

β is the beta

P is the exposure to be hedged (total portfolio value minus portion to be left unhedged)

V is the value of one futures contract and

V= F × Q where, F= futures price and Q is the quantity or size of one market lot of futures.

The above formula will work when the underlying of the futures contract is a broad market index which is assumed to have a beta of one (unity). If the beta value of the index is not one, e.g., if a narrower index is the underlying of the futures contract, then:

N = h × P / V

$$h = \frac{\beta_s}{\beta_f} \text{ and so,}$$

$$N = \frac{\beta_s}{\beta_f} \times \frac{P}{V}$$

Where,

N is the number of future contracts to be bought/sold for hedging,

β_s is the beta of the stock to be hedged,

β_f is the beta of the futures index.

However, it is vital to note (and often overlooked) that while the beta value used in the equation should in theory be the expected beta in the future, the beta value actually used is based on *past data* and therefore backward-looking. Therefore attributing precision or great accuracy to these calculations is somewhat pointless. If the future beta is different from the past, the hedge may prove only partial. It is for this reason that some very successful investors like Warren Buffett have mocked such precision.

For this reason, some market practitioners do not use the historical beta values from a simple CAPM model regression. Instead, they use adjusted betas by bringing them closer to one to prevent extremely low or high beta values distorted by relatively recent and non-recurring events. For example, one widely used calculation of an adjusted beta is:

Adjusted Beta = 1/3 +2/3 calculated historical beta.

No doubt, the adjustment may itself result in an imperfect hedge if the market conforms to the past patterns and so such adjustments carry risks of their own.

Roll over and basis risks

Except in the rare case where the portfolio exactly corresponds to the index which forms the underlying of the futures contract, portfolio hedging is essentially a cross hedge. Every cross hedge of one asset through another always has basis risk. If the portfolio of individual stocks that being hedged is not well diversified or not representative in any form of the broader market, portfolio betas become even more meaningless.

As noted earlier in chapter 4, the maturity date of the liquid futures contract may not exactly match the needs of the hedger, and hence hedging may involve the rollover of futures contracts. This carries its own basis risk because the basis may change during the process of rollover.

It should be noted that stock index futures can only be used to hedge the systematic risk in any equity portfolio, not specific or idiosyncratic risks.

The following examples will illustrate some of the ways in which equity futures can be used and the issues discussed above.

Example 7.1:

XYZ Fund has a long-only (i.e., no short positions) portfolio of 20 diversified stocks listed on the NSE) worth Rs. 10 crores. For the next two weeks, the fund manager wants to eliminate general exposure to the stock market risk (or beta risk) because a big policy announcement is expected, and the manager does not want to risk it as the fund's performance this quarter has been good. She could sell all the stocks and convert to cash, but the fund's investment rules do not allow a high allocation to cash, even temporarily. The rules allow taking positions in derivatives such as futures and options so long as they are exchange-traded and liquid. The average beta of her portfolio (based on the previous three-year average) is 1.2 and Nifty is assumed to have a beta of 1 (i.e., it is taken as representing the market as a whole). The Nifty is at 6000 currently. How should she hedge if,

a. she wants to hedge the whole portfolio?

b. she wants to retain risk on 20 per cent of the portfolio while hedging 80 per cent?

Solution

Using the formula $N = \beta \times P / V$, the number of contracts to be traded is

$N = (\beta \times P) / (F \times Q)$

i.e. $N =$

$$\frac{\beta \times Exposure\ to\ be\ hedged}{Current\ value\ of\ Nifty \times Contract\ size\ (multiple)\ for\ one\ Nifty\ futures\ contract}$$

The exposure to be hedged = Portfolio value − Exposure remaining unhedged.

a. In this case, the entire portfolio value is to be hedged. Assuming that the beta value can be taken for the future, to hedge the entire exposure of ₹10 crores, Nifty futures worth $10 \times 1.2 = ₹12$ crore have to be sold.

One Nifty futures contract is worth 50 times the index value in rupees. Therefore, the number of contracts to be traded is: $= \dfrac{12,00,00,000}{6,000 \times 50} = 400$

That is, XYZ Fund's manager must short 400 relevant index contracts in order to aim for a short term zero-beta portfolio.

b. In this case 20 per cent of the exposure, i.e., ₹2 crores is to remain un-hedged. Thus, only ₹8 crores is to be hedged. To hedge ₹8 crores, Nifty futures worth

₹(8×1.2) crores = ₹9.6 crores

have to be hedged. This can be achieved by selling:

$\dfrac{9,60,00,000}{6000 \times 50} = 320$ Nifty contracts.

Example 7.2

In the above example, since the period was only for two weeks, we assumed the spot price and futures price of Nifty to be the same, and ignored any complications because of dividend yields etc. In a relatively high interest rate environment like India, interest rates have a large influence on pricing. In this example all the facts are as above, except that the target period is two months instead of two weeks. The dividend yield on the Nifty is 2 per cent and the (risk free) interest rate is 12 per cent. For the two-month hedge, the manager decides to use an adjusted beta (with a beta of one having a weight of one-third and the actual beta having a weight of two-thirds) and uses compounding where required. Calculate the number of contracts to be used for hedging.

Solution

To get the number of futures' units to be sold to hedge a long portfolio, we have to divide the value of the portfolio (multiplied by its beta) by the value of the index futures, not the index itself. The question does not give the futures price of the Nifty index. When the index is at 6,000, its futures can be derived from the carrying cost and yield.

$F = S\ (1 + c_t \text{-} y_t)$

Since the carrying cost (interest rate of 12 per cent) is higher than the yield (dividend rate of 2 per cent), C–Y will be positive and the futures price will be higher than the current price because that the interest rate is higher than the dividend yield. In this case, t= 2 months or 2/12 years so

$$c_t\text{-}y_t \;=\; (12\ per\ cent \times 2/12) - (2\ per\ cent \times 2/12)$$
$$=\; (10\ per\ cent \times 2/12)$$
$$=\; 1.67\ per\ cent$$

Therefore, the futures prices is expected to be

$$F \;=\; 6,000\ (1 + 1.67\ per\ cent) = 6,000\ (1.0167) = 6,100.2$$

If continuous compounding is used:

$$F \;=\; Se^{(c-y)t}$$

i.e., $F = 6,000\ (e^{\,(.12-.02)\,(2/12)}) = 6,000\ (e^{\,(.1)\,(.167)})$

This can be solved manually through logarithm tables (inserting a value of 2.718 for e) or through a scientific calculator and it will be seen that

$F = 6,000\ (e^{\,(.1)\,(.167)}) = 6,101.$

The adjusted value of beta,

$\beta = 0.333 + (0.6667 \times 1.2) = 0.333 + 0.8 = 1.133.$

Therefore, the new calculation $N = \beta \times P / V$ becomes

$$N = \frac{1.133 \times 10,00,00,000}{6101 \times 50} = 371.4\ contracts$$

This would be rounded to 371 contracts.

[When compared with Example 7.1 (a), the answer is different because of the change in beta and the change in futures price.]

Example 7.3

A portfolio comprising the shares included in the BSE 30 share index has to be hedged from 1 March to 1 April using Nifty futures. Assume the beta of the Sensex to be 1.1 whereas the beta of the Nifty is .97. The futures contract expiry dates are 18 March and 20 April. What are the alternative ways of hedging and what are the risks remaining?

Solution:

First, the correct equivalency ratio has to be decided upon, considering the correlation and volatility of the BSE Sensex and the Nifty. In this case, the optimal hedge ratio will be as follows:

$$h = \frac{\beta_s}{\beta_f} = \frac{1.1}{.97} = 1.13$$

Once this is decided, there are two ways of achieving the hedge:

a. On 1 March, sell the 18 March futures and then, on 18 March, 'roll over' to the

20 April contract. This rolling over on 18 March will be accomplished by buying back the March futures and simultaneously selling the April futures. On 1 April, the April futures will be bought back to square the transaction. In this case brokerage, transaction taxes etc. will have to be paid twice because two sell-buy transactions are involved.

b. *Directly hedge by selling the 20 April contract on 1 March. Then buy back the April futures on 1 April. In this case the 'bid-ask spread' between the sale price and the buy-back price might be greater than in the case of the two separate contracts as the later contract might be less liquid.*

Though the net gain or loss on the futures can be expected to be the same the relative costs (brokerage vs. bid-ask spread) have to be weighed in choosing the contract in which to hedge.

As seen in chapter 4, cross hedging inevitably involves some basis risk. Basis in the case of a cross hedge is: spot price of the item being hedged – future price of the contract used for hedging.

The basis risk in this case is that the basis on 1 April (at the time of liquidating the hedge) may temporarily be significantly higher or lower compared to what it 'should' be based on expected correlation between BSE Sensex and Nifty and their respective volatilities or on the basis of interest rates, dividend yields etc. This basis risk may mean that the risk borne on the cash portfolio of BSE 30 shares may be under- or over-compensated in the futures market.

Part – III
Swaps

Part III

8

Swaps – Part I
Interest Rate and Currency Swaps

Swaps are contracts in which two separate streams of cash flow are exchanged or 'swapped'. The streams could be two different kinds of interest amounts, two currencies or indeed any two differing streams of cash.

This chapter introduces the conceptual basis of swap contracts and then explains interest rate swaps and currency swaps. The next chapter deals with other types of swaps and some general issues relating to the swaps market.

Definition

A swap transaction is a contract by which two or more parties exchange (swap) one set of pre-determined payments for another.

Some important types of swap are the following:

- An interest rate swap is an agreement between two parties to exchange interest obligations or receipts in the same currency on an agreed amount of notional principal for an agreed period.
- A currency swap is an agreement between two parties to exchange payments or receipts in one currency for payments or receipts in another.
- An equity swap is an agreement between two parties to exchange dividends and/or capital returns on an underlying share with another equity flow or interest flow, in the same or different currencies.

Currency swaps slightly predated interest rate swaps, but the latter now predominate in volume. Equity swaps are more recent but growing fast. Swaps can also combine some of the features of interest rate and, say, currency swaps. Thus, a fixed rate payment in dollars might be swapped for a floating rate payment in yen. Such transactions are more complex.

A key feature of swaps is that they deal with a set of cash flows involving multiple periods, not a one-time cash flow. This is an important distinction between swaps and futures or options, both of which deal with a single expected cash flow at one specified time in the future. In a swap, invariably there are multiple dates involved where one or more income streams would need to exchange hands. Sometimes the two cash flows are paid gross to each other, while in some cases, the amount due is 'netted' and the net amount due from one party to another is transferred.

Interest rate swaps

If one went by just the above definition of swaps, it maybe unclear why the two parties to an interest rate swap would wish to enter into such an agreement. The purpose may be either to achieve mutually beneficial improvements in the cost of borrowing or lending, or to hedge an interest rate risk, or both.

To understand why an interest rate swap can be advantageous to both parties, consider the following example:

Example 8.1

Two companies both wish to borrow ten million pounds. Company A is a giant conglomerate with an excellent credit rating. Company B is a medium sized company of ten years standing with a lower credit rating. Both companies have the option of borrowing either at fixed rates or at floating rates. Company A would prefer a fixed rate obligation, while, Company B prefers a floating rate. The quoted rates of interest to the two companies are as follows:

Company	Interest rate fixed (per cent)	Interest rate floating (per cent)
A	7.5 per cent	LIBOR + 0.5 per cent
B	9.0 per cent	LIBOR + 3.5 per cent

Clearly, B's cost of funds is higher than A whether the loan is on fixed rate or on floating rate basis. However, in the fixed rate case, B's extra cost is 1.5 per cent (9.0 per cent — 7.5 per cent) while in the floating rate market the extra cost is 3 per cent. (In economic terms, A has an absolute advantage over B in both fixed and floating rate markets, but B has a comparative advantage in the fixed rate market[1]).

C Ltd, a broker, comes forward and arranges a swap. Under this arrangement, A actually borrows 10 million pounds from a bank at LIBOR[2] + 0.5 per cent and B borrows 10 million

---

1 Students of international economics will recognise the similarity with international trade theory.

2 LIBOR stands for the London Inter-Bank Offered Rate, which is the rate of interest charged by banks in London on short-term loans to each other. The rate changes from time to time. It is taken as a benchmark for market interest rate and non-bank floating rate borrowers are quoted a rate based on LIBOR plus a margin reflecting their creditworthiness. The more creditworthy the borrower, the lower the margin over LIBOR.

pounds from a bank at 9.0 per cent. As a separate transaction (which constitutes the swap) A, B and C agree as follows:

i.   *A will pay C a fixed rate of 7.0 per cent*

ii.   *A will receive from C a floating rate of LIBOR + 0.5 per cent*

iii. *B will pay C a floating rate of LIBOR + 0.5 per cent*

iv.   *B will receive from C a fixed rate of 6.5 per cent*

The transactions (i) to (iv) constitute the 'swap'. It should be noted that the swap is independent of the borrowing initially undertaken by A and B and the banks which lent the funds to A and B are in no way concerned with the swap. A remains liable for all obligations to its bank and likewise B to its bank. The swap binds only A, B and C.

To understand the benefits from the swap, consider the net cash flows of A, B and C, given in Table 8.1

Table 8.1: *Illustration of a swap*

Party	Outflow on loan from bank (1) per cent	Swap outflow (2) per cent	Swap Inflow (3) per cent	Total (4) [1+2+3] per cent
A	- (LIBOR + 0.5)	- 7.0	+ (LIBOR + 0.5)	- 7.0
B	- 9.0	- (LIBOR + 0.5)	+ 6.5	- (LIBOR + 3.0)
C	NIL	- (LIBOR + 0.5) - 6.5	+ (LIBOR + 0.5) + 7.0	0.5

It may be seen that the net result is:

a.   *for A, a fixed rate obligation at 7 per cent (this is better than the 7.5 per cent which A would have paid if it had directly taken a fixed rate loan); -*

b.   *for B, a floating rate obligation at LIBOR + 3.0 per cent (this is better than the LIBOR + 3.5 per cent which B would have paid if it had directly taken a floating rate loan);*

d.   *for C, a profit of 0.5 per cent for arranging the transaction.*

It was noted earlier that the interest differential on floating rate debt was 3 per cent while on fixed rate debt it was 1.5 per cent. The gap between the differentials was 3 per cent – 1.5 per cent = 1.5 per cent. This 1.5 per cent has been shared as gains by A, B and C, each getting 0.5 per cent.

Terminology of interest rate swaps

The party which pays floating rate in the swap transaction is known as the *floating rate payer* or *seller of the swap*. The party which pays fixed rate in the swap transaction is known as the *fixed rate payer* or *buyer of the swap*.

It should be noted that the terms fixed or floating rate payer refer to the obligations in the swap itself and not the obligations to the original lenders. In Example 8.1, A is the buyer or fixed rate payer while B is the seller or floating rate payer.

The term 'index' is used to denote the benchmark rate of interest which acts as the reference point for the floating rate. LIBOR is the most commonly used index but there are many others.

Asset swap vs. liability swap

In Example 8.1, the parties swapped their interest obligations (i.e., liabilities). Therefore, it is an example of a liability swap. It is also possible to swap interest receipts (i.e., assets), as shown in Example 8.2 below:

Example 8.2

D Ltd is a recipient of floating rate interest through floating rate bonds carrying a coupon of LIBOR + 2 per cent. It apprehends a fall in interest rates and wishes to hedge against it. E Ltd holds fixed rate bonds with a coupon of 7 per cent but expects a rise in interest rates and wishes to hedge this eventuality. (When interest rates rise, the value of fixed rate bonds falls.) At the time, LIBOR is at 5 per cent. D and E enter into a swap through a dealer C, on the following terms.

(i)   D will pay C a floating rate of LIBOR + 2 per cent

(ii) D will receive from C a fixed rate of 6.5 per cent

(iii) E will pay C a fixed rate of 7.0 per cent

(iv) E will receive from C a floating rate of LIBOR + 2 per cent.

The net cash flows are as in Table 4.2.

Table 8.2: *Net cash flows*

Party	Inflow on bond from bank (1) per cent	Swap outflow (2) per cent	Swap inflow (3) per cent	Total (4) per cent
D	+ (LIBOR + 2)	- (LIBOR + 2)	+ 6.5	+ 6.5

Party	Inflow on bond from bank (1) per cent	Swap outflow (2) per cent	Swap inflow (3) per cent	Total (4) per cent
E	+ 7.0	– 7.0	+ (LIBOR + 2)	+(LIBOR + 2)
C	NIL	– (LIBOR + 2) – 6.5	+ (LIBOR + 2) + 7	+ 0.5

After the swap, D is protected against falls in interest rate—it will now receive 6.5 per cent irrespective of the market rate. E is now protected against a fall in bond prices— if rates rise, E's portfolio is hedged because E will now receive the higher LIBOR rate + 2 per cent. To that extent, the loss in the value of bond is offset by the inflow from the swap arrangement.

To see how the hedge works, consider the following scenarios. (To keep the example simple and understandable, it is assumed that the long-term interest rate is identical to LIBOR; this assumption would not hold good in real life. Removing the assumption will not affect the nature of the outcome of the hedges.)

i.   *LIBOR rises from 5 per cent to 7 per cent*

  Effect on D:

  D Ltd. will receive 9 per cent on his floating rate bonds. Thus, it gains in the cash market. In the swap, its inflow remains constant (6.5 per cent) as it is a fixed rate receiver. However, its outflow on the swap increases from 7 per cent to 9 per cent. The net cash flow on the swap is negative and neutralises the gain in the cash market. In essence, since D is hedged it has forgone the gain that would have accrued if it were unhedged.

  Effect on E:

  E Ltd. continues to receive the same amount of interest, but the value of its bonds has fallen. In the swap, its inflow increases from 7 per cent to 9 per cent while its outflow is unchanged. Thus, the swap has a positive cash flow. The capitalised value of this positive flow will compensate for the loss in value of the bonds.

ii. *LIBOR falls from 5 per cent to 4 per cent*

  Effect on D:

  D will receive 6 per cent instead of 7 per cent on its floating rate bonds, and thus loses in the cash market. In the swap, its inflow remains at 6.5 per cent. However, its outflow on the swap falls from 7 per cent to 6 per cent. This exactly compensates it for its cash market loss. Because of the swap, it has avoided the risk of fall in interest rate.

  Effect on E:

  E continues to receive the same amount of interest, but the value of its bonds appreciates. In the swap, however, its inflow falls from 7 per cent to 6 per cent with its outflow staying unchanged at 7 per cent. The net cash flow on the swap is negative. The capitalised value of this loss neutralises the gain in the cash market. By hedging, it has forgone the possible gain in the cash market.

This is an illustration of an asset swap, since the parties end up by exchanging a floating rate asset for a fixed rate asset.

In Example 8.2, the asset swap was used as a hedging device. Earlier, a liability swap was shown where the purpose of the swap was to obtain an advantage in the cost of borrowing. Liability swaps can also be used to hedge existing liabilities (rather than achieve a lower borrowing cost).

Example 8.3

G Ltd has an existing fixed rate liability. It feels that interest rates are going to fall (which will raise the capitalised value of the debt) and wishes to hedge against this. H Ltd has an existing floating rate liability but expects the interest rate to rise, increasing its interest burden. It wishes to hedge against this. G and H enter into a swap through broker M whereby G becomes the floating rate payer and H the fixed rate payer in a swap.

Assume that the interest rate falls as anticipated by G. Its payment under the swap decreases as the floating rate falls, while its receipt remains unchanged. There is a positive cash flow which offsets the increase in the value of the fixed rate debt. As for H, the fall in rates reduces its receipt under the swap while leaving its payment unchanged. There is a negative cash flow in the swap, which offsets H's gain in the cash market.

On the other hand, if the interest rate rises (as anticipated by H), G's payment under the swap increases with its receipt unchanged. The resulting negative swap cash flow offsets the reduction in the value of the cash market liability. For H, the rise in interest rates means an increased receipt under the swap with unchanged payments. The resulting positive cash flow offsets H's loss in the cash market.

Currency swaps

As in the case of interest rate swaps, currency swaps may be entered into either for mutual benefit of two parties or in order to hedge currency risks, or both.

It was seen earlier that interest rate swaps can be mutually profitable if there is a comparative advantage for the two parties in one loan market over another. The rationale for currency swaps is similar: one party has a comparative advantage in borrowing in one currency while another has an advantage in the other.

For example, suppose an Indian company (say, Sundaram Finance) wants to raise funds in the USA. At the same time, an American company, say, Jacobs Engineering wants to borrow in Indian rupees for a project in India. Sundaram, though reputed in India, may not be as well regarded in the US debt market and would therefore have to pay a higher rate of interest than its credentials would otherwise warrant. Similarly, Jacobs Engineering may not receive a rate of interest in India that truly reflects its creditworthiness because of the obscurity of the 'name' in India. It would be beneficial to both companies if Sundaram borrows in rupees, Jacobs in dollars and the two then swap the liabilities.

Sometimes, comparative advantage could run in the opposite direction. A British company might have already borrowed heavily in the sterling bond market. As a result, the market may demand a premium on further borrowings, as they would not prefer a concentration of holdings in one company. On the other hand, say because it is a well-known multinational, it may be able to raise funds relatively cheaply in the Indian rupee debt market because it has no previous exposure.

Example 8.4

S, an Indian company and J, an American company are both contemplating raising of funds. J, by virtue of its larger size, greater diversification etc. has a better credit rating than S in both markets. The rates at which the companies can borrow are as follows:

Company	Quoted interest rate	
	₹ *(per cent)*	$ *(per cent)*
S	9	7
J	8	4

S needs dollars, while J needs rupees. The differential in cost of borrowing is 1 per cent in India but 3 per cent in America. Both parties stand to gain by the following arrangement through M, a middleman. (Assume ₹55 = $1)

a.   *S will borrow in India, a sum of ₹55 crore at 9 per cent*

b.   *J will borrow $10 million in the USA at 4 per cent*

c.   *Both parties enter into a swap on the following terms:*

　　 i.　 *The principal sums are exchanged, i.e., S pays J ₹55 crore and receives $10 million*

　　 ii.　 *S will pay M dollar interest at 6.5 per cent and receive rupee interest at 9 per cent*

　　 iii.　 *J will pay M rupee interest at 7.5 per cent and receive from M dollar interest at 4 per cent.*

The cash flows are shown in Table 8.3.

Table 8.3: *Cash flows*

Party	Interest outflow on loan (per cent) (1)	Swap outflow (per cent) (2)	Swap inflow (per cent) (3)	Net flow (per cent) (4)= (1+2+3)
S	₹ -9	$ -6.5	₹ +9	$ -6.5
J	$ -4	₹ -7.5	$ +4	₹ -7.5
M	–	₹ -9 $ -4	+ ₹ 7.5 $ + 6.5	₹ -1.5 $ + 2.5

S and J have both achieved a lower cost of capital than if they had borrowed directly in the other currency. M gains 2.5 per cent in dollars and loses 1.5 per cent in rupees, producing a net gain of 1 per cent. (However, it should be noted that M bears an exchange rate risk. It is possible to arrange the payments differently with the swap parties bearing some or all of the risk.)

The differential in rates was 3 per cent in USA and 1 per cent in India; this left a gap of 2 per cent to be shared as gains by the parties to the swap transaction. In the above transaction, S gains 0.5 per cent (by effectively borrowing at 6.5 per cent instead of 7 per cent), J gains 0.5 per cent (by borrowing at an effective rate of 7.5 per cent instead of 8 per cent) and M gains 1 per cent (+ 2.5 per cent in dollars, – 1.5 per cent in rupees).

Terminology of currency swaps

In Example 8.4, a fixed interest obligation in one currency was exchanged for a fixed interest obligation in another currency. This is known as a fixed-to-fixed currency swap.

Another type of currency swap involves exchange of a fixed rate obligation in one currency for a floating rate obligation in another currency. This is known as a 'fixed-to-floating currency swap' or a 'circus swap' or 'currency coupon swap'.

Hedging through currency swaps

Just as interest rate swaps can be used to hedge interest exposures, currency swaps can be used to hedge exchange rate risk. Suppose an Indian company has a dollar debt liability. If the dollar appreciates, it suffers exchange losses. If it becomes the rupee payer (dollar receiver) in a rupee-dollar currency swap, whenever the dollar rises, there will be a profit on the swap position which will offset the loss on the initial (cash market) liability.

9

Swaps – Part II
Other Swaps

This chapter looks at some more kinds of swap transactions and at certain general issues relating to swap markets.

Equity swaps

An equity swap is an arrangement by which one party pays to the counter-party an amount based on the value of the shares in a company, and receives from the counter-party an amount of fixed or floating interest on an equivalent notional value. In effect, an equity position is converted into a deposit or debenture.

Example 9.1

X Ltd owns a large stake of one lakh shares in Y Ltd, a quoted sister company. The shares are currently quoted at ₹ 1,000 per share. X is apprehensive that the price of Y's shares may fall, but does not want to sell its stake as that would mean relinquishing its say over the management of Y Ltd. Instead it enters into an equity swap with Z Ltd, a financial institution, whereby

i.   *X will pay Z annually the value of all dividends declared by Y plus or minus any net appreciation or depreciation in the share price (from the base value of ₹ 1,000) on its one lakh shares.*

ii. *Z will pay X annually the market floating rate of interest on a sum of ₹ 10 crore, being the market value of X's holding at the time of the swap.*

Financially, the effect of an equity swap is the same as that of selling the shares outright. However, the shareholder may wish to retain the shares for reasons of control (as in the Example above) or to avoid capital gains tax, or to avoid giving a negative signal to the market. (For example, a sale of Tata Motors shares by Tata Sons might provoke general bearishness in Tata Motors shares, which can be avoided through an equity swap.) The disadvantage is that there is a transaction cost. Depending on the prevailing market sentiment, a premium may have to be paid by one or other party to attract the counterparty and there will usually be a margin for the intermediary.

Commodity swaps

A commodity swap is an arrangement or a contract by which one party (a commodity user/buyer) agrees to pay a fixed price for a designated quantity of a commodity to the counter party (commodity producer/seller), who in turn pays the first party a market-based price (or an accepted index thereof) for the same quantity. Commodity swaps are a means of hedging commodity price risk, over a long period.

Example 9.2

B Ltd, a British chocolate manufacturer, is apprehensive of adverse fluctuations in cocoa prices. G Ltd, a Ghanaian cocoa producer, wishes to ensure a steady income over a five-year horizon. B and G enter into a commodity swap through an intermediary on the following terms:

i.   *B will pay quarterly to G a fixed price of $2,700/tonne over the five-year period, for a quantity of 5000 tonnes per quarter.*

ii. *G will pay quarterly to B a floating price for 5,000 tonnes which shall be the price of the nearest London cocoa futures contract as on the last day of the previous quarter.*

It should be noted that no cocoa is actually delivered – only a financial payment is made.

Assume cocoa prices fall. G will get a reduced income from its cocoa exports to various buyers; however the amount it has to pay to B under the swap will also fall, whereas the amount it receives from B is unchanged. Thus, it gains on the swap, compensating for its loss on actual physical sales.

Now suppose cocoa prices rise. B will be forced to pay more to its various suppliers of cocoa. However, it will also receive more from G under the swap, with its payment to G remaining unchanged. Thus, it gains on the swap, compensating for the loss in physical purchases.

Readers will notice in Example 9.2 that effectively the commodity swap is equivalent to a long-term fixed price contract between B and G. Why not then just enter into such a contract instead of all the complicated transactions involved in a swap? The advantage is that the swap leaves B and G free to buy/sell their actual cocoa supplies from/to other parties. Perhaps the variety produced by G may not be the one B needs at a future date, or G may have a transport cost disadvantage and so on. Thus, the swap leaves both parties with full operational flexibility in the spot market, but without price risk. The disadvantage is the transaction cost, fees etc. Depending on prevailing sentiment, one of the parties may also have to pay a 'premium' to attract the counterparty.

Example 9.3

A conglomerate, C needs 1 million barrels each of oil two years from now and three years from now. It wishes to hedge the price risk. The forward price for two years is $100 per barrel, and for three years is $105 per barrel. An oil-trading firm Z offers to pay the prevailing market price at the desired time in exchange for either a lump sum paid now or two equal payments in years two and three. The interest rate (yield to maturity) on two year and three year bonds are 7 per cent and 8 per cent respectively. How much can C pay to the swap counterparty Z without suffering a loss?

Solution:

If the risk is hedged on the forward market, the price that C will pay is:

$100 million after two years + $105 million after three years.

The present value of that amount is:

$100/(1.07)^2 + 105/(1.08)^3$

or $170.69 million.

If the conglomerate had to make equal (nominal) payments for year two and three, then the payment which would be equivalent to the sum of $170.69 million (denoted by 'P') would be:

$(P/1.07^2 + P/1.08^3) = P(1/1.07^2 + 1/1.08^3) = 170.69$

i.e., P = $102.38 million.

Therefore, C can afford to pay either one lumpsum of $170.69 million now or pay two equal instalments of $102.38 m in years two and three; C would be insulated from any changes in the price of oil in the interim, no matter what the oil prices would be then. In this example, the fixed rate payer is the conglomerate and the floating rate payer is the oil trader.

If the lump sum is paid up front, such an instrument is known as a pre-paid swap. Apart from the need for C to put up the cash up front, the disadvantage of this is the credit risk of the counterparty to C, i.e., what if Z fails to perform the obligation at the due date? On the other hand, if no pre-payment is made, there is a credit risk for Z – what if C defaults on the obligation even though Z has incurred risks?

In practice, the counterparties rarely deal with each other – instead they deal with broker-dealers. The broker-dealer is usually a well-known institution and this makes it easier for the counter-parties to go through with the transaction without having to worry about the risks of dealing with an unknown, and possibly foreign, entity. Such a situation is called a back-to-back transaction and the broker-dealer does bear the credit risk, though no price risk. There is still a credit risk to the swap parties – the risk of the broker itself defaulting. After the financial crisis of 2008, this risk can no longer be completely dismissed, but it is usually easier to assess than the risk of a less-known counterparty.

Commodity swaps vs futures as hedges

The main advantage of commodity swaps over futures is that these are long-term hedging instruments. Swaps may, however, be costlier to arrange. An additional reason for using swaps could be non-availability of liquid futures markets in some commodities. For instance, in the previous example, there was an assumption that there was a known forward price for oil for delivery three years from now. If such a market were not available, then swaps might offer the only means of hedging.

Exotic swaps

The kind of swap transactions depicted in the previous chapter under interest rate swaps are known as 'plain vanilla' or plain swaps. More complicated swaps have evolved to meet specialised needs. Some of these are discussed below. (While exotic swaps are described below in terms of interest rate swaps, for most of them there is an equivalent in the currency swap market and other swap markets also.)

Basis swaps

A basis swap is one where two parties swap floating rate payments but the two floating rate payments are determined by different indices. (Readers may recall that in the context of swaps, the term 'index' refers to the benchmark rate of interest for determining the floating rate.) For example, one party may have payments dominated at LIBOR + 2 per cent, while the other's payments are dominated at treasury bill rate + 1 per cent.

Forward swaps

A forward swap is an arrangement by which a swap is entered into with a commencement date in the future. It is like a forward or a future contract on a swap (which itself is the conceptual equivalent of a strip of forwards or futures – see below).

Callable swaps

In a callable swap, the fixed rate payer has an option to terminate it before maturity. The right to terminate comes at a price reflected in a higher fixed rate than an ordinary swap, and possibly a termination fee.

Puttable swaps

In a puttable swap, the floating rate payer has an option to terminate a swap before maturity. The price for this option is reflected through a higher floating rate and in some cases a termination fee. (Puttable and callable swaps are also known as cancellable or terminable swaps.)

Extendible swaps

An extendible swap is one in which the fixed rate payer is given an option to extend the maturity date of the swap. This additional facility is reflected in a higher fixed rate and/or an extension fee.

Rate capped swaps

A rate capped swap is one where the maximum rate payable by the floating rate payer has a ceiling or 'cap'. This cap reduces the risk to the floating rate payer but reduces the benefit to the fixed rate payer. For this facility, the floating rate payer has to pay a premium to the fixed rate payer.

Amortising swaps

In such cases, the notional principal amount diminishes during the life of the transaction. This is in contrast to the plain or plain vanilla swap (the type covered in the examples) in which the principal amount remains the same. This type of swap is more suitable when a loan is repaid in several instalments.

There are various other types of swaps as there is no limit to the ingenuity of the financial markets in evolving more and more sophisticated instruments.

Swaps as a collection of consecutive futures

It can be shown that a swap is conceptually the equivalent of buying a string or 'strip' of futures contracts. A strip of futures is a set of futures of identical value but different maturities. (For example if one were to simultaneously buy one lot of April gold futures + 1 lot of June gold futures + 1 lot of August gold futures, this is called a 'futures strip'.)

A simple illustration of this can be found in Example 9.2 above. It was seen that the same hedge could be achieved either by a purchase of a strip of futures for a present value of $170.69 million or by a prepaid swap of $170.69 million or a post-paid swap of $102.38 million per annum in years two and three.

We can see that the swap price is not $102.50 (the simple average of the two forward prices) across different years, despite the same amount being bought. This is because of the time value of money, which pushes the swap price closer to the nearer term price rather than farther term price.

Example 9.4

F Ltd. owns 9 per cent perpetual bonds. In mid-2014, it apprehends a rise in interest rates which will reduce the bond price. To protect itself, it sells a strip of bond futures, i.e., one contract each of 10,000 Pounds of January 2015, January 2016 and January 2017 maturity[1] At the time – of sale of futures, the perpetual bond futures are priced at 100, since the prevailing long-term interest rate is 9 per cent. At the same time, LIBOR is 7 per cent. The actual rates of interest during the three years are as follows:

Time	Market interest rate (per cent)	Perpetual bond price
January 2015	8	112.50
January 2016	10	90.00
January 2017	11	81.82

The profit/loss on the bond futures is as follows:

Month	Contract value	Sale price	Purchase price	Profit/Loss per bond	TOTAL
Jan. 2015	10000	100	112.5	-12.50	-1250
Jan. 2016	10000	100	90.00	+10.00	+1000
Jan. 2017	10000	100	81.82	+18.18	+1818

---

1   In practice, bond futures for such long maturities may not exist. They are given here to illustrate the concept.

Alternatively, suppose F had entered into a swap for 1,000 pounds and become the fixed rate payer at 9 per cent, receiving floating rate. Assume also that the floating rate index is the long-term bond rate and swap cash flows are perpetual.

The cash flows and the discounted present value of the swap position would be as follows:

Month	Market interest rate (long-term) in per cent	Receipt at prevailing interest rate	Payment at 9 per cent	Net cash flow	Discounted value of swap at prevailing interest rate
Jan. 2013	8	800	-900	-100	-1250
Jan. 2014	10	1000	-900	+100	+1000
Jan. 2015	11	1100	-900	+200	+1818

It may be seen that the value of the swap position exactly mirrors the profit/loss on the bond futures. (This example makes a number of simplifying assumptions to bring out clearly and simply the similarity between the two hedging instruments. The principle that a swap is equivalent to a string of future contracts, however, remains valid without these assumptions.)

Though a futures strip may, in theory, be equivalent to a swap, in practice there are usually no futures contracts running beyond two-three years (at the very most). Therefore, swaps occupy a niche position: they provide long-term hedging facilities.

Some features of the swaps market

Over the counter trading

Swaps are customised instruments and not standardised. Therefore, the swaps market is an over-the-counter market and there are no exchange-traded swaps. Because they are not traded through exchanges, the total volume of transactions cannot be quickly assessed. However, in some countries like Brazil, swaps are required to be registered through an exchange to enhance transparency and reduce counter-party risk.

Confirmations

The confirmation is the legal agreement that forms the basis of the relevant swap. The drafting is facilitated by the International Swaps and Derivatives

Association (ISDA) in New York. A number of master agreements (or standard templates) can be used and customised. Regulatory pressure towards standardisation has increased since the financial crisis. The Dodd-Frank Act in the United States of America modified the Commodity Exchange Act by adding a new section – 'Confirmation, Portfolio Reconciliation, Portfolio Compression, and Swap Trading Relationship Documentation, Requirements for Swap Dealers and Major Swap Participants.' This mandates the Commission to prescribe standards for Swap Dealers and Major Swap Participants with respect to the timely/accurate confirmation, processing, netting, documentation and valuation of swaps.

Settlement of net amount

In the various examples, it was assumed that each party to the swap makes one payment and receives another. In practice, only the net amount due from one party to the other is actually paid. If the payment falls on a holiday, it is generally made on the next business day.

Mark to market valuation of swaps

When the purchaser first initiates a swap transaction, the market value of the swap instrument is invariably zero. That means that if the market does not move, both the parties can end up exiting the agreement – ignoring the transaction costs for now. Thereafter, the swap is valued at each settlement date based on the level of the index at that date.

Warehousing and market-making

When a company wants to enter into a swap, it goes through an intermediary, which is usually a special purpose subsidiary of a bank or major stockbroker. In order to enable them to respond quickly to clients' needs and earn their commissions, these intermediaries generally engage in 'warehousing'. They enter into one side of the swap transaction, say as fixed rate payer to a client who wants to be a floating rate payer. They then wait for a suitable counterparty and offload the swap to him. This means that users of the swap market need not wait for locating a suitable counterparty. The 'warehousing' activity enables the intermediary to become a 'market maker'. This enhances the liquidity of the swap market.

Secondary market in swaps

It is possible to 'sell' a swap to another party with the agreement of the intermediary. The secondary market is, however, not very active and rather illiquid. The obligations in a swap can also be extinguished by 'unwinding' it, i.e., by reversing the transaction. The consent of the intermediary is, of course, necessary.

Credit default swaps

An important component of the present day swap market is the 'credit default swap'. However, while this is called a 'swap', it is not really an exchange of cash flows and is akin to a guarantee from one party in the event of another party defaulting on a credit risk. These instruments are therefore discussed in the chapter on Other Derivatives.

Economic functions of swap transactions

Financing function

Swaps, by exploiting comparative advantage, make funds available to borrowers at cheaper rates than would otherwise be possible. They therefore perform a financing function by making investment capital cheaper.

Arbitrage function

Interest rate swaps can reduce borrowing costs for both parties by exploiting the differences in the interest spreads in different segments (i.e., fixed vs., floating). Similarly, currency swaps exploit the differences in interest spreads between different currency segments. The availability of swaps tends to:

a.   increase demand or reduce supply in the underpriced segment; and

b.   reduce demand or increase supply in the overpriced segment.

By so doing, it actually tends to narrow the gap between the two segments. Swaps therefore act as an arbitrage mechanism which helps market integration and reduces interest rate distortions.

Hedging function

It was shown that swaps are analytically equivalent to a strip of futures transactions and that they can act as a hedge. Because of this, swaps perform the hedging function. Also, whereas futures only provide a short-term hedging facility, *swaps provide a long-term hedging facility which may not be available through other instruments.*

Part – IV
Options

10

Options – I

Introduction to Options

The evolution and growth of options trading has already been touched upon in the first chapter. This chapter explains the various features of different kinds of options. The next chapter deals with pricing of options. Chapter 12 looks more closely at options with specific reference to equity markets and outlines some hedging and trading strategies. Chapter 13 deals with some more advanced options strategies. (The term 'strategy' is used in the loose sense of a planned set of transactions carried out with a pre-determined objective in mind. While the strategies in chapters 12 and 13 are explained through equity options, they are also applicable to options on other underlyings.) Real options and employee stock options are covered in chapter 14.

The bulk of options trading happens through exchanges and the major options exchanges in the world are listed in Table 10.1.

Table 10.1: Major options exchanges

Location	Name of exchange	Main underlyings traded
London	London International Financial Futures and Options Exchange (LIFFE)	Short term interest rates (sterling, dollar, Euro, Swiss franc), German gilts, stock index, equities
London	London Commodity Exchange (LCE)	coffee, sugar, wheat, baltic freight index
Chicago	Chicago Board Options Exchange (CBOE)	stocks indices, t-bonds, t-notes and currencies
Chicago	CME	commodities
New York	American Stock Exchange (AMEX)	stocks and stock indices
Hong Kong	Hong Kong Futures Exchange	stock indices

Location	Name of exchange	Main underlyings traded
Singapore	Singapore Exchange (SGX) and Singapore Mercantile Exchange (SME)	Various securities; Singapore is also a big market for OTC currency transactions
Mumbai	NSE	equity and currency options
Korea	Korea Exchange (KRX)	equity
Dubai	Dubai Mercantile Exchange and NASDAQ Dubai	equity, commodities

Terminology

An option is a contract between two parties whereby one party acquires the right, but not the obligation, to buy or sell a particular commodity or instrument or asset, at a specified price, on or before a specified date. The person who acquires the right is known as the option buyer or holder while the counter-party (who confers the right) is known as the seller or writer. In return for giving such an option to the buyer, the seller charges an amount, which is known as the option premium. The specified price is called the exercise price or strike price. The commodity or instrument or asset covered by the contract is called the 'underlying' commodity or instrument or asset or simply 'the underlying'. The specified date is called the 'expiration date' or 'expiry date' or 'maturity date'. In this chapter, wherever the term 'commodity' is used, it should be construed as covering financial instruments also.

A feature of the jargon of derivatives in general, but particularly visible in the case of options, is the tendency to use colloquial abbreviations for certain terms. The newcomer to these markets may find them confusing. A common tendency is to shorten the terms. For instance, exercise price or strike price may be shortened to 'exercise' or 'strike', put or call options may be simply called 'puts' or 'calls', and so on. The term 'price' is sometimes used to refer to the market price of the option itself rather than the price of the underlying. One has to observe the context in which the word is used and deduce the correct meaning from it.

Option types: Call and put

Options may be of two types, i.e., call options and put options. In a call option, the option buyer has the right (but not the obligation) to buy the underlying commodity at the pre-determined price (in a sense, 'call' for the item from the market, hence the term). In put options, the option buyer has the right to sell the asset (in a sense, 'put' the item in the market). Before commodity options were banned in India in 1952, the same two types of options were traded as *teji* (call) and *mandi* (put). India now has options trading in equities and currencies, but commodity options were still banned as of early 2017. The following examples illustrate simple call and put options.

Example 10.1

A enters into a contract with B whereby A has the right to purchase 100 ounces of gold from B for $1400 per ounce at any time prior to 1 August. For granting this option A pays B an option premium of $15 per ounce. This is a call option.

Example 10.2

A enters into a contract with B whereby A has the option to sell 100 ounces of gold to B at a price of $1400 any time before August 1. For granting him this option, A pays B $16 per ounce as premium. This is a put option.

In both the above examples, A is the buyer (holder) of the option while B is the writer, or grantor. The term 'writer' (or 'grantor') is used for the original seller, while the term seller could refer to a reseller also (e.g., a person selling to square up an earlier purchase).

Simple or plain put and call options are often called 'plain vanilla' options using the analogy of ice cream.

A third type is the double option, which is a call-cum-put (or *teji-mandi*) option, whereby the option buyer acquires the right (but not obligation) to buy or sell the underlying commodity. (In the examples above, gold is the underlying commodity.)

Example 10.3

A enters into a contract with B, whereby he has the option to buy or sell 100 ounces of gold at $1400 per ounce any time before 1 August. For granting this option, B charges a premium of $31.

It may be noted that the premium for a double option is the sum of the premia for a call and put option at the same strike price for the same duration.

There are many other types of options, called exotic options, which will be described later. One type which looks similar to (but is different from) a double option, is the chooser option in which the buyer has the right to decide by a certain date what 'type' of option he will possess – call or put, but not both. The different types of option may have different exercise prices. While the double option is a call-cum-put, the chooser option is a call-or-put, with the choice of type being deferred.

Example 10.4

A hedge fund buys a chooser option on the S&P 500 which enables it to choose one month from now whether to convert this option into a call option or a put option (both of which expire three months from now). The S&P is currently at 1,100, and the call exercise (i.e., exercise price) is at 1,200 and the put exercise is at 1,000.

The buyer has one month to observe the market trend and decide whether a bullish or a bearish outlook is more plausible. On the other hand, once the choice has already been made, the fund cannot benefit from the type of option that was not chosen. Hence, the price must be less than a double option, but more than a plain vanilla call or put option (because the buyer has more flexibility).

Traded vs. over-the-counter (OTC) options

If option contracts are standardised, i.e., with standard contract sizes, standard strike prices and standard contract terms, and are traded through an exchange, they are known as traded options. Most traded options markets use a clearing house system. Where an options contract is not executed through an exchange, it is an OTC option. Some OTC options markets, though not exchange-traded, have standard legal terms.

Closing out in lieu of exercise

In a traded options market, it is not necessary to exercise an option in order to realise its value. Since options can be resold in the market, it is sufficient to take an offsetting position; a call buyer will sell a call, a put seller will buy a put, etc. The difference between the premium received and premium paid will be the profit or loss. Thus, the 'squaring up' approach used in futures is also used in traded options. For this reason, in traded options markets, the term 'price' is often used to refer to the premium.

Example 10.5

On May 1, the price of gold is $1395. X, a gold jewellery manufacturer requires a certain volume of gold in the month of September. He has an apprehension that the price may rise considerably by then. He therefore purchases a call option on gold with a strike price of $ 1,400. (The strike price is the price which the option buyer has to pay the option seller for the commodity, if and when he exercises his right to buy or sell.) In the instant case, X acquires the right to buy gold at the pre-determined price (strike price or exercise price) of $1,400. On September 1, the price of gold has risen to $1,450. Clearly, it is to the advantage of X to exercise his option. X has two alternatives. The first and obvious alternative is to exercise his option and purchase the gold at the pre-determined strike price of $1,400 per ounce. If there is a liquid market (e.g., in a traded options market) there is a second alternative - that is to 'close out' or 'square up' the position by reselling the option in the exchange, and then buy the physical gold separately. An expiring option would have a premium of approximately nil. The difference in premium represents the profit. Either way, by entering into the options contract, he has gained $50 per ounce. No doubt, the final net gain is lower by the amount of premium paid to the option seller when the jeweller purchased the option. (The option writer correspondingly would have lost $50 but the loss would be reduced by the amount of the premium he collected.)

Example 10.6

All the facts are as in Example 10.5 except that on 1 September the price of gold is $1,350. At this price, it is cheaper for X to purchase gold from the market at the prevailing rate than to exercise his call option and pay $1,400. He therefore allows the option to lapse. The net cost of the option is the amount of premium. Since the option is not exercised, the premium amount represents an income for the option seller and a loss for the buyer (who would have been better off without buying the option – just as a person who never makes a claim would have been better off by not insuring. But, that is with the benefit of hindsight).

Example 10.7

On 1 May, the price of gold is $1,395. C is a gold mine owner whose income increases with the price of gold. C has an apprehension that the price may fall, by the time his production comes to market in July. Accordingly, C purchases a put option from D whereby C has the right to sell 100 ounces of gold at the predetermined price of $1,385 up to 1 July. On 1 July, the price of gold is $1,330. If C were to sell gold in the market, he would only get $1,330 per ounce. Since he has an option contract to sell at $1,385 he exercises the option and gets a price of $1,385. In this case, C has gained $55 per ounce by entering into the options contract. His gain is reduced by the amount of premium that he has paid to D. D has correspondingly *lost $55 per ounce, but the loss is offset by the premium he has earned. (Alternatively, if the market were liquid, C could have closed out the position with the same net financial result.)*

Example 10.8

The facts are as in Example 10.7 except that the price of gold on 1 July is $ 1400. In this case, C will get a better price by selling his gold in the market than by exercising his option. Therefore, he allows the option to lapse. The amount of option premium is a loss to C and gain to D.

Various option styles – American, European and Asian options

Options can be classified into American, European, Asian and Bermudan style options. This classification (known as 'option style') has nothing to do with the location of the options trade – 'American' options are traded in Europe and vice versa. They are only varieties of contracts.

- In an American style option, the option can be exercised any time up to the maturity date.

- In a European option, the right can be exercised only on the maturity date.

- Asian options (also known as 'average rate options') do not have a fixed strike price. Instead, they have a formula for determining the strike price, which would be the average of the spot price over a given period of time.

- Bermudan options can be exercised only on certain dates.

Asian and Bermudan options are relatively rare. The following examples illustrate some of the features of different styles.

Example 10.9

On 1 March, the price of copper is $9,800 per ton. Person A expects a rise in price and buys an American option on June Copper (maturity date of 15 June and a strike price of $9,800). The prices subsequently are as follows:

15 May: $ 10,100

15 June: $ 9,700

As the option is an American option, A exercises it on 15 May (well before the expiry date), takes delivery of the copper at the strike price of $9,800 and then sells the copper in the spot market at a profit of $300 per ton. (It should be noted that in practice, if an American option *is a traded option or has an active OTC market, it will usually be more cost effective to sell it than to exercise it, because the transaction costs of giving/taking delivery can be avoided.)*

Example 10.10

All the other facts are as above, but the option is a European option. In this case, A cannot exercise the option on 15 May because he only has the right to do so on the maturity date. If it is not a traded option, he therefore does not have the profit opportunity that he had in the previous example. Therefore , an American option may have a higher profit potential than a European option for the buyer. This often leads to slightly higher premia for American options.

Example 10.11

Q Limited is an oil importer, requiring a regular monthly supply of oil. In August, it anticipates a drop in the price of oil, but wants to be hedged against a possible rise. It buys an Asian option on Brent Crude by which it has the right to buy from Y, 10,000 barrels at the average spot price from 15 August to 15 December. If the spot price on 15 December is lower than the three-month average, it is not worth exercising the option and vice versa.

Relationship between strike price and market price

It would have been clear from Examples 10.5 to 10.8 that the decision of an option buyer on option exercise depends on whether the strike price is above or below the market price. In market terminology:

- An option is said to be 'at-the-money' (abbreviated to ATM) if the current market price of the underlying is exactly equal to the option strike price.

- An option is said to be 'in-the-money' (abbreviated to ITM) when the strike price relates to the market price in such a way that there is an advantage in exercising the option. A call option will be 'in-the-money' if the strike price is below the current price (of the underlying). A put option will be 'in-the-money' if the strike price is above the current market price.

- An option is said to be 'out-of-the-money' (abbreviated to OTM) if the strike price relates to the market price in such a way that the buyer has no advantage in exercising the option. A call option is 'out-of-the- money' when the strike price is above the current market price, while a put option is 'out-of-the-money' when the strike price is below the current market price.

The premium for an option is the sum of intrinsic value and time value. An option is said to have intrinsic value when it is ITM. The more in-the-money an option is, the higher the intrinsic value. Intrinsic value is nil for ATM and OTM options. The time value, on the other hand, depends on the time to expiry, the volatility of the underlying asset, and the risk-free interest rate. Generally speaking, the longer the time remaining for expiry and the higher the volatility, the higher the time value.

As a simplification, the amount of intrinsic value is simply the *difference between the strike price and the current market price* of an in-the-money option. However, for a more precise formulation, it is necessary to take into account the fact that a European option can only be exercised *on* the maturity date and not before; this requires an adjustment for the discounted present value of the exercise price. By doing this and taking into account various arbitrage possibilities, it can be shown that:

- The intrinsic value of a call option (whether American or European) is the difference between the market price of the underlying and the discounted present value of the exercise price.
- The intrinsic value of an American put option is the difference between the exercise price and the market price of the underlying.
- The intrinsic value of a European put option is the difference between the discounted present-value of the exercise price and the market price of the underlying.

(The discount rate to be used is the risk-free interest rate; the yield on Treasury Bills can be taken for this purpose, because Treasury securities issued by the government are free of the risk of default.)

Options on futures

In many traded options markets, instead of the underlying asset being the spot commodity, a futures contract is used as the underlying. For instance, in the earlier examples a call option would give the right to buy 'one May futures gold contract' (rather than gold itself), while a put option would give the right to sell one gold futures contract.

Comparison of options and futures: Options as one-sided hedges

Under a futures contract, the buyer or seller acquires both the right and the obligation to buy or sell, whereas in an options contract there is only a right without obligation. An options contract is therefore one sided or unilateral and the purchaser has more rights than the seller of the option. However, in order to acquire this right the option buyer has to pay a premium to the option seller, which is not required in a futures contract.

Options are conceptually very similar to insurance contracts where a fixed premium is paid in return for cover against adverse risks. (The key differences between an option and an insurance contract are the absence of need for an 'insurable interest' and the fact that options can be used to earn profits and not just to protect against an eventual loss, as in insurance contracts.) From the buyer's viewpoint, an option has a certain and limited loss (the amount of premium) with unlimited profit potential. From the point of view of options sellers, an option has a certain and limited profit potential with virtually unlimited loss potential.[1] A futures contract has an unlimited loss and profit potential for both parties.

Earlier we saw that futures and forward contracts could be used as hedges. Options can also be used as hedges. Hedging through options has different payoffs (i.e., profit/ loss outcomes) as compared to hedging with futures or forwards, or 'linear' derivatives in general.[2] A farmer hedging his crops by selling futures 'locks in' the future price. While he is protected against price falls, he also misses out on any increase in prices. The same farmer can have protection as well as keep the 'upside' (i.e., profit potential) by buying a put option. If, for the purposes of simplicity, we assume that a farmer buys an ATM European put (that is, where the current price is equal to the strike price[3]), then any decrease in prices is compensated for by the increasing value of the put option. On the other hand, any increase in prices is welcome and only the premium is lost. An option is thus a one-sided hedge. Table 10.2 makes a comparison between futures and options as hedging instruments.

---

1   Mathematically, the loss potential for call sellers is unlimited since the price can rise to infinity, while for put sellers it is limited only by the fact that the price cannot fall below zero.

2   Linear derivatives are those where the relationship between the profit/loss and the price of the underlying can be expressed as, or approximates to, a linear equation.

3   In practice, an adjustment for the time value of money has to be made, but for short periods of time and at low interest rates, this can be ignored.

Table 10.2: Comparison between futures/forwards and options as hedging instruments

Issue	Futures	Options
Unfavourable (downside) price risk	Is avoided	Is avoided
Favourable (upside) price risk	Is forgone (hedger gets no net benefit if the price of the underlying moves in a favourable direction).	Is retained (hedger gets the benefit if the price of the underlying moves in a favourable direction).
Premium	Does not arise.	Is payable and hedger has to forgo the interest that could have been earned on this amount.
Initial margin	Is payable: hedger has to pay a portion of the value of the contract as margin and has to forgo the interest that could have been earned on this amount.	Does not arise.
Risk of additional margin calls	Hedger may have to pay additional margin when a margin call is made, i.e., when the price moves in an adverse direction. Thus, the hedger will have to be able to come up with more cash when necessary in order to sustain the hedge; if he is not able to provide the margin call, the position will be closed out and the hedge will no longer be effective.	Does not arise. Hedge remains effective for the duration of the contract.

Options as speculative instruments

While the examples above had depicted the options buyer as a hedger, options can also be used purely as speculative vehicles. The simplest options trading strategies involve the purchase or sale of 'naked' options. (A naked option is one which is not accompanied by an opposite or 'covering' position in the underlying or in some other option.) More complex strategies involve combinations of an option with a position in the underlying itself or a combination of different options.

Speculation through options purchase

Buying options is a 'limited liability' method of speculating on price. The profit potential ('upside') on buying an option is unlimited whereas the loss potential ('downside') is limited to the premium.

It is sometimes felt that an option is nothing but a futures contract accompanied by a 'stop loss' order. However, an option is actually safer than a futures contract with a stop loss order for three reasons. Firstly, stop losses may not actually be executed at the prescribed price because markets sometimes move so fast that it may not be possible to carry out the stop loss order at the stipulated price.

Example 10.12

X purchases one gold futures contract at $1,400 with a stop loss order to sell it if the price falls to $1,300. On a particular day, the price falls suddenly from $1,310 to $1,265 without any trade being executed at $1,300. In this case, despite the stop loss order, A will suffer a much bigger loss than he has anticipated, since the stop loss will be executed only at $1,265.

The second difference is that once a stop loss order is activated, the participant cannot share in any subsequent beneficial price move. In Example 10.12, we saw that the price had dropped to $ 1,265. If it subsequently moves up to $ 1,420, the speculator will not get any benefit because he has already closed out his transaction. (This is sometimes known as the 'whipsaw' risk.) This risk does not occur in an options contract.

Thirdly, in a futures contract, one may have to pay margin calls if there are adverse charges in price. This creates uncertainty in cash flows. In an options contract, no margin calls are levied on the buyer, once the premium has been paid.

Among the option buying strategies, the speculator has some choices to make. If she expects a major price move, she can get 'more bang for her buck' by buying out-of-the-money puts and calls which will be relatively cheap (the more deeply out-of-the-money the cheaper), with no extra downside risk.

For a speculator who buys options, the nominal break-even prices (i.e., the price at which the option premium is recovered) are as follows:

a. For call purchase:

Break-even price of underlying = Strike price + Premium

b. For put purchase:

Break-even price of underlying = Strike price – Premium.

Speculation through options selling

Speculators *can also sell options* but the key difference is that it involves unlimited loss potential with a limited and fixed potential for gain. Naked option selling is thus unsuitable for most investors.

Basic options strategies

The following table lists the strategy that would generally be apt for various expectations of a speculator:

Speculator's opinion on market prices	Appropriate option strategy
Very bullish	Buy a call
Moderately bullish	Write a put
Moderately bearish	Write a call
Very bearish	Buy a put

Of these strategies, it is worth repeating that *those involving writing an option carry unlimited risk.*

Table 10.3 illustrates the position of the (speculative) buyer and seller in a put option and call option, *vis-à-vis* a short and long position in futures respectively.

Table 10.3: Options vs. futures: Gains and losses in different circumstances

	Call buyer	Long futures	Call seller	Put buyer	Short futures	Put seller
Price rises	Unlimited gain	Unlimited gain	Unlimited loss	Limited loss	Unlimited loss	Limited gain
Price falls	Limited loss	Unlimited loss*	Limited gain	Unlimited gain	Unlimited gain	Unlimited loss*
Price unchanged	Limited loss	No gain or loss	Limited gain	Limited loss	No gain or loss	Limited gain

Transaction costs are ignored.

*Since the price of any asset cannot go below zero, there is technically a 'limit' to the gain/loss when the price falls. For practical purposes, this is largely irrelevant.

Options price tables

For all traded options and for active OTC options, price quotations are published.

Table 10.4 is an example of an option 'chain' with the Nifty share index as the underlying. The table shows the prices on end of day 12 August 2016 for index options having an expiry date of 26 August 2016. For ease of reference for the reader, column numbers from one to 15 have been added.

- Column eight is the key column giving the strike prices of the various options being traded in the exchange for the 30 August maturity.

- To the left of column eight are the values relating to call options.

- On the right of column eight are the values pertaining to put options.

- Column one reflects the open interest (OI). This figure is the total number of call options with a given strike price and expiry that were not settled as of 12 August 2016, i.e., options that are still 'open'. (Higher open interest generally represents higher liquidity.)

- The 'LTP' in column two refers to the last traded price (i.e., price of the option, not the underlying) for the different strike prices (of the underlying). For example, the LTP of the call option for a strike price of 8700 is 62.55. This means that as on 12 August, the premium (price) payable by a buyer/receivable by a seller of a call option on Nifty with a strike price of 8700 and exercise date of 26 August is ₹ 62.55.

- Similarly, on the right hand side, LTP (column 14) for a put option can be seen, and the OI is reflected in column 15.

The calls in the shaded boxes (on the left and top of the image) are the 'in-the-money' (ITM) calls. The puts in the shaded boxes (on the right and bottom of the image) are the ITM puts.

The various bid and ask prices and quantities are also shown in the table. The 'ask' price is the price payable by buyers while the 'bid' price is the price receivable by sellers. The difference between these two (known as the 'bid-ask spread') is the profit margin of the dealers. The bid quantities in columns four and nine are the volumes (in number of contracts of standard size) of bids for calls and puts respectively while the ask quantity in columns seven and 12 are the ask quantities for calls and puts respectively.

Below, in Tables 10.5 and 10.6, are abridged tables for the Microsoft

Table 10.4: NIFTY option as on 12 August 2016 for options
with expiry 25 August 2016
(Underlying price: 8,672.15)

1	2	3	4	5	6	7	8	9	10	11	12	13	14	15
OI	LTP	Net chng	Bid qty	Bid pr	Ask pr	Ask qty	Strike pr	Bid qty	Bid pr	Ask pr	Ask qty	Net chng	LTP	OI
1500	331.15	54.75	75	311.1	343.65	75	8350	225	9.7	9.85	375	-7.2	9.8	205650
649800	278	46.85	75	278.05	279.9	75	8400	375	13.35	13.4	75	-10.15	13.7	5050425
5925	238.35	43.85	750	225.8	243.3	750	8450	75	17.4	17.7	375	-14.5	17.55	782850
1497675	192	39.7	150	191.6	192.3	225	8500	5100	25.2	25.3	2175	-18.45	25.45	5617125
62700	155	35.35	75	151.4	154.95	150	8550	2850	34.5	34.55	300	-24.15	35	712200
2529225	117.45	27.45	75	118.7	119	150	8600	75	49.25	49.4	225	-29.7	49.65	4476375
507150	87.95	22.5	75	87.05	87.8	75	8650	75	66.9	67.85	600	-35.25	67	480075
4571625	62.55	16.25	10275	63	63.2	600	8700	75	90.8	90.9	600	-40.25	91.9	2095125
631950	42.35	10.15	75	42.55	42.65	75	8750	825	118.35	120.3	75	-42.95	122.95	66075
5668875	28.85	8.1	75	28.45	28.6	3750	8800	150	153.6	154.35	375	-52.4	154	1011150
372450	18.55	4.8	225	17.8	18	300	8850	300	192.2	196.05	600	-55.85	192.95	10875
3934650	11.65	2.7	2550	11.5	11.6	1725	8900	2250	236.1	236.95	75	-56.15	237	221475
232125	7.1	1.2	75	6.95	7	150	8950	5250	235.65	308.1	2925	-	-	-
6320175	4.95	0.8	12225	4.8	4.9	5250	9000	75	325.7	327	75	-59	326	778425

Source: NSE website, nseindia.com.

stock option in the United States (August 2016 and September 2016 expiries respectively) as on 12 August 2016. On that day, Microsoft shares were quoted at approximately $57.94 per share.

Table 10.5: Microsoft (MSFT) option chain, August 2016 expiry

Last trade	Change	Call bid	Call ask	Strike price	Last trade	Change	Put bid	Put ask
3.92	0.48	3.25	3.45	54.5	0.09	0.01	0.03	0.08
2.7	-0.59	2.92	2.95	55	0.11	0.04	0.07	0.1
2.35	-0.33	2.42	2.45	55.5	0.16	-0.03	0.09	0.14
1.77	-0.54	1.92	1.95	56	0.22	-0.01	0.17	0.2
1.39	-0.57	1.44	1.47	56.5	0.3	0.08	0.25	0.28
1	-0.4	1	1.03	57	0.46	0.12	0.4	0.42
0.58	-0.43	0.65	0.7	57.5	0.66	0.15	0.58	0.6
0.37	-0.23	0.39	0.41	58	0.99	0.29	0.85	0.88
0.21	-0.19	0.2	0.23	58.5	0.95	-0.02	1.19	1.22
0.1	-0.11	0.09	0.13	59	1.7	0.22	1.57	1.61
0.16	0.08	0.04	0.07	59.5	0	0	1.96	2.03
0.03	-0.04	0.02	0.04	60	2.5	0.47	2.43	2.47
0.04	0.01	0.02	0.04	60.5	0	0	2.97	3.05
0.05	0	0.01	0.03	61	5.35	0.45	3.45	3.55

Source: Marketwatch.com website.

The market value of the underlying Microsoft stock (US$57.94) must be kept in mind. The August call in Table 10.5 with a strike price of 55 can be bought at 2.95, and its intrinsic value is $(57.94–55.00) =$ 2.94 per share. Therefore, the time value is just $0.01 per share. However, the time value for September expiry is higher as expected. It can be calculated by subtracting the intrinsic value from the option price. Checking the figures in Table 10.6, that comes to (3.10 - (57.94-55.00)) = (3.10-2.94) =US$ 0.16.

Table 10.6: Microsoft (MSFT) option chain, September 2016 expiry

Last trade	Change	Call bid	Call ask	Strike price	Last trade	Change	Put bid	Put ask
0	0	3.4	3.55	54.5	0.46	0	0.42	0.45
3.05	0	3	3.1	55	0.53	0	0.48	0.52
2.69	0	2.68	2.75	55.5	0.66	0	0.58	0.62
0	0	2.29	2.33	56	0.78	0	0.7	0.74
1.94	-0.29	1.93	1.98	56.5	0.93	0	0.88	0.9
1.49	0	1.62	1.67	57	0	0	1.04	1.08
1.28	-0.28	1.29	1.32	57.5	1.39	0	1.22	1.26
1.03	-0.27	1.05	1.09	58	1.6	0	1.46	1.49
0.79	-0.26	0.82	0.84	58.5	0	0	1.76	1.79
0.61	-0.3	0.63	0.66	59	0	0	2.03	2.13
0.47	-0.12	0.46	0.56	59.5	0	0	2.36	2.43
0.35	-0.2	0.33	0.38	60	0	0	2.79	2.85
0.4	0	0.23	0.28	60.5	0	0	3.15	3.3
0.29	0	0.15	0.24	61	3.82	0	3.55	3.75

Source: Marketwatch.com website.

The August put for the same strike (55) is out-of-the-money and so has a premium (entirely time value) of around $0.10 per share. For September expiry, the put option for the same strike (55) can be bought for $0.52. Intrinsic value is still the same (zero) but time value has now increased. This is because there is a longer time left for expiry.

Yet another format of options price table is given in Table 10.7. In this format, for a single strike price, options premia for different expiry months are given.

Table 10.7: Index options with same strike and varying expiry

LTP	Net chng	Call bid qty	Call bid price	Call ask price	Call ask qty	Expiry date	Put bid qty	Put bid price	Put ask price	Put ask qty	Net chng	LTP
62.55	16.25	10,275	63	63.2	600	25-Aug-16	75	90.8	90.9	600	-40.25	91.9
169	26.95	150	169.4	170.35	75	29-Sep-16	75	152	152.85	75	-29.35	153

LTP	Net chng	Call bid qty	Call bid price	Call ask price	Call ask qty	Expiry date	Put bid qty	Put bid price	Put ask price	Put ask qty	Net chng	LTP
235	26.3	225	231.3	238	150	27-Oct-16	150	174.05	185.45	150	-37.15	176
350	-	750	333.05	-	-	29-Dec-16	1,500	185.5	-	-	-	-
1,530.00	-	-	-	-	-	29-Jun-17	750	210.05	-	-	-	332
750	-	-	-	-	-	28-Dec-17	-	-	-	-	-	580
1,354.50	-	-	-	-	-	28-Jun-18	75	318.6	-	-	-	900
2,569.45	-	-	-	-	-	27-Dec-18	75	295.45	-	-	-	-
-	-	-	-	-	-	27-Jun-19	75	530	590	7,500	-5	590
2,002.85	-	-	-	-	-	26-Dec-19	-	-	-	-	-	-

Source: nseindia.com. Underlying NIFTY 8672.15 12/8/16. STRIKE 8700.

Quotations are arranged in ascending order of expiry for the 8,700 strike price (NIFTY: with the underlying at 8,672), with maturity months arranged vertically. The reader will notice that premia tend to increase from top to bottom for both calls and puts - this reflects the time value of the option. The prices for the December 2018 and June 2019 options are exceptions; they may indicate illiquidity (poor trading volume) and the prices may reflect the situation on earlier dates when the underlying price was different.

Exotic options

Apart from the 'straightforward' put and call options enumerated above, several 'exotic' options have been developed which have special features. Some of these (like capped options on shares – see below) are exchange-traded while others are custom-made or OTC options.

Limit-dependent or barrier options

These are options, which come into force /go out of force if and when a particular price limit is reached, as illustrated in examples below.

Example 10.13

In July, the price of gold is $1,400. X, who needs gold in October, wants protection against a rising gold price. However, he feels (based on his technical analysis) that if the price falls below $1,390, then it will not rise above $1,400 before October. He therefore buys an October barrier call option on gold with a strike price of $1,400 with a 'knock-out' price of $1,390. If, any time before expiry, the gold price touches $1,390, the call option will be automatically cancelled – this is known as the knock-out feature as the option gets 'knocked out'.

Example 10.14

In July, the price of gold is $1,400. Y, who needs gold in October, feels the price is not likely to rise, and he feels he can absorb minor price increases. However, his technical analysis shows that if the price rises above $1,415, then a bull run is likely to commence which would be too much for him to absorb. He therefore buys an October barrier call option with a strike price of $1,400 but a 'knock-in' price of $1,415. If at any time before expiry, the gold price touches $4,115, he will automatically get a call option.

Barrier options are cheaper than ordinary options (which is the advantage to the buyer) because they offer less risk protection. However, the risk to the buyer, particularly in knock-out options, is that the price may move in an erratic manner, i.e., 'hit' the barrier but then reverse the trend. (This is the whipsaw risk referred to earlier.) In the previous example, suppose the price drops to $1,385 in August; the option is 'knocked out'. If, suddenly, in September the price soars to $1,420, X would be unprotected. Because the existence/extinction of the option depends on the path taken by the price, these are known as path-dependent barrier options.

Capped options

A capped option is an option, which will be automatically exercised if the underlying (commodity or financial instrument) touches a particular predetermined price prior to the expiry of the option. If the 'cap' is not reached during the validity of the option, it can be exercised at the end of the period like a European option.'

Example 10.15

The share price of XYZ Limited is trading at ₹460 in May. An investor purchases a capped September call option with an exercise price of 460 and a cap price of 490. This means that if any time before September the price of the share of XYZ Limited touches the 490 level, the capped option will get automatically exercised. On 6 June, the share price touches ₹491. The option is exercised on that day.

There is a specialised terminology applicable to capped options. The 'cap interval' is the difference between the exercise price and the cap price. In the above example, the cap interval is ₹ 30. In exchange- traded capped options, there are standardised cap intervals fixed by the options exchange and capped options can only be purchased/sold using these standardised intervals.

In the above example, it was simply assumed that the underlying price had 'touched' a pre-determined cap price. The precise method of determining whether the cap has been touched or not, is specified by the options exchange. The exchange would decide, which is the 'automatic exercise value.' For example, it may be decided that the closing price of the share in a specified stock exchange is the automatic exercise value; if the cap value is reached during the day, but the closing price does not exceed the cap, then the cap is deemed not to have been touched.

Most capped options are 'cash settled', i.e., instead of delivering the underlying interest, the cash value of the difference between market price and exercise price on the date of exercise is paid. The advantage of a capped (cash-settled) option for the buyer is that exercise takes place automatically once a pre-determined level of profit has occurred, without risk of reversal in the price trend later. From the point of view of the option seller, a capped option has the advantage of limiting the maximum risk possible. The disadvantage to the buyer is that the option is exercised automatically even if the option buyer would like to hold on to it in the anticipation of further favourable price changes in the underlying interest.

Flexibly structured options

Flexibly structured options are those in which some of the terms are not standardised. When a flexibly structured option is purchased and sold, the parties have the flexibility (subject to the limits decided by the options exchange) to decide certain terms of the options. In flexibly structured options, some of the terms are standardised while the others are to be decided by the parties. The terms which are left to be decided by the parties are called 'variable terms'.

As an example of a flexibly structured option, a company may be able to engage in an option transaction with a maturity date of a non-standard nature. For example, the standard September Gold option may have a maturity date of 30 September , while the August option has a maturity date of 31 August. A particular company may require an option expiring on 12 September. Normally the company will have to use either the August or September option for hedging with resulting timing differences. However, if flexibly structured options are available, the company may be able to get an option with an expiry date of 12 September. In this case, the expiration date is the 'variable term'.

Normally, the options exchange itself will decide which of the terms can be treated as variable terms in a flexibly structured option. Since flexibly structured options are not standardised, there is a lesser likelihood of having a secondary market in such options. This means they are more risky in terms of marketability. Options exchanges generally fix a higher minimum monetary value for flexibly structured options. Sophisticated investors or hedgers seeking to manage highly specific portfolio or trading risks may use these options.

Rainbow options

These are options where, in return for payment of a premium, the purchaser of the option gets the right to buy or sell the best performer out of a number of different assets. For example, a rainbow call option on stock indices might give the buyer the right to buy either the FTSE 100 index or the Standard and Poor's 500 index at predetermined prices, depending on which had performed better during the option period. This is called a two-colour rainbow option. If the same option gave the investor the right to buy the best out of three indices it would be called a three-colour rainbow option and so on. These options are relatively rare, and are custom-made OTC options.

Real options

While this book will be dealing primarily with financial options,[4] it is important to realise that one is always surrounded by various options in real life, quite separate from the derivative markets. 'Real options' are discussed in chapter 13.

---

4   In the context of this paragraph, 'financial' options include options on commodities.

Appendix 10.1

Options and 'complete markets'

A discussion of the theory of complete markets and its relationship to derivatives is beyond the scope of this book, but a very brief conceptual introduction may be useful.

To understand the terminology let us take the example of a bet on a die throw. If the outcome is guessed correctly you win hundred rupees (say), otherwise you lose twenty. A bet on any number is a 'state-contingent claim', often simplified to 'state claim', i.e., a claim which is contingent on the state of the world.[5] In this case, there is a state claim with payoff of a hundred rupees if that number is the outcome, and payoff of minus twenty rupees if it is not. One, two, three, four, five and six are the 'states of the world' in this example. If you feel that the next throw will be a six, then that is your 'market view' and you can place a bet accordingly. When the dice is actually thrown, the actual state of the world will materialize and you will know whether your view was correct or wrong, and depending on that, you will gain a hundred or lose twenty rupees.

States of the world can be defined even more elaborately to take into account the time, place or environment. Cricketing records are an interesting example of state-contingent measurement. Take the case of a high score by a batsman. The score may be the 'highest score ever' or the 'highest score by an opener' or the 'highest score by an opener in an overseas game' or the 'highest score by an opener on this ground' or' the highest score by an opener in the second innings' or 'the highest score by an opener in the second innings on this ground' or the 'highest score by an opener in the second innings while playing overseas' and so on.

In economic terms, the price of a good or service is always somewhat dependent on the prevailing state of the world – time, place, environment etc. It can be shown by complex mathematics that in a perfectly competitive world with perfect information and complete markets and where certain other assumptions are fulfilled, economic welfare is maximized. (Complete markets

---

5   The word state in this context refers to condition (e.g., 'what is the state of a person's health'), rather than to a political or geographic unit.

imply that a market exists in every possible good or service for every possible state of the world; thus not only would there be a market for potatoes, but there would be a market for potatoes for each time,[6] place and environment.) On this basis, some influential economists argued that economic welfare is improved whenever there is an incremental move towards more complete markets and hence that the creation of new derivatives markets is, by definition, beneficial to the economy.

Derivatives have allowed all kinds of 'states of the world' to be 'bet' on or against. Futures contracts themselves introduce new (more complete) markets by allowing bets on prices at future dates. Options go even further. Options allow speculators to bet on the probability distribution of the expected future price. Other derivatives allow claims to be based on specific circumstances or combinations of circumstances, i.e., based on various states of the world.

For example, consider a pharmaceutical stock in the United States that is awaiting a crucial decision on some clinical trials by the Food and Drug Administration (FDA). The result is expected to either increase the stock price by around 30 per cent or decrease it by 30 per cent. Changes, in absolute magnitude of less than 20 per cent or more than 40 per cent are very improbable. In such a case, the futures contract with the shortest maturity (the 'nearest' futures contract) could be near the stock price, but the options at 30 per cent ITM and OTM could be more expensive than usual, and the options at 20 per cent or 40 per cent ITM/OTM could be much cheaper than usual. 'Usual' here refers to option prices calculated based on an approximately normal distribution of stock returns, whereas the return distribution expected in this special case is bimodal. Thus, not only do options allow market participants to hedge and leverage, they allow them to express very specific and unique views on each market for different states of the world.

However, the theory that derivatives markets are automatically beneficial because they incrementally lead to 'completion of markets' stands on a weak footing. The underlying assumption is that since 'complete markets' are desirable in a perfect or ideal world, any incremental improvement towards complete markets is also always good. Contrary to such an assumption propagated by some economists, other economists have shown clearly (in the 'Theory of Second Best') that if the utopian conditions of perfection are

---

6   And for all times in the future.

not attained, then a partial movement towards more complete markets is not necessarily beneficial and can even be harmful. Hence, one cannot conclude automatically that creating new derivatives markets is necessarily beneficial to the economy as a whole. For a detailed discussion of this topic, readers may refer to Chapter 4 of The Economics of Derivatives by Somanathan and Nageswaran, cited in the Bibliography.

11

Options – II
Pricing of Options

As briefly mentioned in chapter 10, the price of an option is the sum of two components: intrinsic value and time value.

Intrinsic value

To recapitulate, the *intrinsic value* of an American option is:
- For call options: The difference, if positive, between the current price of the underlying and the strike price of the option.
- For put options: The difference, if positive, between the strike price of the option and the current price of the underlying.

The intrinsic value of a European option is the difference, if positive, between the current price of the underlying and the *discounted present value* of the strike price for calls and vice versa for puts.

As was seen in chapter 10, an option which has intrinsic value is said to be 'in-the-money' and one with no intrinsic value is either 'at-the-money' or 'out-of-the-money'. In the case of traded options the premium is usually referred to as the 'price' of the option and hence the term pricing refers to how the premium is determined.

Time value

As regards the second component, *time value*, this is due to the fact that even if the price may be unattractive today, future fluctuations may make the option profitable. The time value depends on the interplay of a number of factors:

Time

It is obvious that the longer the period of time, the greater are the chances of price fluctuations and vice-versa. Thus, time value generally varies directly with amount of time left to maturity. This leads to the fact that options are wasting assets: as an option's expiration date approaches, its time value diminishes and eventually becomes nil. The only value remaining is the intrinsic worth, if any. Therefore, if an option is not sold or exercised by the expiration date, it becomes worthless. (This is important from an investor's point of view: in contrast to options, underlying assets like shares can be held indefinitely.)

Extent of the difference between current price and strike price

An option which is deeply out-of-the-money has a lower time value than an option which is only slightly out-of-the-money. A deep OTM option has a much lower probability of ever becoming profitable than one which is slightly OTM for the same maturity period.

Example 11.1

The current market price of shares in X Ltd. is ₹ 300. The 200 put for August is priced at ₹ 5 while the 250 put is priced at ₹ 14 and the ₹ 290 put is priced at ₹ 30. Note that none of them has intrinsic value because in all cases, the option is not worth exercising at the current market price but the deep OTM option (200) is worth much less than the near-the-money (290) option.

Interest rate

Generally, increases in interest rates tend to cause higher premia for calls and lower premia for puts, while decreases in interest rates tend to cause lower premia for calls and higher premia for puts.[1]

This is because a call option represents a contingent payment of money for the holder while a put option represents a contingent receipt of money. Higher interest rates reduce the present value of future cash flows: for a call option holder, this reduces the future payment making the option more valuable, while for a put option holder this reduces the future receipt making it less valuable.

---

1   In some rare cases (when interest rates are relatively high compared to price volatility), the interest rate factor (which reduces the value of longer maturity receipts) may overwhelm the 'longer profit opportunity' factor, thereby resulting in prices of long duration put options being lower than those of shorter duration put options.

Volatility (price variability) of the underlying

If the commodity (or share or financial instrument) normally has a very stable price, then the time value would be relatively smaller. If it has a high degree of volatility, then the time value will be relatively greater because there is a greater likelihood that the price will move to ITM.

Dividends

Pricing of options on dividend-yielding securities is more complex than pricing of options on commodities. In the case of a share, the expected dividend has to be factored into the calculation of the time value. As a general rule, the higher the dividends expected, the lower the value of call options (compared to a similar situation with no dividends), and the higher the value of put options. This is because, *ceteris paribus*, the price of the stock is expected to fall by the amount of dividend pay-out on the ex-dividend date (adjusted for time value of money).

Here it is important to note that only expected dividends reduce the value of calls *vis-à-vis* a situation where no dividend is paid. Unexpected dividends could increase the price of the stock and hence the call. After the unexpected dividend is declared and the new stock price level is established, the Black-Scholes value (see later in this chapter) of the call would again be relatively cheaper than a hypothetical situation of no dividend.

Absolute value of underlying

Lastly, the absolute amount of time value also varies with the absolute value of the underlying. In absolute terms, a given percentage swing can result in differing amounts of losses for the writer depending on the price of the underlying. The absolute value of loss to the writer of a naked (i.e., uncovered) call option from a 10 per cent rise in the price of a ₹ 40 share is clearly less than that from a 10 per cent rise in a ₹ 400 share. Hence, time value of an option on a ₹ 40 share will obviously be lower than on a ₹ 400 share.

Summary

a.   The premium for an option is the intrinsic value plus the time value.

b. Intrinsic value is nil for OTM/ATM options.

c. The intrinsic value of an ITM American option can be calculated in a straightforward manner: strike price minus market price of underlying for a put and vice versa for calls. (For ITM European options, precision requires that the strike price be discounted to present value, but for short term options and at low interest rates, the discounting can be ignored for most purposes and the intrinsic value can be taken as roughly the same as that of an American option.)

d. Calculating the time value is more complicated. All unexpired options (whether OTM/ATM or ITM) have time value. Time value is affected by:

    i. the time remaining till expiry;

    ii. the extent of the difference between strike price and market price;

    iii. the prevailing rate of interest;

    iv. the volatility (i.e., variability of the price) of the underlying;

    v. the amount of dividend if any; and

    vi. the absolute value of the underlying.

Put-call parity (PCP)

It has been shown[2] that in markets where short sales of the underlying asset are possible, the premium for a call and a put with the same maturity date and an at-the-money strike price will be equal because of arbitrage. If there is any deviation, risk free arbitrage profits can be earned by simultaneously:

- buying the underlying asset (if the call is higher priced) or short selling the underlying asset (if the put is higher priced) by;

- selling the option with higher premium; and

- buying the option with lower premium.

Obviously only one of the two (call or put) will be exercised depending on the price. The purchase or sale of the underlying asset cancels this out leaving the difference in premium as profit. For strike prices other than at-the-money,

---

2   H. R. Stoll, 'The Relationship between Put and Call Option Prices,' *Journal of Finance*, December, 1969.

the put and call premia are not equal due to the differing implications of the gap between the two prices. However, even in such cases it has been shown that there is predictable relationship between put and call premia for the same strike price which is explained below.

To understand PCP in a simple and relatively non-mathematical way, the reader should work through Example 11.2.

Example 11.2

Consider two portfolios of investment. One portfolio (Portfolio 1) consists of two elements:-

- *A European call option on 100 oz. of gold with a strike price of $1,600 and maturity date of 30 September.*
- *An amount of cash equal to the strike price of the option, viz., $1,600.*[3]

The second portfolio (Portfolio 2) comprises two elements:

- *A European put option on 100 oz. of gold at the same strike price ($1,600) and maturity date (30 September)*
- *Equal quantity of underlying (in this case Gold equivalent in value to 100 oz.*[4]*) at the current price, say, $1,570.*

In portfolio 1, when the gold price falls, the value of the call option will also fall but the cash will remain intact. Alternatively, if the gold price rises, the call option will also rise in value while the cash remains unchanged.

In portfolio 2, when the price of gold falls, the put option will appreciate while the value of the gold (underlying) would fall. If the gold price rises, the put option declines in value but the underlying (gold) appreciates. These payoffs are shown in Figure 11.1:

Portfolio 1 = Call + Cash, where Cash amount = Call strike price

Portfolio 2 = Put + Underlying asset

Figure 11.1: *Pay off diagrams for PCP*

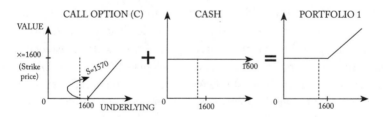

---

3   For simplicity, interest is ignored at this stage or taken as zero (incidentally, in recessionary times this has sometimes actually been close to the truth—e.g., in Japan or lately in the United States as well.)

4   Storage cost of gold is assumed to be zero.

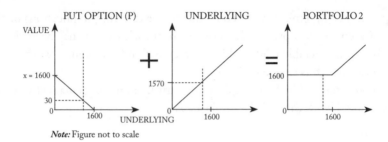

Note: Figure not to scale

Note that the combined pay off diagram for both portfolios in Example 11.3 is identical. From this it will be clear that the two portfolios are identical in terms of their payoff structure, i.e., (Call + Cash) has the same pay off as (Put + Stock) i.e.,

$C+X=P+S$

Where,

C = *call premium*

P = *put premium*

S = *value of the underlying security or asset*

X = *exercise price (also known as strike price) for both the call and the put option*

This (Call premium plus exercise price= Put option premium for the same exercise price plus value of the underlying security) is the PCP relationship when the interest rate is assumed to be nil. If there were a difference in the pay off, then it would be advantageous for an investor to do arbitrage, e.g., buy the cheaper portfolio, simultaneously sell the costlier portfolio and thereby earn a risk free profit. In liquid and well-traded markets any such opportunity would lead to quick and massive arbitrage until the parity is restored. For example, if puts are under-priced, traders would buy puts until the premium on puts increases and the parity is reached. *Hence, normally the two portfolios should have an identical value viz., should be at parity.*

In Example 11.2, the interest rate was assumed to be nil. If interest rates are taken into account, then the amount of cash required in portfolio 1 of Example 11.2 has to be adjusted so that with interest it would yield the strike price on the maturity date. Instead of an amount X, a smaller amount is needed. Accounting for this, mathematically the PCP relationship becomes:

$C + Xe^{-rt} = P + S$

Or

$P = C + Xe^{-rt} - S$

Where,

C = call premium

e= 2.71828 (Euler's number or exponential constant)

P = put premium

S= value of the underlying security or asset

X= exercise price (also known as strike price)

r= risk-free interest rate

PCP for ATM European options and American options

It may be noted that a European call is in-the-money when S> Xe^{-rt} and a European put is in-the-money when S< Xe^{-rt}. In the special case of an at-the-money European option, the current market price is equal to the discounted value of the strike price, i.e., S= Xe^{-rt}.

We know that,

$P = C + Xe^{-rt} - S$

But S= Xe^{-rt} Substituting S for Xe^{-rt},

P= C+S-S

i.e., P= C.

Thus, a put and a call have identical premia when the option is ATM.

For American options, the term Xe^{-rt} simply becomes X. Even for European options, Xe^{-rt} can be replaced by X for approximate calculations in respect of short term options when interest rates are very low because the difference between X and Xe^{-rt} is small.

The PCP can be used to derive approximate prices for calls or puts if the price of puts or calls (respectively) is known.

Example 11.3

The current stock price is ₹ 730 for Company XYZ, and the risk-free interest rate is 7.5 percent. A two month (European) put option with an exercise price of ₹ 500 has a price (premium) of ₹ 10, but due to low liquidity, there was no listed quote for the two month, ₹ 500 call. What is a good estimate of its value?

Rearranging the call-put parity equation,

$C = P + S - Xe^{-rt}$

Call value = 10 + 730 – 500(e-0.0125) = 740-493.8   [rt = (7.5/100)*(2/12)=0.0125]

= ₹ 246.2

Options pricing models

Over the years, several mathematical formulae have been evolved for calculating the composite (intrinsic plus time) value of options. Explaining the derivation of these formulae or how they work would be beyond the scope of this book, which explicitly aims to provide a non-mathematical approach. In practice, market participants need not do these calculations themselves as they can be programmed into a computer. However, a basic conceptual understanding of the methods is important for sellers and writers, to prevent mispricing, and for buyers in assessing the correctness of a given price. Accordingly, a short introduction to the main formulae is provided so that readers are aware of the most important techniques in use and as a basis for further reading.

Black-Scholes option pricing model

The most important options pricing model is known as the Black-Scholes option-pricing model.[5] This model (which was evolved by the economists Fischer Black and Myron Scholes) gives a formula by which the premium can be worked out.

The value of a European call option on shares under the Black-Scholes option pricing model is:

$c = SN(d_1) - Ke^{-rT} N(d_2)$

where,

c = European call premium

S = current market price of underlying asset or security

T = time left till maturity

K = strike price

$N(d_1)$, $N(d_2)$ = cumulative normal distribution function of d_1 and d_2 respectively.

e = 2.71828 (Euler's number or exponential constant)

$d_1 = [\ln (S/K) + (r + s^2/2)T] \div [s\sqrt{T}]$

$d_2 = d_1 - s\sqrt{T}$

Ln = natural logarithm

---

5   F. Black and M. J. Scholes, 'The Pricing of Options and Corporate Liabilities', *Journal of Political Economy*, May, 1973. This seminal paper became the starting point for a whole body of literature on options pricing.

s = standard deviation of price changes of the underlying (i.e., volatility)

r = risk-free interest rate

This basic formula can be adapted to price European puts, for which the formula is:

$p = Xe^{-rT} N(-d_2) - SN(d_1)$,

where, p is the put premium.

There are adaptations of the Black-Scholes formula to price options on futures, American options, barrier options, commodity options and currency options (where there are two interest rates to be considered), etc. For some of these, the formulae are only approximate.

Binomial distribution or binomial options pricing model

This model is an alternative to Black-Scholes that is considered more accurate when dealing with options that may be exercised over a period of time rather than on a single date. It is often used to price American and Bermudan options, particularly for dividend-paying stocks. This alternative is only suitable when path dependence is not an issue, that is when it does not matter what path a security took to reach its present price or condition (see below).

Monte Carlo method

The Monte Carlo method[6] is a method which uses computer-generated algorithms that rely on a huge number of repeated random samples to compute the final results of various scenarios and hence generate a distribution. The sheer size of the iterations provides fairly robust results since all possible scenarios are tested. The disadvantage is that the sheer volume of computation and computational time involved makes this impractical for use on a real-time basis for actively traded markets. It is primarily used for one-off valuations of real or financial options (as in Example 11.4 below) rather than for repeated use in a trading desk.

The Monte Carlo method is often used for valuation of certain kinds of

---

6   The physicists John von Neumann, Stanislaw Ulam and Nichols Metropolis first used the Monte Carlo method in the 1940s while they were working on the nuclear weapon project (Manhattan Project) in the Los Alamos National Laboratory. The method was named after the Monte Carlo casinos.

financial options, (complex options involving multiple parameters including Asian options) and for real options. This method is particularly suited for situations involving 'path dependency'.

Example 11.4

A bank has a portfolio of fixed rate mortgages with different maturities and interest rates. The mortgages contain a pre-payment option which allows the borrower to pre-pay the loan. For purposes of securitising and selling this portfolio as a method of refinance, the Bank needs to be able to value the cost of the 'pre-payment option'. The option is more likely to be exercised when market rates of interest go down. Whether the options would be exercised by borrowers is 'path-dependent', i.e., the outcome depends on the exact path or sequence of events. If the same events happen but in a different sequence, the outcome may be different. (For instance, if interest rates rise and then fall after a few years, the outcome will be beneficial to the bank vis-à-vis a situation where they first fall for a few years and then rise, even if the average interest rate is the same in both cases.) This can be modelled with the Monte Carlo method and a price of the mortgage portfolio can thus be calculated. Then the calculation can be repeated without the pre-payment option. The difference in the portfolio values in the two cases represents the value of the pre-payment option in the mortgage.

Estimating volatility

Earlier, when describing the Black-Scholes option pricing model, we saw that one of the terms is: s = standard deviation of price changes of the underlying.

This is also known as volatility. Volatility is thus clearly a crucial input to the Black-Scholes model. The other inputs – risk-free interest rate, time to expiry, strike price, underlying price – are all known or easily discernible. Theoretically the volatility to be used is the future volatility but this is obviously not known. The question arises as to the best way of estimating the future volatility, based on extrapolating the past. There are various possibilities which have advantages and disadvantages.

Current volatility

The 'current' volatility – volatility in say the last trading day – is easy to obtain and reflects the current situation but is subject to large fluctuations (i.e., the volatility itself is volatile!). Another alternative is the average daily volatility of a longer period - say the last month. Even this can sometimes exhibit a large fluctuation when an exceptionally volatile trading day falls out of the sample.

Another alternative is to take a weighted-average of the volatilities of a specified number of trading days, with a higher weight being given to the 'nearer' days (so long as the total of the probabilities add up to one).

Historical average volatility over a long period can also be combined with the weighted-average probability of the last few days (such that the sum of the weight of the historical average and all the different weights for volatility of the last N days add up to one). Depending on the parameters used, adding a historical average to the current weighted average can imply a mean-reverting volatility model. ('Mean reversion' is an assumption or belief that a variable will eventually revert to its historical mean and is often empirically borne out. For instance, if the price-earnings ratio of the Indian stock market has historically been at, say, 15 and is currently at 20, mean reversion would imply that the ratio will be expected to fall and come back to its historic level.) Such models for estimating volatility are various versions of the 'generalised autoregressive conditional heteroskedasticity' (GARCH) model.

Implied volatility

Implied volatility (i.v.) is the volatility implicit in the market prices of traded options according to a certain valuation model (like Black-Scholes). Instead of trying to estimate volatility based on historical data or some other method, the volatility becomes the unknown in the equation in which all other parameters (including put and call prices) are known. The volatility that emerges from the pricing model is the 'implied volatility', which (if it had been used in the formula) would have resulted in the current price structure.

Of course, to estimate volatility for a stock option's 'true value' one cannot use the volatility implied by the current trading price of that stock's existing options, as that would be assuming that the stock is fairly valued, and the model would simply return the market price! It would be an exercise is tautology. However, implied volatility can be used for valuing other kinds of options – employee stock options, over-the-counter exotic options, and so on. If traded options (long term or short term) exist comparable to ESOPs then a company can use the i.v., instead of estimating volatility from scratch to know the true cost (for accounting and other purposes) of these employee incentives.

Example 11.5

A NIFTY 5,000 call trades for ₹ 200 for a certain month's expiry date. ₹ 200 as call premium would be returned by the Black Scholes value only if the input parameter of volatility is 23 per cent annualised. The i.v., of this call option is 23 per cent.

The problem with using i.v., to estimate volatility is the assumption of 'market knows best' or in more technical terms, that a very strong form of market efficiency holds true. Experience has demonstrated that this assumption is often invalid.

Moreover, if an investor wants to do 'volatility arbitrage' or 'vol arb' (statistical arbitrage[7] on the volatility – see later in this chapter), he obviously cannot rely directly on implied volatility because that would be a tautological error. If the i.v. of some option is 23 per cent and we assume that to be the true volatility, then there is no scope for profitable statistical arbitrage trading left, because the current market price itself gave us that number of 23 per cent! However, having the i.v. of similar options can be useful in 'vol arb' too: one could look for unusual patterns in the way the i.v., changes at different strike prices or different maturities and then trade on the basis that the i.v. will return to its 'normal' pattern. (The assumption that a pattern will revert to its previous average or mean is known as 'mean reversion'.)

Skews and smiles

On the basis of the conventional option pricing models, implied volatility should be the same across various strike prices. In other words, a graph of the volatility of a particular option at different strike prices should be a straight line parallel to the x-axis. However, this is rarely the case. Currency options are an example where it is often found that volatility-as-a-function-of-strike-price displays a 'smile' or a flat U-shaped structure (see Figure 11.2 below). This means that market participants do not expect currency movements to be 'normal', instead they expect the distribution to have a higher frequency or probability of more extreme currency movements (up or down) compared to movements suggested by a normal distribution. The presence of a 'smile' gives rise to an inference that the distribution of currency fluctuations is leptokurtic (that is, having thicker tails than a normal distribution). Non-normality strikes at the heart of options pricing models.

---

7   Note that this type of 'arbitrage' is not riskless.

Figure 11.2: Implied volatilities in a 'smile' pattern

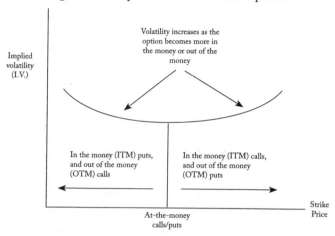

Equity options on the other hand often exhibit a **skew** structure (see Figure 11.3 below which shows how the 'smile' converted into a skew for US equity markets after the 1987 crash); this implies that market participants feel that the probability of really big down moves is higher than the probability of really big up moves (beyond 2 or 3 standard deviations).

Figure 11.3: Implied volatility showing a skew

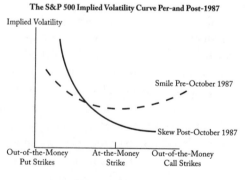

Source: CBOE (Chicago Board Options Exchange).

Another reason for the volatility structure to be skewed (instead of flat or 'smiling') could be the existence of portfolio insurance. Large institutions often take 'portfolio insurance' against downward price moves through the purchase of deep OTM put options, to protect themselves against large crashes. In so far as the second factor (i.e., skew due to need for insurance) dominates the first factor (expectation of more frequent down moves), there is scope for statistical and/or volatility arbitrage to make the structure more symmetrical – that is, by buying options at strike prices with relatively lower volatility, and selling those with higher volatility.

Risks in using option pricing models

The Black and Scholes Model owes its popularity to the fact that unlike many theoretical models, it can be applied to real life on the basis of observable statistics. The volatility of the underlying asset can be estimated from data on past price behaviour. Every other variable in the formula is directly observable. Over the years, several refinements to the model have been made on the basis of advanced theoretical research using complicated mathematical techniques. To a large extent, option writers base their price quotes on one or other version of the model (which may include modified versions involving the Monte Carlo, Binomial etc. methods outlined above). Theoretically, the use of the model is expected to yield a price for each option that exactly compensates the writer for the expected risks over a period of time, so that on the average, taking gains with losses, the writer incurs no net loss. (The actual cost to the buyer would of course include a margin for the writer.)

It is however crucial for the reader to understand that, notwithstanding the apparent precision of the Black–Scholes formula, option pricing is not an exact science. The Achilles' heel of the formula is the fact that while the volatility in the theoretical model is the volatility over the (future) period covered by the option, the figure of volatility actually 'plugged in' to the model for real-life calculations is based on a study of the past. In a sense, it is like driving a car by looking backwards. If future volatility mirrors or closely follows past volatility, the model gives good results. If, however, the volatility undergoes a big change, due to an unexpected fundamental change in the underlying market (say), the formula can produce inaccurate results causing losses to writers. Also certain assumptions are used in the derivation of the formula, which may not always hold in practice. The existence of smiles and skews is an example of this. Therefore, while formulae and models are useful guides to pricing, they should not be taken as fool-proof rules.

Option price sensitivity and option Greeks

As seen in earlier chapters, the option price or premium depends on the price of the underlying, the interest rate, the time left to expiration, and the volatility of the underlying.

A change in any of these factors will lead to a change in option premia. The *sensitivity or rate of change of the option premium due to a change in these variables* is a parameter that options market participants monitor closely. A distinctive letter of the Greek alphabet denotes the sensitivity of the option premium to each of these factors. These are therefore called 'option Greeks'. The option Greeks are listed in Table 11.1 below:

Table 11.1: Option price sensitivities

Rate of change of option premium due to change in	..... is known as:
Price of the underlying	Delta
Time left to expiration	Theta
Volatility	Vega
Interest rate	Rho

Source: CBOE.

The delta itself changes in value at different prices. When an option is deeply OTM, a given change in the price of the underlying produces only a small change in the option premium; thus the delta is small. As the underlying price moves closer to the strike price, the option premium becomes more sensitive to changes in the price of the underlying. For instance, when the price of a share changes from ₹ 100 to ₹ 101 (i.e. 1 per cent), the premium on an ₹ 200 call may change by only 0.05 per cent. When the price of the share changes from ₹ 175 to ₹ 176.75 (1 per cent) with other parameters unchanged, the option premium on the same ₹ 200 call might change by 0.4 per cent. Thus, the delta itself has changed. The delta for deeply out-of-money options will be close to zero, for ATM options close to 0.5, and for deeply in-the money options, close to 1. Another Greek letter, gamma, is used to denote the rate of change of the delta. Mathematically speaking, delta, theta, vega and rho are the first derivatives[8] of the option premium with respect to underlying price, time, underlying volatility and interest rate, while gamma is the second derivative of the option premium with respect to underlying price.

---

8   The word derivative is used here in a mathematical sense and hence a different meaning from the rest of the book.

12

Options – III

Equity Options Strategies[1]

Options trading in equities has grown rapidly in India since the beginning of this century and has had a very big impact on the Indian stock markets. This chapter introduces some methods by which options can be used for hedging and speculation on equities. It should be noted that most of these 'strategies' can also be used with other kinds of options. This chapter will start with an example of a simple speculative strategy and one example of a hedging strategy before getting into more details. More advanced strategies are covered in chapter 13.

Speculative strategy: Long call

Example 12.1

It is the month of May. Mohan expects to receive a bequest in July. He is bullish about SBI, and wants to buy the stock. But he does not yet have the money. He cannot use the futures contract because he would be exposed to mark to market loss: If the stock price falls by a large amount (e.g., 50 per cent), he would have to pay up, and he does not have that much money. So he buys the call option that expires after he expects to receive the cash. The call option allows him to invest in the market in anticipation of getting his bequest. Buying a call allows him to effectively own SBI stock without having all the money now. In essence, Mohan is borrowing from the writer of the call. By buying a call option, Mohan now has a 'long call'.

Prevailing prices are as follows:

Current Spot price of SBI shares (in May) = ₹ 1,900

Premium for July SBI Call (with 1,900 strike) = ₹ 100[2]

The pay-off for the position is, depicted diagrammatically in Figure 12.1.

---

1   The term 'strategy' is used in the investment analyst's sense of a set of investment transactions, rather than in the management sense of a long term plan of action.

2   Assuming no dividend, and approximately 12 per cent interest, this implies an annualised volatility of 25 per cent which seems reasonable for a blue chip stock (using the Black Scholes calculator; free versions can be found online).

Table 12.1: *Pay off from long call*

SBI Stock Price at expiry [1]	Premium paid* [2]	Gain on exercising the option [3]	Net Gain / (Loss) [4]
1500	-100	0	-100
1700	-100	0	-100
1900	-100	0	-100
2100	-100	200	100
2300	-100	400	300
2500	-100	600	500

Note: me value of money is ignored here.

Figure 12.1: *Net gain on SBI call option at or after July expiry (equivalent to column [4] in Table 12.1)*

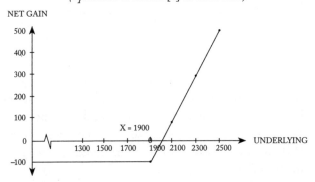

The pay-off diagram in Figure 12.1, as in Table 12.1, represents the pay-offs at the expiry date in July. If the position is closed earlier than July, the pay-offs would be different. In this case, the option would be closed by selling it rather than by exercise or by expiry unexercised. When it is sold, the selling price will always be positive (since every unexpired option has some time value even if it has no intrinsic value.) Since the selling price will be greater than zero, the net premium incurred (purchase price minus selling price) will be less than the premium paid initially. The pay-off for a closure of the position before expiry is depicted by the curved line in Figure 12.2. The pre-expiry pay-off line is a smoothed version of the expiry pay-off line. As the position approaches expiry, the distance between the two lines will narrow and the shape will also become closer to the expiry pay-off line, till eventually (on the last day) the two curves merge.

Figure 12.2: Net gain on SBI call option before July expiry (equivalent to option's market value, assuming a liquid near-efficient market, minus option premium paid)

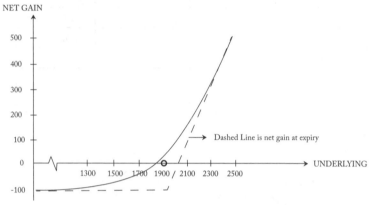

Notes: 1. Exact curve depends on interest rate, time to expiry, market volatility and whether option is American or European.
  2. The dashed line represents intrinsic value of the option minus call premium.

As the Table 12.1 and Figures 12.1 and 12.2 show, this strategy limits the potential loss to ₹ 100, while leaving unlimited potential for gain. Readers may note that because the option underlying is identical to the spot market equivalent which is the purpose of the transaction, there is no need to adjust for any 'beta' factor. On the other hand if the Nifty index were being used as a substitute for SBI shares, the size of the options transaction would have to be weighted by the beta factor.

In the above case, Mohan had no short position in SBI shares and was speculating – he wanted to profit from a rise in SBI share prices rather than protect himself from a fall. If, on the other hand, he had started out with a short position in SBI shares and then purchased the call option, it would be a hedging transaction. In that case, the pay-off diagram for the combined position (i.e., a short position in the underlying plus a long call) would be the same as for simply having a put option on the underlying, If a put option is purchased, then at expiry, there would be a profit if the price of the underlying is below the strike price and a loss equal to the premium if the underlying is at or above the strike price. In other words, the gains and losses from holding a short position in the underlying along with a long call option are the same as just holding a naked put option on the same underlying. Therefore, this combination of positions (short position in the underlying with the purchase of a call option) is sometimes, rather confusingly, called a '*synthetic put*'.

Hedging strategy – protective put buying or long put

Example 12.2

Abdul already has a substantial holding in SBI shares and desires to hedge against a fall in prices between May and July. The price, as in the previous example, is ₹ 1,900 in May with a July put (at-the-money) priced at say ₹ 100.

Abdul now hedges by buying a put option (hence the term 'long put') at the money. If SBI's stock price rises, he gains in the spot market but does not lose in the options market – he can simply let the option expire unexercised. If the price falls, he loses in the spot market but the value of the option rises. The position is summarised in Table 12.2:

Table 12.2: *Pay off table: Protective long put*

(All figures in rupees)

SBI share price at the time of options expiry	Spot market gain/(loss)	Options position			Combined spot plus options position
		Premium	Gain on option	Gain/ (Loss)	
[1]	[2]	[3]	[4]	[5] =[4+3]	[6]=[2+5]
1500	(400)	(100)	400	300	(100)
1600	(300)	(100)	300	200	(100)
1700	(200)	(100)	200	100	(100)
1800	(100)	(100)	100	0	(100)
1900	0	(100)	0	(100)	(100)
2000	100	(100)	0	(100)	0
2100	200	(100)	0	(100)	100
2200	300	(100)	0	(100)	200
2300	400	(100)	0	(100)	300

Figure 12.3: Gain on SBI put option at or after July expiry
(corresponding to column 5 in Table 12.2)

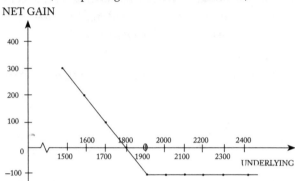

The pay-off diagram in Figure 12.3, as in Table 12.2, represents the pay-offs at the expiry date in July. If the position is closed earlier than July, the pay-offs would be different. In this case, the option would be closed by selling it rather than by exercise or by expiry unexercised. When it is sold, the selling price will always be positive (since every unexpired option has some time value even if it has no intrinsic value.) Since the selling price will be greater than zero, the net premium incurred (purchase price minus selling price) will be less than the premium paid initially. The pay-off for a closure of the position before expiry is depicted in Figure 12.4. As with Figure 12.2, here again the pre-expiry pay-off line is a smoothed version of the expiry pay-off line. As the position approaches expiry, the distance between the two lines will narrow and the shape will also become closer to the expiry pay-off line, till eventually (on the last day) the two curves merge.

Figure 12.4: Net gain on SBI put option before July expiry

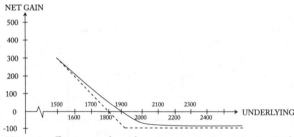

Notes: 1. Exact curve depends on interest rate, time to expiry, market volatility and whether option is American or European.
2. The dashed line represents intrinsic value of the option minus put premium.

The strategy limits the potential loss to ₹ 100, even while maintaining the upside potential. But this hedge may not be worthwhile if only a marginal decline in price is anticipated. In such a situation, it may be better to absorb the smaller price decline, rather than to hedge at a greater cost (i.e., premium).

The pay-off diagram for the *combined position* (i.e., a long position in the underlying plus a long put) is the same as for *simply buying a (naked) call option* on the same stock: if a call option is purchased, then at expiry, there would be a profit if the price of the underlying is above the strike price and a loss equal to the premium if the underlying is at or below the strike price. Therefore, this combination of positions is sometimes, rather confusingly, called a '*synthetic call*'.

Other strategies[3]

Covered calls or buy-write strategies

Investors and traders often use limit orders to sell equities (with limit price above market price). A limit order is one where the broker is instructed to buy or sell a security or commodity if, and only if, a particular price is reached. Options can offer an alternative to limit orders where the investor can not only retain the discipline of a limit order but even get paid for it by receiving options premium or the variance risk premium. Of course, there may (depending on the specific circumstances) be some transaction costs and / or margin requirements *vis-à-vis* limit orders.

Example 12.3: Selling covered calls

In the earlier example a holder of SBI stocks decided to hedge by buying a put which involved payment of a premium. Raman, another holder of SBI shares, feels the price is unlikely to fall much and would like to earn some premium income. He writes a call option (hence a 'short call') at-the-money, thereby earning a premium of ₹100. If the price remains at or below the present level, the option will not be exercised, and the premium will be a clear profit. The outcome at various prices is as in Table 12.3 below:

---

3   These have not been classified as 'speculative' or 'hedging' because some of them could, in some cases, be used for either purpose depending on specific circumstances.

Table 12.3: *Selling covered calls*
(All figures in rupees)

Price of SBI shares	Options position			Combined spot plus options position
	Premium	Market gain / (loss)	Net position	
1500	100	0	100	1600
1600	100	0	100	1700
1700	100	0	100	1800
1800	100	0	100	1900
1900	100	0	100	2000
2000	100	(100)	0	2000
2100	100	(200)	(100)	2000
2200	100	(300)	(200)	2000
2300	100	(400)	(300)	2000

The pay-off diagram for the combined position alone is shown below:

Figure 12.5: *Pay off for a 'covered call' at expiry (long underlying plus short call option) based on the last column in Table 12.3*

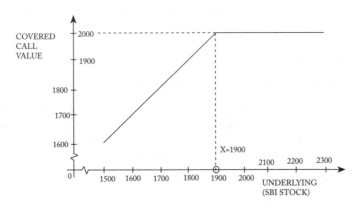

The pay-off for a closure of the position before expiry is depicted by the curved line in Figure 12.6.

Figure 12.6: *Pay off for a 'covered call' before expiry*

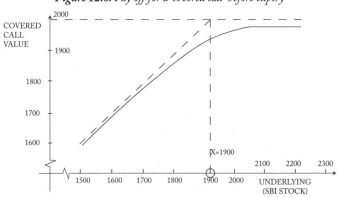

Note: Exact curve depends on interest rate, time to expiry, market volatility and whether option is American or European.

Selling covered calls is a limited gain and unlimited[4] potential loss strategy, involving an un-hedged adverse price risk. But this downside risk is present even if one merely holds the stock. Therefore, taking the holding of the relevant stock as a given, the real trade-off is the earning of a premium (₹ 100 in this case) compared to letting go of any upside during the maturity of the option.

Another use of a covered call, as referred in the introduction above, is to effectively set an exit price for a holding of the underlying. Instead of selling an ATM call, Raman could have sold an out-of-the-money call with an exercise price of ₹ 2,000 per share. He would have earned a smaller premium. If the price rose by less than ₹ 100 during the period remaining till maturity, the call would expire without being exercised. If the price rose above ₹ 2,000, the option would be exercised and Raman would have to sell his holding at ₹ 2,000.

When used in this manner, selling a covered call (which forces the holder of the stock to sell the stock if it rises by a specified amount within a specified period) is equivalent to, but not the same as, a limit order to sell at ₹ 2,000. If Raman wanted to give a limit order to sell his shares at ₹ 2,000 per share, then the above options strategy may (depending on transaction costs) be a superior way of doing it. If the price rose as expected, Raman would achieve the expected sale price. If the price fell, he would be slightly better off than by simply giving

---

4   More precisely, the risk is limited by the fact that the stock price cannot fall below zero. Thus, in Example 12.3, the loss is limited to ₹ 1,800; of course this is 18 times the option premium of ₹ 100 .

a limit order, because he would have earned a premium. However, there may be some transaction costs.

Selling puts while keeping requisite cash (cash-secured put)

Example 12.4

Bhagat is interested in buying SBI shares. SBI is currently trading at ₹ 1,900. He thinks buying SBI at a net cost of ₹1,750 or below is worth it, but above that it is too expensive. He sells a July SBI 1,800 put for ₹ 50. In this way, if SBI trades at above ₹1,800 later, he will retain ₹ 50. If the put trades below 1,800, the purchaser of the put option will exercise the option and Bhagat will have to buy it. He was ready to buy SBI at ₹1,750 in any case; the cost to him if the price falls below ₹ 1,800 is effectively ₹ 1,750 (strike price of ₹1,800 minus put premium received of ₹ 50). Hence he has nothing to lose from this outcome. However, Bhagat has to retain enough cash to buy the shares in case the option is exercised, and the interest on the margin locked up represents a cost. The payoff is shown in Table 12.4.

Table 12.4: *Cash-covered short put*
(All figures in rupees)

SBI share price in July	Put option premium received	Gain (loss) on put option	Balance from cash cover of ₹1800 i.e., strike price	Value of stock bought	Overall portfolio
	(1)	(2)	(3)	(4)	(1+2+3+4)
1500	50	−300	300	1500	1550
1600	50	−200	200	1600	1650
1700	50	−100	100	1700	1750
1800	50	0	0	1800	1850
1900	50	0	1800	0	1850
2000	50	0	1800	0	1850
2100	50	0	1800	0	1850

In essence, if an investor wants to buy shares in case they fall to a particular level, he or she can sell a put option at the desired level. Similarly, if an investor wants to short-sell a stock in case it rises to a particular level, he can sell a call option at that level. If an investor already has a short position in a stock, he can sell a put option; any losses on selling the option will be compensated by the gain on the short position.

In short, options can be used to hedge existing holdings or expected purchases. They can also be used to earn income while continuing to hold the underlying shares, or (if one is prepared to purchase the stock) even without holding the stock. To summarise:

- One can buy a put along with an existing holding, or purchase, of the underlying. This is called a *protective put buying*. This is appropriate when one is bullish but wants to protect against unexpected downward price movements.

- One can sell a call option while holding the underlying – this is called a *covered call selling*. If the option is exercised, the holder already has the shares to deliver – hence the term 'covered'.

- *Selling puts and keeping requisite cash* can be used to earn income if the price rises, or to buy the underlying security if the price falls (while pocketing a premium)

Portfolio hedging through options

Portfolio managers who are net long on equities can partially or fully hedge themselves by selling stock index futures. However, while this avoids future losses, it also implies giving up any future gains. As an alternative, they can hedge by buying stock index put options and/or entering into 'spreads'. Consider a fund manager who runs a well-diversified portfolio which mirrors the stock market and therefore has a beta of close to one. The fund manager can buy downside 'insurance' by buying an appropriate number of stock index put options without sacrificing any upside. That is, the portfolio has not been immunised or 'frozen', but it has been insured.

However, hedging through a futures contract incurs no expense (except margin collateral deposit and transaction costs), but buying options involves paying a premium which will never be returned – just like an insurance policy. If the risk materialises, the returns could be many times the original premium but otherwise the premium may be a 'waste' – the answer will only be known *ex post facto*. More advanced strategies often involve spreads (i.e., multiple option positions or 'legs') to minimise premium outflow (or to increase net inflow) and the overall risk, given a certain market outlook. Examples of such strategies are presented and examined in the next chapter.

13

Advanced Options Strategies

The basic options techniques used by speculators or investors are buying naked calls and puts to profit from an increase or decrease in the price of the underlying, respectively. These were introduced in chapter 10. The preceding chapter looked at more complicated scenarios such as protective puts and covered calls where options were used in conjunction with holdings of the underlying.

This chapter explains some more advanced applications of options:

• Strategies in which more than one option is used at the same time on the same underlying, i.e., strategies where options are *combined* in various ways;

• Arbitrage and statistical arbitrage strategies.

Collars, cylinders and spreads

Options strategies that combine more than one option often come with interesting names, usually reflecting the graphical shape of the pay-off.

Zero cost collar or fence/cylinder: Combination of selling calls and buying puts while holding the underlying security.

Example 13.1

Sarojini feels that the SBI shares she owns may fall from the present level of ₹ 1,900 and wishes to protect herself from such a decline. At the same time she does not want to incur any option premia. Option premia are quoted as follows (say):

Strike Price (₹)	Premium (₹)	
	Call	Put
1700	300	70
1800	200	82
1900	100	100
2000	80	200
2100	70	295

Note that the 1,800 call and the 2,000 put are both quoted at 200 (in real life, premia on equidistant strikes, one being a call and another a put, are unlikely to be exactly the same but it is assumed here to simplify the example). Sarojini can adopt the following strategy:

a.   *Buy a 1,800 put at 200, and*

b.   *Write a 2,000 call at 200*

The premium paid on the put is offset by the premium received on the call. Thus, the net premium is zero (hence 'zero cost'). In assessing this strategy, the point to remember (ignoring the premium which is nil in net terms) is:

a.   *If the market price at expiry is above 1,800, Sarojini will earn a profit on the call.*

b.   *If the market price at expiry is below 2,000 the put will be exercised, creating a loss for Sarojini, on the put.*

The pay-off is depicted in Table 13.1 and Figure 13.1.

Table 13.1: Pay-off table for zero cost collar at expiry

Price	Spot gain on long underlying	Gain (ignoring premium) from buying 1,800 put	Loss (ignoring premium) from selling 2,000 call	Net position (option premia cancel each other)
1500	-400	300	0	-100
1600	-300	200	0	-100
1700	-200	100	0	-100
1800	-100	0	0	-100
1900	0	0	0	0
2000	100	0	0	100
2100	200	0	-100	100
2200	300	0	-200	100
2300	400	0	-300	100

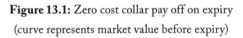

Figure 13.1: Zero cost collar pay off on expiry
(curve represents market value before expiry)

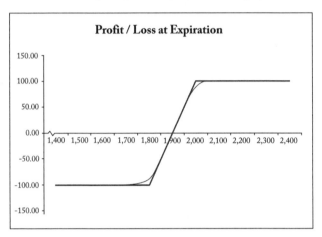

This combination of trades places a ceiling and a floor on the profit/loss, while allowing participation in profits and losses within a certain range. This strategy is known as a collar (based on the shape of the pay-off graph) and also as a fence or cylinder. It puts limits on the range of values a position can take. Because of the 'hedged' nature of the position, margin requirements for the combined position are much lower than for the individual positions.

This approach was used by some investors to effectively sell shares without paying the capital gains taxes (see Box 13.1). With the advent of tax provisions like 'constructive sale' in the USA and other similar laws elsewhere (see chapter 17), this has become less common. A constructive sale is one where, even though an actual sale has not taken place, a sale is deemed to have occurred through legal 'construction'. Under these rules, the range of position values after the implementation of a collar or similar strategy should be wide (say, above 15 per cent) to avoid paying the capital gains tax.

Box 13.1: Using options to avoid contracts and taxes?

During the dot-com 'bubble' in the late 90s when shares of internet-based companies rose to very high levels, many founder-owners were required to not sell their stock after the Initial Public Offering (IPO).

Some owners used options strategies to circumvent these provisions. A collar mechanism (shown above in Example 13.1) is a way of effectively fixing the sale price within a range without actually selling the shares. A shareholder could effectively sell the share from a financial point of view, while nominally and legally remaining a shareholder. Of course, such a situation would mean that the owner of the shares would no longer have a real stake in the success of the company, thereby defeating the purpose of the ownership requirement.

Others used options to defer payment of capital gains tax by selling deep-in-the-money options with expiry dates in the future (beyond the current tax period). These were also called 'Low Exercise Price Options' (LEPOs). Under this strategy, the holder sells a deep-in-the-money call, generally OTC, on his or her underlying stock holding. Since the option is ITM, it is almost certain to be exercised, but that will happen in the future. The holder can effectively sell the shares this year but defer the actual sale to the next. Das quotes the example of Lend Lease Corporation which, in 1996 wanted to sell its 9 per cent holding in Westpac and used LEPOs. According to Das, at a time when Westpac shares were trading at 5.40 Australian dollars, the strike price of the LEPOs was 0.01 Australian dollars. 'The low exercise price ensured that the options were certain to be exercised. Lend Lease had effectively sold the shares... deferred its substantial capital gains...'.[1]

The LEPO strategy is less useful if the share yields dividends. In this case, the difference between the stock price and a long-term call option (with a strike price just above zero) can be substantial. Conceptually the two strategies – collar and LEPO – are very similar. A LEPO, in terms of its pay-off, is equivalent to a short collar where the long put strike is 0 and the short call strike is just above 0. Thus, collars can also be used to defer taxes. The main difference is that LEPOs result in an immediate cash inflow while a collar is usually zero cost. However, even a zero-cost collar can enable an investor to obtain a cash inflow because by buying such a collar, one can 'freeze' the value of the overall portfolio and thereby

---

1   Satyajit Das, 'Traders, Guns and Money: Knowns and Unknowns in the Dazzling World of Derivatives', *Financial Times*, Prentice Hall, 2006, 261.

margin requirements can be reduced to almost nil (if the arrangement is so recognised by the broker); hence the margin money can be withdrawn. However, this is usually only feasible for large investors for whom brokers may be willing to structure such a deal.

Theoretically, a similar *de facto* sale can be effected through futures by selling the futures and rolling over.

Apart from tax implications, these strategies may be unethical depending on the circumstances (for instance, when used to evade prescribed ownership levels).

Selling 'bull call spreads' on existing holding to gain income without sacrificing entire upside

Example 13.2

George owns 100 stocks of Microsoft (MSFT). The current price is $29.30 (therefore the position is worth $2930). He has a target price for the stock of about $32 (10 per cent appreciation) in about five weeks' time which he feels would be a fair value based on long term fundamentals. He intends to sell if that price is reached. Microsoft's next quarterly results announcement is expected within that period, and there is a plausible, though not likely, chance that Microsoft shares could shoot up significantly. He does not want to take the risk of any significant fall in MSFT. He is considering the use of options to protect himself against a large drop while retaining as much upside as possible. What approaches can he use? The various option prices for the relevant period are as in Table 13.2.

Table 13.2: Microsoft option prices

Call bid	Call ask	MSFT price	Put bid	Put ask
7.35	7.45	22.00	0.02	0.03
6.40	6.45	23.00	0.04	0.05
5.40	5.45	24.00	0.06	0.07
4.45	4.50	25.00	0.11	0.12
3.50	3.60	26.00	0.18	0.19
2.62	2.64	27.00	0.29	0.31
1.85	1.88	28.00	0.49	0.51

Call bid	Call ask	MSFT price	Put bid	Put ask
1.19	1.20	29.00	0.81	0.83
0.65	0.67	30.00	1.29	1.32
0.31	0.33	31.00	1.96	2.00
0.14	0.15	32.00	2.78	2.82
0.06	0.07	33.00	3.65	3.75
0.01	0.03	34.00	4.65	4.75
0.01	0.02	35.00	5.60	5.75
0.01	0.01	36.00	6.60	6.70
0.01	0.02	37.00	7.35	8.40

Solution:

a.   *Covered calls:*

A simple approach could be to sell covered calls as in Example 12.4. George could sell one lot of call options with a strike price of $32 per share expiring five weeks from now for about $15. (Each call option is worth about $0.15—assuming that the trade is executed at 0.15, and not 0.14 - and each option lot is a multiple of 100. The options are assumed to be European options, i.e,. exercisable only at expiry.) $15 received from an option expiring in 5 weeks on an underlying position of $2930 means a rough annualised yield of

(52/5) x (15/2930)=5.32 per cent

There are three possibilities after five weeks depending on whether MSFT shares end below, at, or above 32 USD.

i.   *If the share price is below 32, then the call option will lapse without being exercised. George will get the 5.32 per cent annualised yield as a 'bonus' over and above, any dividends and capital gains or losses.*

ii.   *If MSFT ends at exactly 32, George gets this 5.32 per cent annualised yield. In addition he retains the dividends and the 9.22 per cent capital gain over five weeks (95.88 per cent yield annualised) that he would have got by just holding the shares.*

iii. *If MSFT ends at a price higher than 32 the option will be exercised and he will have to sell the shares at $32 per share. He will get the same amount of money as in item (ii) above but if the price of MSFT shares goes above $32.15 ($32 plus the premium of $0.15 he earned) he could have made more money by not selling the call.*

b. *Another approach is a 'bull call spread'. George could:*

- *sell the call option with a $32 strike price; and*

- *simultaneously buy the call option with a $33 strike price.*

Selling the former would get him about $15 for one lot of 100 options, but buying the latter would cost him about $7 (as seen from the option price table above). His net income from option premium would thus be $8. This represents an annualised yield of

(52/5) x (8/2930) = 2.84 per cent.

If the MSFT share price ends at or below $32, he would earn a smaller yield than in the covered call, but if it rises above $33, he can continue to benefit from the appreciation. Compared to strategy (A) (simply selling a covered call), George will receive 8 cents less in strategy (B) which involves selling a covered call and simultaneously buying a deeper-out-of-the-money call. Since (in this particular example) the next higher strike price for tradable options is $33 (there are no options available at, say, $32.75) and there is a net option income of $.08 per share, Strategy (B) would turn out to be superior to Strategy (A) only if MSFT ends higher than 33.08. [It should be noted that if the price ends above $33.08 then George would have been better off simply holding the shares without entering into any options transaction and with hindsight he would have been better off not trying to protect against a fall in price – but that is like saying that not paying an insurance premium is good if the risk does not materialise.]

The bull call spread shown in Example 13.2 is a lower risk / lower return strategy compared to the covered call. The scenarios are compared below in Table 13.3:

Table 13.3: Comparison between covered (short) call and bull call spread

Characteristic	Uncovered stock holding	Covered call	Bull call spread
Yield from option premium	Nil	High	Low
Gain if price rises above expected level	High (no opportunity loss)	Nil (opportunity loss)	Low (partial opportunity loss)

Example 13.3

Devi holds Reliance Industries (RIL) shares and she is considering appropriate options strategies to protect herself from a fall in price. RIL closed on May 17 at ₹ 686. The 31 May expiry ₹ 700 strike price call option is priced at ₹ 7, and the ₹ 720 call is priced at ₹ 3. Depending on her view and circumstances, there are various possible strategies:

a. *Covered short call: If she thinks RIL shares are likely to be mildly bearish to range-bound but does not want to sell for taxation or other reasons, then she could sell the 700 call for an income of ₹ 7 per share. She would be protected from a fall in price but would have forgone any major appreciation beyond 700.*

b. *Bull call spread: If her views range from neutral to mildly bullish, she could sell the 700 call and buy the 720 call (creating a bull call spread) for a net income of ₹ 4 per stock; she would retain upside potential if RIL rises above ₹ 720 while remaining protected from a fall.*

c. *If she is very bullish, then she is clearly no longer in a defensive mood and she should not sell any calls. She could just hold the stock, or (if she wants to increase her stake) perhaps even buy the 720 or other OTM calls.*

Selling 'bear put spreads' to gain income while retaining downside protection

Bull call spreads enable downside protection without missing the upside of the underlying stock; the obverse is the bear put spread. One can also sell bear put spreads instead of put options to instil buying discipline while protecting the downside of the stock that is to be bought.

Example 13.4

George wants to buy 100 shares of Microsoft (MSFT). The current price is $29.30. He believes that MSFT's fair valuation according to fundamentals is about 10 per cent lower than the current price and is interested in buying if it falls that far. Microsoft's next quarterly results announcement is expected in five weeks, and there is a plausible, though not very likely, possibility that Microsoft shares could fall significantly. If those results portend an unexpected slowdown and the shares fall much more than 10 per cent that would signify a change in fundamentals and his current outlook would no longer hold true; in that case he would not want to hold the stock.

What put option strategies could he use? Assume option prices for expiry in five weeks are as given in Table 13.2.

Solution

a. *Cash covered puts: George could sell $26 strike price puts (for 19 cents each). He would earn $19 in income (since each stock option lot consists of 100 options in the United*

States, where MSFT trades). He has to set aside $2600 to be able to buy the shares if the option is exercised (hence he is 'covered'). If at expiry the shares are above $26 the put option will not be exercised and he would have earned a yield of:

(19/2600) x (52/5) = 6.2 per cent per annum.

This is over and above any interest that this liquid fund position was earning. If the price of MSFT shares closes below 26, the option will be exercised. He will be left owning MSFT at an effective price of $(26−0.19) = $25.81 per share which is approximately the target level he wanted.

b. *Bear put spread: George could sell $26 strike price puts (for 19 cents each) and simultaneously buy $22 strike price puts (for 3 cents each), for a net credit of $16 dollars. He should keep about $2,600 ready to buy 100 shares of MSFT if that stock price ends between 22 and 26 five weeks from now, at expiry. There are three possibilities for the price of MSFT on the expiry date which are analysed below:*

  i.   *Above $26: Here, George does not have to buy anything. He has effectively earned 16 dollars on his cash of $2600 i.e. 6.2 per cent annualised return.*

  ii. *Between $22 and $26: George will have to buy MSFT at 26 (assuming the person who bought 26 strike price put options from him is rational enough to exercise them, which is almost a certainty). Say, MSFT is at 23 at expiry. Taking into account the 16 cents per share put spread premium, the effective cost price for Tom is $26 − 0.16 = $25.84. Ex post facto, George may regret paying $25.84 for this stock at a time when its price is lower than that, but ex ante, this position would have looked very favourable (since at the time the option was sold the stock was at $29.30.*

  iii. *Below $22: In this case, George can buy the stock at 26 (because of the put he sold), and sell the stock at 22 (because of the put he bought). He therefore suffers a loss of $4 per stock, which (after adjusting the premium earned of $19) is $381 net. But the fact that the price is below $22 signifies a change in his fundamental long view of MSFT. He is still better off compared to directly buying at $29.30 because then he would have lost $730.*

Example 13.5

Mala is a stock market investor considering purchase of RIL shares. RIL closed on 17 May at 686. The 31 May 680 Put is priced around ₹ 15, and the 640 put at ₹ 3.50. Depending on her view and circumstances, there are different options strategies she could consider:

a. *If she wants to hold RIL in the long run but does not expect any sharp rise in the short run, selling puts would be a good approach. She could sell the 680 put and earn ₹15 per share if she is ready to buy RIL. If the option gets exercised her nett price would be ₹ 680−15= ₹ 665. If the option is not exercised, she would have earned ₹ 15 and she can still buy the shares from the market if she wishes. So long as the price does not rise substantially, she would be better off this way than directly buying the share, ignoring transaction costs.*

b. *If she intends to buy but also feels that any steep fall in the said stock's price would imply some adverse information that others know but she does not, she could not only sell the 680 put, but also buy the ₹ 640 put as a downside hedge by paying ₹ 3.50 and earn a net income of ₹ (15 – 3.50) = Rs. 11.50. This way, she will be able to limit her loss in case there is a sharp fall in the interim.*

To summarise, Examples 13.2 and 13.3 illustrated the selling of bull call spreads instead of selling stock-covered calls; this enabled the investor to exchange a lower call premium for keeping the upside on the underlying stock positions. Examples 13.4 and 13.5 illustrated the selling of bear put spreads instead of selling cash-covered puts; this fetches the investor a relatively lower premium but limits the downside on stock positions that the investor wants to buy at slightly lower prices. Similarly investors can use spreads instead of single options in virtually all options strategies: buying outright calls, buying outright puts, selling covered calls and short-covered puts etc.

Arbitrage and statistical arbitrage strategies

As discussed in chapter 2, arbitrage is the practice of buying and simultaneously selling the same asset in different markets or different forms to profit from price differences. Conventional or pure arbitrage is risk-free. Because of this, traders who spot such an opportunity try to trade as much as possible and this action helps, in and of itself, to eliminate the price difference between the two markets or two forms of the asset involved.

Such risk-free arbitrage is a major contributor to efficiency of markets. It ensures that the same asset cannot have unjustified differences in price in two different markets. Arbitrage between futures and spot of an asset which can be delivered in the futures market is risk-free. Similarly, arbitrage may be possible with options using the put-call parity: if margin costs are properly factored in where applicable, such a trade can also be considered risk-free and hence pure arbitrage.

Arbitrage through put call parity application

Example 13.6

Qasim, an investor, is considering an arbitrage possibility. The quarterly results of Reliance will be out next week and the implied volatility of a 1,000 put for Reliance options expiring one month from now expiry is around 40 per cent and the implied volatility of the 1,000 call with same expiry is at 45 per cent. Reliance is also currently trading at 1,000. The annual interest rate is 12 per cent so the discount factor for time value of money for one month is 0.99. Assume 100 options have to be bought at a minimum, and there is no dividend involved. The 1,000 call is trading at ₹ 55 and the put at ₹ 40, reflecting these differing volatilities. Is there a profit potential through arbitrage and if so how much?

Solution

The Put Call Parity (PCP) equation states that:

Put Market Price + Underlying Stock Price

= Call Market Price + Cash deposit equivalent to Present Time Value of the Strike Price

➡ *P (X) +Stock = C (X) + Xe-rt*

➡ *C (X) = P (X) + S - Xe-rt...............…..… (i)*

Given that here both the put and the call are of the same strike, having different implied volatilities means that theoretically, there is a possibility for an arbitrage trade. Whether the arbitrage is worth executing in practice depends on whether the difference in implied volatility is high enough for the various transaction costs (brokerage, etc.) to be covered.

Here, therefore as shown in Equation (i) to effect an arbitrage trade Qasim can:

- *SELL the relevant strike's call. That is, sell 100 calls for ₹ 5,500.*

- *BUY the put of the same strike and expiry (here, the strike being ₹ 1,000, and the expiry being in one month). That is, buy 100 puts for ₹ 4,000.*

- *BUY the underlying stock. That is, buy 100 Reliance shares at ₹ 1,000 for ₹ 100,000.*

- *BORROW an amount equivalent to the present value of the strike price under consideration. That is, borrow ₹ 99,000.*

Cash outflow today is = ₹ 100,000 + ₹ 4,000 – ₹ 5,500 – ₹ 99,000 = - ₹ 500, i.e., an inflow of ₹ 500.

The option positions are closed just before expiry. Assume three scenarios whereby the price of Reliance shares is I) ₹ 900 II) ₹ 1,000 or III) ₹ 1,100 one month from now.

a. *In case I, when stock price goes to 900, the calls sold have no value, the puts are worth ₹ (1,000-900) x 100 = ₹ 10,000. The stock is worth ₹ 90,000.*

   i. *Qasim's assets are worth ₹ 90,000 + 10,000 = ₹ 100,000.*

   ii. *He has to repay ₹ 99,000 plus interest thereon of 1 per cent i.e., ₹ 1,000. Thus, he has to repay ₹ 100,000.*

   iii. *Item b offsets item a, and his total portfolio is worth 0.*

   iv. *He can retain the ₹ 500 cash received one month ago which is now worth ₹ 505 with interest.*

b. In case II, when stock price remains same, calls and puts have no value. The shares are worth ₹ 100,000 but Qasim has to pay back ₹ 100,000; again the two offset each other. But the cash received plus interest (₹ 505) is still retained.

c. In case III, when stock price goes to ₹ 1,100, the calls sold will carry a loss of ₹ 10,000. The puts are worthless. The stock portfolio is worth ₹ 110,000. Qasim has to repay ₹ 100,000. The net position is once again nil, i.e.,

$$-10,000 + 110,000 - 100,000 = 0$$

Again, the initial cash flow received remains as a profit.

In all cases, no matter what the stock price the arbitrageur gets to keep ₹ 500. So long as the transaction costs are lower than this, there is a profitable arbitrage possibility. Also, because a broker can see this overall position is a perfect arbitrage one, the arbitrageur may have to pay considerably less margin for carrying out this trade than for a normal options trade. Such arbitrage opportunities are rare and usually arbitrage margins are narrower. Nonetheless, the point is that professional arbitrageurs may be able to make small but riskless profits.

Arbitrage through box spreads

A box spread, in options' terminology, is a combination of transactions that involves a synthetic long position and a synthetic short position on the same underlying but at different strike prices. This involves *being long a call and short a put (at one strike price), and being short a call and long a put (at a higher strike price), all on the same underlying.* In other words, a box spread is a combination of a bull spread and a bear spread with the same expiry dates.

This strategy will always yield a fixed return on expiry date based on the value of the four options on the day of trading. Buying a box spread means buying the call at a lower strike and selling the call at a higher strike, with the opposite position in puts, requiring payment of net premium. Selling a box spread means selling the call at a lower strike and buying a call at a higher strike with the opposite position in puts, involving receipt of net premium. This is called a spread[2] since the net exposure to the underlying is a pre-fixed amount equal to the gap between the two strike prices. It is called a box because of the shape of the pay-off diagram (see Figure 13.2). Due to the four 'legs' to this strategy, some traders also call this the 'alligator spread' because of the resemblance to the legs of an alligator. (In Figure 13.2, as in similar diagrams, the horizontal axis represents the price of the underlying and the vertical axis represents the net profit or loss on the position.)

---

2   The term 'spread' here has a different meaning here *vis-à-vis* the chapters on futures where it is used as a synonym for 'basis' (difference between spot and futures price).

Figure 13.2: Bull spread (2,000 and 2,100 are the exercise prices of the call options, former being a long position and latter short)

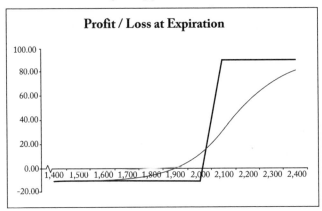

The thick line represents the combined position's payoff at expiry and the curved line represents the market value before expiry. We can see that a net call option premium of around ten was paid, and therefore a maximum profit of 90 (2,100-2,000-10) can be made.

Figure 13.3: Bear spread (1,700 and 1,800 are the exercise prices of the put options, former being a short position and latter long)

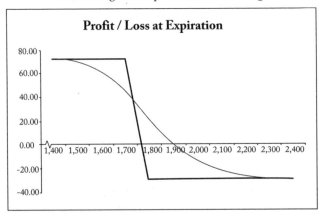

The thick line represents the combined position's payoff at expiry and the curved line represents the market value before expiry. We can see that a net put option premium of around 30 was paid. Therefore, a maximum profit of 70 (1,800-1,700-30) can be made.

Figure 13.4: 'Box spread' pay off on expiry

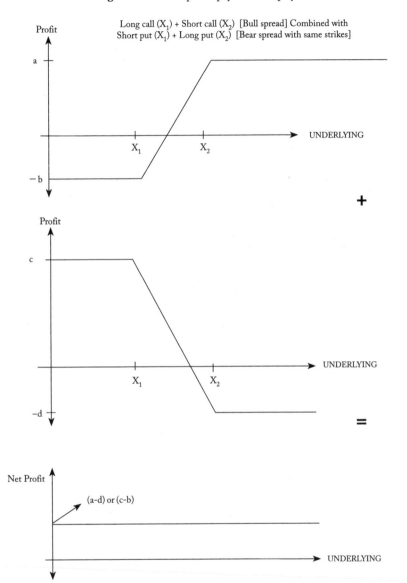

Note: If a-d ≠ c-b, then there is a possibility of arbitrage.
Also, a - d ≠ 0 because there is a time value of money.

Depending on the premium spent/earned on buying/selling the box and the pre-determined fixed gain or loss based on the difference in strike prices, there may be an arbitrage opportunity. This is illustrated in the following example.

Example 13.7

Eshwar is considering an arbitrage opportunity in MSFT shares. One month MSFT options are priced as in Table 13.2. Is there an opportunity for Eshwar to profitably sell a box?

Solution:

Selling a box means selling the call with lower strike and buying a call with higher strike while buying a put with lower strike and selling a put with higher strike. If Eshwar sells a 29 call and buys a 29 put (for say 1.19 and 0.83 respectively as per the price table) he will get a net inflow of 36 dollars per option contract (each contract corresponds to 100 stocks). By buying a 30 call for 0.67 and selling a 30 put for 1.29, he will get a net inflow of 62 dollars. Overall, he gets an initial inflow of $98. The outcome of this strategy on the expiry date, at various market prices of the underlying is shown in Table 13.4.

Table 13.4: *Pay-offs on each leg of box spread sold (per share; market lot=100 shares)*
[Figures in brackets denote losses]

Scenario	Price of MSFT on expiry date ($)	Gain/ (loss) on 29 call sold	Gain/ (loss) on 29 put bought	Gain/ (loss) on 30 call bought	Gain/ (loss) on 30 put sold	Combined gain/loss on all 4 options
1	28	0 Call will not be exercised	1 Put will be exercised by Eshwar – causing a profit of 29-28=1.	0 Call will not be exercised	(2) Put will be exercised by the other party causing a loss of 28-30= (2)	(1)

Scenario	Price of MSFT on expiry date ($)	Gain / (loss) on 29 call sold	Gain / (loss) on 29 put bought	Gain / (loss) on 30 call bought	Gain / (loss) on 30 put sold	Combined gain/loss on all 4 options
2	29	0 Call will not be exercised / if exercised will not entail any gain / loss	0 Put will not be exercised	0 Call will not be exercised.	(1) Put will be exercised by the other party causing a loss of 29–30=(1)	(1)
3	30	(1) Call will be exercised by the other party causing a loss of 29–30=(1)	0 Put will not be exercised	0 Call will not be exercised.	0 Put will not be exercised / if exercised will not entail any gain /loss	(1)
4	31	(2) Call will be exercised by the other party causing a loss of 29–31=(2)	0 Put will not be exercised	1 Call will be exercised by Eshwar, causing a profit of 31–30=1	0 Put will not be exercised	(1)

What the table shows is that regardless of the price of MSFT on the expiry date, Eshwar will make a net loss of $1 per share on the box, which is exactly equal to the difference between the two strike prices. Since the lot size is 100, the aggregate loss will be $100. The total cash flows from the box strategy can now be summarised:

- *At the time of selling the box (i.e., entering into the four options trades), Eshwar receives $98.*

- *One month later, he has to pay $100.*

He makes a net loss of $2 on this box, ignoring the interest element. There is a loss of approximately 2 per cent in one month. Hence, there is no profitable arbitrage opportunity in this case.

However, suppose the option prices were such that the premium income earned in the beginning was $101 instead of $98, then the selling of the box would have yielded a riskless arbitrage profit. Even if the premium income was such that along with interest for a month it would exceed the pre-determined and fixed loss of $100 on the box, there may be a profitable arbitrage opportunity subject to transaction costs.

Box spread selling as a means of borrowing

In Example 13.7, Eshwar was able to get money now with a payment later. In a way, this is equivalent to borrowing money for one month. The effective interest rate was 2/98 = 2.04 per cent per month. This shows that, apart from its use as an arbitrage strategy, selling boxes is also a way to borrow money from the market. Depending on the option prices, the implicit rate of interest on such borrowings may or may not be economical. However, it illustrates the manner in which some companies can use derivative markets as a source of off-balance sheet short term financing.

Example 13.8: Box spread buying

Reliance stock is trading at 1,000 and, as in the Example 13.6 the call option with a strike price of 1,000 for a given expiry has an implied volatility (i.v.) of 45 per cent and the put option with a strike price of 1,000 for the same expiry has an i.v., of 40 per cent. The other option contract for the same expiry with good liquidity is the one with a strike price of 950; this has both call and put with implied volatilities of 45 per cent. The volatility figures imply that the 1,000 call is overvalued. An arbitrageur does the following:

- *Buys the 950 call and sells the 950 put (creating a synthetic long at 950), and*

- *Sells the 1,000 call and buys the 1,000 put (creating a synthetic short at 1,000).*

Thus she buys a box spread. Since she is short the overvalued 'vol' (1,000 call), if the valuation returns to normal this call will fall in price disproportionately compared to the other legs of the spread. Therefore she can expect to realise a net risk-free profit from this strategy, assuming the interest cost on the margin and transaction costs do not exceed the profit.

Statistical arbitrage

Examples 13.6, 13.7 and 13.8 are true or conventional (riskless) arbitrage. The next two examples are of statistical arbitrage in the context of volatility trading.[3] They are not free of risk and profitability depends on the future conforming to expectations based on the past.

Example 13.9: Mean reversion application (similar to, but distinct from, put call parity application)

Qasim is considering options strategies on RIL shares. The quarterly results of RIL are not for another two months. The implied volatility of a 1,000 put for RIL options expiring one month from now is around 40 per cent and the implied volatility of the 1,100 call with same expiry is at 45 per cent. This is a blue-chip stock where sudden large movements are unlikely.

RIL is currently trading at 1,000, the annual interest rate is 12 per cent and the discount factor for the time value of money sense for one month ahead is 0.99. Assume a market lot of 100 shares. have to be bought at a minimum, and there is no dividend involved. The relevant call is trading at ₹ 20 and the put at ₹ 40.

What can Qasim do and how?

Solution:

The Put Call Parity (PCP) equation only applies for the same strike price. In this case, the options under consideration are at different strike prices so there is no pure arbitrage. What can be attempted is statistical arbitrage or mean reversion. Essentially, it represents an assumption that prices which have deviated from their mean or normal level, will revert to that mean.

In this example, a higher strike price (i.e., the call option) has a higher implied volatility. It can be assumed that the put option at the higher strike price (₹ 1,100) will also have a very similar implied volatility as explained in the last example (implied volatility is simply reverse-calculated based on the Black–Scholes equation by putting in the option market price, time to expiry, interest rate, dividend if any, and current underlying price).

The implied volatilities at different strikes would be the same if the probability distributions of an up or down move in the stock price in any given unit of time were symmetrical, and the

---

3   Note that 'statistical' arbitrage may not be riskless and thus differs from classic economic 'arbitrage'.

market was efficient. Even assuming the latter in a broad sense, in real life (based on past data), the distribution of equity returns is only approximately symmetrical at best. Assume that, as a general pattern, the market tends to display a skew or smirk, whereby implied volatilities for options at lower strikes tend to be higher (Note: This volatility structure of a skew or 'smirk' occurs when implied volatilities of ITM calls are higher than out-of-the-money calls. This is in contrast to a symmetrical 'smile'.)

Figure 13.5: *Smile pattern (symmetrical) and Skew or Smirk pattern (asymmetrical)*

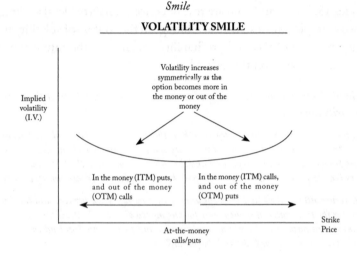

In the given example, the higher-strike call has a higher annualised implied volatility than that of the lower-strike put which is not 'normal' vis-à-vis the generally observed pattern of a skew. So while there is no conventional arbitrage profit, it may be reasonable to assume that this 'reverse skew' will become a 'skew' or at least a 'smile' in one month, or at least there is a high enough chance of the same if historical data shows that to be the case (for which the necessary analysis would have to be done).

Qasim can sell the higher 'vol' (by selling the 1,100 call options, in a lot of 100), while buying the lower 'vol' (1,000 put), and buying 100 stocks of RIL. If the expected correction or mean reversion happens, the strategy will yield a profit.

Example 13.10: Statistical arbitrage.

Assume that, the implied volatility of RIL at-the-money options has averaged, say, 35 per cent. Assume implied Nifty volatility is currently near its historical average of say 20 per cent i.e., there is no excess volatility or fear in the general market. The market also does not expect any major results from, or significant corporate news about RIL, i.e., there is no prima facie reason to expect unusually high volatility in the spot. RIL stock is trading at 1,000 and the 1,000 call has an i.v., of 50 per cent and the 1,000 put has an i.v., of 50 per cent also (For simplicity, assume that RIL's share price is perfectly correlated with the market index, i.e. the correlation is 100 per cent and the correlation coefficient or beta is one). The Nifty is trading at 5,000.

Sandeep, a statistical arbitrageur, observes that the ratio of the implied volatility of RIL to the implied volatility of the Nifty (50:20) is higher than usual (35:20). He gathers information to make sure that no news is around the corner that could sharply increase or decrease the relevant stock price. In the absence of such news, the higher-than-normal i.v., of the RIL shares becomes a statistical arbitrage opportunity. He sells five RIL 1,000 calls and five 1,000 puts, and buys one Nifty 5,000 call and one Nifty 5,000 put (with the Nifty and RIL expiry coinciding), basically short selling ('shorting') the RIL 'vols' and buying the market 'vols' (after suitable numerical adjustments, ignored here for simplicity.) He can, on average and going by the past, expect to make money from this four-leg strategy.

In the above example, going by the past, prices are expected to change in such a manner that the ratio returns to its expected level. However, any one such transaction could make a profit or a loss. The only way to increase the chance of making profits (but always with uncertainty and a chance of making a loss) is to replicate this strategy across many different stocks and expiries. If volatility has empirically been seen to be mean-reverting, statistical arbitrageurs can expect to make money on average. *However, the reader should be cautioned that mean-reversion may not always take place and it is even possible that a 'new mean' gets established!* Large hedge funds have found this out at huge cost to themselves and to investors.

Notes regarding examples:

a. The use of examples using specific companies such as State Bank of India, Microsoft or Reliance Industries does not imply any endorsement or criticism of those companies; they are used for illustration simply because they are large companies whose shares are, at the time of writing, highly liquid in their respective markets.

b. The prices, volatilities and scenarios mentioned are purely hypothetical and the cases described are imaginary.

14

Options – IV

Real and Other Options

This chapter concludes the treatment of options with a brief discussion of real options and employee stock options.

Real options

Independently of the derivatives markets, life is full of situations involving 'options' in the conventional English language meaning of the term. These situations often do have financial consequences, as shown in Example 14.1.

Example 14.1

A Professor in a university who has a tenured (i.e., permanent) post is contemplating a new offer from a private company that offers her a much higher salary. She is not expecting to return to the University. However, there is always some uncertainty and less security of tenure in the private sector. She can retain a lien on her university post for three years by applying for leave without pay (sabbatical) but this involves paying a pension contribution which will not bring any extra pension benefit. If she is successful in the private sector, the amount she pays will be a waste. However, if she is unsuccessful, she can get back her University post. In this situation, retaining her lien would be the equivalent of buying a call option on the job—the premium is the amount of pension contribution. This is an example of a real option.

More formally and quantitatively, the concept of real options is used in corporate finance and capital budgeting. Stewart Myers coined the term 'real option' in 1977.

Example 14.2

M Ltd. proposes to acquire a copper mine. The mine is already in production and has some reserves, which are profitable to exploit at any price above $3,000. Current prices are approximately $6,000 per ton. Traditional discounted cash flow techniques have been used to arrive at a valuation of the cash flow from the production expected each year. However, there are also some reserves that will be viable to extract only at prices higher than $9,000. The seller is insisting that the price must include a premium to reflect this potential future value. There is no certainty that the price of $9,000 would ever be reached; however if it *is reached then a substantial additional cash flow will arise. Intuitively, it is obvious that this potential has some value but X Ltd. is not clear how to value this.*

This is another example of a real option. In this case, an options-based valuation approach would be to make estimations and calculations about the quantity of viable resources as a function of future price, the expected volatility of the mineral's price and various other factors. The tools used for calculating the price of this real option would be very similar to that for financial options (Black-Scholes, binomial, Monte Carlo etc.) Then, after appropriately discounting for time, the value of this option would be added to a net present value (NPV) calculation. The seller and/or buyer might use this calculation in their price negotiations.

The discounted value of future cash flows is an important consideration when companies and entrepreneurs decide whether to invest in specific projects. The NPV is the sum of the future cash flows generated by the project adjusted for the time value of money (gross present value), minus the investment(s), also adjusted for time value of money. The time value of money is essentially the fact that a rupee received today is worth more than a rupee received in future, because it can earn interest. The appropriate interest rate is the cost of capital to the firm. In some cases, the cost of capital is increased to reflect a risk premium.

Theoretically, there may be no limit to borrowing, and therefore 'rational' investors would never pass over any positive NPV project; but realistically there are limits to taking out loans and hence projects are often ranked by NPV or IRR (internal rate of return) or some simpler measures which do not entertain the pretence of precision. In practice, companies sometimes undertake investments on the basis of criteria other than cash flow or profitability, for various reasons including managerial empire-building, thwarting hostile takeovers or – in the case of breakthrough technologies or highly risky ideas – because future cash flows may be highly speculative or impossible to estimate. However, subject to these caveats, the following discussion of real options assumes that choices are driven by NPV.

Example 14.3
A mining company is considering leasing a gold mine for the next three years, and the mine has four broadly discernible deposits. One deposit has 100,000 ounces and the other three have 50,000 ounces each. Assume that the cost of extraction within each deposit is homogenous.

Cost of extraction	Estimate of extractable resources
1,100 USD/ounce	100,000 ounces
1,300 USD/ounce	50,000 ounces more
1,500 USD/ounce	50,000 ounces more
1,700 USD/ounce	25,000 ounces more

Currently the price of gold is $1,600 per ounce. Assume there are very low interest rates and storage costs. Because gold is a 'continuous storage' good with large stocks, futures prices are determined by the storage cost rather than expected prices. Therefore, the futures prices of gold in one, two, three years from now are also $1,600 in each case (ignoring storage costs). The following simplifying assumptions are made:

- *There will be no major change in the cost or technology of gold extraction in the next few years.*

- *There are only three possible scenarios for gold prices in the coming three years:*
  - *Scenario 1: Price increases by 10 per cent at the end of every year – 30 per cent probability*
  - *Scenario 2: Price remains constant – 40 per cent probability*
  - *Scenario 3: Price decreases by 10 per cent at the end of every year – 30 per cent probability*

In all three scenarios it is assumed that the price stabilises after year three, and that a discount rate of 10 per cent should be used for all calculations.

(N.B. More detailed and sophisticated calculations could be done through the Monte Carlo and other techniques like Binomial modeling, if these simplifying assumptions were not present.) The expected prices in the different scenarios are as follows:

Price (of gold in USD/ounce)	Year 1	Year 2	Year 3	Year 4 onwards
Scenario 1	1600	1760	1936	2129.6
Scenario 2	1600	1600	1600	1600
Scenario 3	1600	1440	1296	1166.4

Scenario 1

- *Scenario 1- Profits in Year 1: Since the price is $1,600, only reserves costing less than $1,600 to extract are worth extracting. Hence profits are: $[100,000 (1,600-1,100)+50,000 (1,600-1300)+50,000 (1,600-1,500)] = $70 million*

- *Scenario 1- Profits in Year 2: Since the price is $1,760, all the reserves are worth extracting. Hence profits are: $[100,000 (1,760-1,100)+50,000 (1,760-1,300)+50,000 (1,760-1,500)+25,000 (1,760-1,700)] = $103.5 million*

- *Scenario 1- Profits in Year 3: Since the price is $1,760, all the reserves are worth extracting. Hence profits are: $[100,000 (1,936–1,100)+50,000 (1,936–1,300)+50,000 (1,936–1,500)+25,000 (1,936–1,700)] = $143.1 million.*

The future cash flows have to be discounted; since the interest rate is 10 per cent (or 0.1), amounts received in year two will be valued at 1/ (1+ 0.1), those in year three at 1/(1+0.1) (1+0.1) = 1/1.21.

Present value (PV) of profits = (70 + 103.5/1.1 + 143.1/1.21) = $282.35 million

Scenario 2

Since the price is $1,600, only reserves costing less than that to extract are worth extracting. The price remains unchanged for all three years. Hence, profits are:
- *Year 1: $ [100,000 (1,600–1,100)+50,000 (1,600–1,300)+50,000 (1,600–1,500)] = $70 million*
- *Year 2: $[100,000 (1,600–1,100)+50,000 (1,600–1,300) + 50,000 (1,600 – 1,500)] = $70 million*
- *Year 3: $[100,000 (1,600–1,100)+50,000 (1,600–1,300)+50,000 (1,600–1,500)] = $70 million*

PV of profits = (70 + 70/1.1 + 70/1.21) = $191.48 million

Scenario 3
- *Scenario 3- Profits in Year 1: Since the price is $1,600, only reserves costing less than that to extract are worth extracting. $[100,000 (1,600–1,100)+50,000 (1,600–1,300)+50,000 (1,600–1,500)] = $70 million*
- *Scenario 3- Profits in Year 2: Since the price is $1,440, only reserves costing less than that to extract are worth extracting. $100,000 (1,440–1,100)+50,000 (1,440–1,300) = $41 million*
- *Scenario 3- Profits in Year 3: Since the price is $1296, only reserves costing less than that to extract are worth extracting. $100,000 (1,296–1,100) = $19.6 million*

PV of profits = $(70 + 41/1.1 + 19.6/1.21) = $123.47 million

Expected value (without taking the lease expense) = $ (0.3 x 282.35 + 0.4 x 191.48 + 0.3 x 138.02) million= $202.7 million.

However, if the analysis had taken into account only static prices, the lease would not be worth more than $191.5 m, whereas now it is worth 202.7 m, i.e., 11.2 million dollars more. This extra 'premium' is in effect what the mining company is paying for the 'real option' of using the more difficult and expensive to extract deposits the lifetime of the lease of the entire mine. It is the difference in value between a mine which has only deposits which are profitable now and a mine which also has some deposits which are not profitable now, but may possibly become profitable in the future.

Abandonment options

A corollary and mirror image of the real option to expand is the equally real option to abandon. Wherever such flexibility exists, management could apply the economic concept of 'sunk cost', curb operations and minimise variable costs. In the above gold mine and deposits' example, for instance, the investor need not even run the biggest deposit of 100,000 ounces if the price of gold falls below 1,100 USD per ounce (which was not in any of the three scenarios – but could well be in another scenario analysis). The value of this option may become clear if one considers two scenarios confronting a multi-national mining company: a mine in a socialist country where permission to cease operations may be needed and may not be given, versus another country where no permission is needed. Even if both mines have identical deposits and costs, the latter has a better 'abandonment option value'.

Inter-temporal comparison of positive NPV projects using real options

Any NPV project is good for the investor, but in real life borrowing is constrained so the investor has to choose. She must choose not only between projects, but also *across time of initiation and execution* for a given project. Suppose an investor is building a large hotel-cum-mall complex in a city where the next Olympics are likely to take place seven years from now. The investor can buy the land now, but delay the project execution enough to maximise NPV especially if the major portion of 'footfalls' and tourists are likely to come only with the sporting event. The different starting times are 'real options'.

Executive and employee stock options

Companies face a fundamental agent-principal problem – the shareholders (the principals who in theory own the company) want the profits to be maximised, but the managers (in theory, agents of the principals) too want their own 'profits' (i.e., income, remuneration and perhaps non-monetary benefits like prestige) to be maximised. The board of directors is in theory supposed to represent the shareholders and the management are supposed to be accountable to them – but this is almost never fully attained in practice.

For example, a CEO with no equity stake (or insignificant equity stake compared to his base pay and benefits) is likely to have other factors than the company's long term and sustainable profit growth in mind. He may want to focus on revenue growth and sacrifice margins because that may justify a bigger pay to manage a bigger and hence more prestigious, 'empire'. Similarly, he may initiate mergers and acquisitions (especially the latter) without due diligence about the probable synergies in cost-reductions and value-additions.

The result of such managerial behaviour could be that shareholders investments are eroded or do not keep up with better-run companies. This is a variation on the theme of conflict between labour and capital – albeit with the labour here being the rather well off bourgeoisie rather than the hand-to-mouth proletariat.

The question that arises is how to solve this 'principal-agent problem' and align the incentives of managers with those of the shareholders. One way is through performance-related variable, non-guaranteed bonus pay. This is generally useful for mid-level managers and lower-level workers. But, what about the top management? One solution is to make the top management part owners. However, the shareholders may not want to give stock to a CEO and his or her lieutenants at the time of joining: what is to stop them from resigning and just collecting their newfound wealth? Moreover, the stock ought not to be given for bad or even average performance. There ought to be this 'reward' only for good performance by the top management for the shareholders. One theoretically elegant solution which was evolved to combat this principal-agent problem in the corporate world was the concept of stock options.

The company gives senior management, and increasingly workers down the line, some stock options with an appropriate exercise price and an appropriate expiry date. The options can be structured in line with the aims in terms of retention of key staff. If the idea is to incentivise and prioritise length of stay, then the stock call options can have a low exercise price, and hence be in-the-money, but have an exercise date far in the future. To promote loyalty and length of service, the options 'vest' or can be exercised only if, as of the expiry date, the manager is still a bona fide employee of the company. (In practice, many more clauses can and are brought into stock option grants and contracts.)

If the objective is to create incentives for extraordinary growth and super-profits, top executives could be given 'deep out of the money' options which will only become profitable if the share price rises substantially above current levels. If the idea is to incentivise good performance without too much risk taking, then the exercise price can be at-the-money or near the current stock price (generally slightly above). This has the disadvantage of perhaps being too 'easy' compensation for the top management, whereas the advantage of this approach is that (unlike deep OTM options), slightly-out-of-the-money options do not goad the managers to go for an overly aggressive all-or-nothing approach, which could be catastrophic for the owners of the company i.e., shareholders (and possibly even for the senior bondholders).

Other approaches can also be tried – whereby the exercise price or the strike price can be a moving function of the broader market, with or without some adjustments for the beta of the company in question. The board of directors can try to ensure that the management is only compensated for outperforming the stock market over a given period of time rather than be beneficiaries of a broad rally even if the company has significantly under-performed. Other combinations and permutations can also be attempted.

Setting the 'ideal' expiry date and exercise price for stock options is more art than science.

Real life experience has shown that options are not as effective as their proponents thought in aligning the incentives of managers with those of shareholders.

Part – V
Other Derivatives and Derivative-like Instruments

15

Other Derivatives

The three main derivative securities (futures, swaps and options) have been discussed at length in preceding chapters. This chapter covers other derivatives, in brief. Analytically, many of these derivatives can also be viewed as being constructed from the basic building blocks of futures and options, an exception being event-based derivatives which are closer conceptually to insurance contracts.

Forward rate agreements

A forward rate agreement is a contract, generally entered into between a bank and a customer, which gives the latter a guaranteed future rate of interest to cover a specified sum of money over a specified period of time in the future. A forward rate agreement (FRA) does not involve actual lending or borrowing of sums of money. It is merely an agreement which fixes a rate of interest for a future transaction. At the time when the customer actually requires funds, he has to separately borrow the money in the cash market at the rate of interest prevailing then. If the rate of interest payable in the cash market turns out to be higher than the rate of interest fixed in the FRA (entered into earlier), the bank which signed the FRA will pay to the customer the difference in the interest rate. However, if the rate of interest payable in the cash market turns out to be lower than that fixed in the FRA, the customer has to pay the difference in the rate of interest. This transaction is known as purchase of a FRA from the bank.

It is worth repeating that no actual lending or borrowing is involved in the FRA. If the customer eventually decides not to borrow the sum of money, no amount is payable from or to the bank. While reference was made to a customer intending to borrow, it is also possible for a customer to enter into an FRA for his deposits. A customer may wish to have a guaranteed rate of interest for a sum of money which he intends to deposit at a future point of time. He can enter into an FRA with a bank. He has to separately make a deposit in the cash market at the appropriate point of time. If the market rate on his deposit turns out to be lower than that guaranteed in the FRA, the bank will compensate him for the difference. On the other hand, if the deposit interest rate turns out to be higher than what was fixed in the FRA the customer has to pay the difference to the bank. This transaction is known as sale of a FRA to the bank.

For this reason, purchase of a FRA protects against a rise in interest rate where a company needs to borrow from a bank. Sale of a FRA protects against a fall in the interest rate where a company needs to deposit money with the bank. The bank charges different interest rates for borrowers and lenders and the spread between the two constitutes its profit margin. Generally, no other fee is payable for FRA contracts.

As hedging instruments, FRAs are substitutes for short term debt futures, but being OTC, the size and terms can be customised.

Range forwards

Range forwards are an instrument found in the foreign exchange markets. They are essentially a variation on the standard forward exchange contracts and are also known as flexible forward contracts. In such contracts, instead of quoting a single forward rate (for example three months forward rupee at ₹ 59.8 per $), a quotation is given in terms of a range. The forward rupee would be quoted at '₹ 59 to 61'. If the spot exchange rate on the maturity date is between these two levels, then the actual spot rate is used. If the spot rate rises above the maximum, then the maximum level is used. If the spot rate falls below the minimum, the minimum rate is used. Range forwards differ from normal forward contracts because they:

a.   give the customer a range within which he can benefit or lose from exchange fluctuations; and

b.   provide protection from extreme variation in exchange rates.

The risk-return profile of range forwards is very similar to that of a 'foreign exchange collar' in the currency options market. For an illustration of the collar mechanism, albeit in the context of equity options, see Example 13.1.

Swaptions

A 'swaption' is a contract by which a party acquires an option to enter into a swap. A call swaption gives the purchaser a right to enter into a swap as the fixed rate payer. A put swaption gives the purchaser of the swaption the option of entering into a swap as a floating rate payer. A swaption has got a strike rate (denominated in terms of the fixed rate payable) and a maturity date which can be either on European or American terms. Swaptions can be used to hedge uncertain cash flows. For example, a company may not be sure whether a tender which it has bid for will be awarded to it. If the bid is successful it may have to enter into a swap. To hedge such *contingent borrowing*, it can enter into a swaption.

Commodity-linked loans and bonds

These are instruments, first designed in the eighties, primarily to meet the needs of companies and countries whose earnings are closely linked to commodity prices. A commodity-linked bond would involve a loan to a borrower in which the interest payable and/or repayment schedule is linked to a commodity price. If the commodity price rises, the debt service obligation increases by a predetermined margin. If the commodity price falls, then the debt service obligation is also reduced, though there is often a minimum debt service obligation. The positive correlation between the commodity price and debt service, reduces hardship to the commodity producer. For the lender, the bond reduces the risk of default since repayment is linked to 'ability to pay'. These bonds are (analytically) equivalent to a combination of a conventional loan and an option on the commodity price.

Interest-only (IO)/principal-only (PO) strips

These are synthetic securities which split up the interest and principal elements of a security, and allow the holder to receive a return based on one component alone. Thus, an IO strip holder receives *interest only* on a particular type of asset (say a securitised pool of mortgage loans or treasury bonds), but *no principal payments*. A PO strip or IO strip costs much less than the underlying asset itself. These instruments are useful to financial institutions in matching their assets with their liabilities. For this reason, these and similar derivatives are sometimes known collectively as 'asset/liability-based derivatives'.

Equity-linked bonds and notes

These are bonds linked to a *specified equity index*. If the equity index rises, the bond earns higher return and vice versa. In *protected equity linked bonds* both principal repayments and a pre-set minimum coupon rate are fixed (i.e., 'protected') but additional returns are payable depending on the performance of a specified index or indices. The protected (minimum) coupon interest rate is lower than the normal bond interest rate – the sacrifice is the consideration paid for the opportunity of higher earnings through equity index appreciation. These instruments are usually used by pension funds, insurance companies, etc. Analytically, they are a combination of a conventional loan with equity options.

Event-based derivatives

Event-based derivatives are those where the pay-off is based on the occurrence of a specified event. If the event does not occur, one of the parties may not receive a pay-off.

Credit derivatives

Credit derivatives are an example of event-based derivatives. The event in question is the occurrence of default in servicing of a loan. The interest rate on a loan has three components:

a.   the borrowing cost for the bank or institution (e.g., deposit interest rate prevailing in the market);
b.   loan-deposit spread, being the normal profit margin of the bank; and
c.   a credit risk premium or spread depending on the credit-worthiness of the borrower.

Credit derivatives involve the third element, i.e., the credit risk premium. A typical credit derivative is a 'credit default swap' (CDS) in which one party 'swaps' the *default risk (credit risk) alone* with a counterparty; the latter agrees to pay the first party in the event of a default by the borrower, but receives a regular payment in return. (Conceptually this is equivalent to a guarantee in return for guarantee commission.)

Example 15.1

B, a bank, has lent heavily to D, a developing country. D has asked for further loans. B is worried at 'having too many eggs in one basket', but at the same time does not want to forgo the business and the profits therein especially as its rival bank may get an entry into the country if it does not lend. It therefore gives the loan to D at 10 per cent but enters into a default swap with C, an institution with no exposure to D so far. It agrees to pay C 2 per cent per annum in exchange for C covering the default risk.

Credit derivatives are a useful means of spreading default risks. They do not alter the lender-borrower relationship. In the above example, the borrower is in no way involved in the swap. Credit derivatives allow lenders to continue to lend and earn normal banking profits (deposit-to-loan spread) without assuming the credit risk.

CDS are called swaps, but analytically are not really swaps because there is no exchange of cash flows. Rather, there is a fixed cash flow in one direction; in the other direction there may or may not be a cash flow depending on whether or not a particular event happens. If the event does not happen, the cash flow remains one-sided. The use of the term 'swap' is linked to the desire of CDS buyers and sellers in the USA to keep them out of the scope of insurance regulation. CDS played a role in the global financial crisis of 2008 (see Appendix 1.1).

Weather and catastrophe derivatives

In recent years, derivatives linked to specified weather events and to natural disasters have been developed. For example, a weather derivative contract may specify that if the rainfall in a specified area exceeds a pre-set level, then a pre-specified payment will be triggered. A catastrophe derivative contract may specify that if an earthquake occurs in a particular area, a payment will be triggered. Catastrophe bonds – sometimes but not always considered as derivatives – are bonds where the borrower is allowed to reduce or defer debt servicing when a specified catastrophe occurs. Because of this, they would normally have a higher coupon than an ordinary bond.

Like CDS, these are also event-based derivatives: one of the parties makes a fixed payment. The other party may or may not make any payment depending on the occurrence or non-occurrence of the specified event. Weather and catastrophe derivatives are alternatives to traditional insurance.

Other complex and synthetic derivatives

Using the building blocks of futures and options it is possible to construct a number of complex derivative instruments. Complex derivatives can be designed to suit the particular needs and circumstances of a particular client. International banks and brokers structure such specialised derivatives, known as 'synthetic' (or custom-made) derivatives. A number of such instruments have been churned out by derivatives specialists (especially those in Wall Street who became known as the 'rocket scientists' because of the complexity of their designs). Some such complex instruments have subsequently become widely used and available OTC from financial intermediaries. The precise financial implications of a complex or custom-made derivative can be quite difficult to unravel. A client entering into a complex or custom-made derivative transaction should be very careful in understanding in advance the likely financial outcomes in various circumstances.

The commodity-linked and equity-linked bonds referred to in this chapter are examples of complex derivatives which started off as custom-made instruments for particular clients. The 'rainbow options', 'barrier options', amortising swaps etc., referred to in earlier chapters are other examples of complex derivatives.

16

Exchange Traded Funds and Structured Products

This chapter examines exchange traded funds (ETFs) and 'structured products'. Some, but not all, ETFs and structured products are effectively derivatives.

Exchange traded funds

ETFs are investment funds that can be bought or sold on an exchange like a share. They may be of two types:

- 'Index mutual funds' or 'Cash ETFs' whose composition and performance matches a specified equity or other price index; such funds may hold the actual underlying asset in the same proportion as the index. For example, an ETF mirroring the Nifty index might hold the shares comprised in the Nifty in exactly those proportions; a gold ETF will hold gold. Cash ETFs may be geared up by borrowing.

- Synthetic funds whose performance matches a specified underlying without actual ownership of the underlying.

ETFs usually trade close to, but not exactly at, their Net Asset Value (NAV) although depending on demand and supply they can trade at significant premia/ discounts. The NAV is the value of the assets owned by the fund but the shares of the fund may trade at values higher or lower than that underlying value. To the extent the fund actually owns income-earning assets; ETFs may have a yield through dividends.

Most ETFs have an annualised expense ratio – ranging from 0.1 per cent of the price or NAV to around 2 per cent, depending on the liquidity, quantity of assets under management and strategy. (A strategy requiring more frequent trading or 'rolling over' of underlying assets will require higher costs than one involving passive holding of a fixed set of assets.) In this respect, the cost of holding the index fund is different from an actual holding of the underlying.

As with company shares, unless there is an Initial Public Offering (IPO) or Follow-on Public Offering (FPO), most trading takes place in the secondary market. Only some dealers buy ETF units in large blocks called 'creation units' directly from the ETF distributor. The rest of the trading is between secondary market participants. ETFs were first successfully introduced in the United States in 1993.

Table 16.1 below lists examples of the ETFs traded on Indian bourses to give readers a flavour of the kinds of schemes available.

Table 16.1: ETFs traded in India
(Top 50 by AUM, as of August 2016) along with their annualised returns

Schemes	Latest price	Percentage change	Asset size ₹ cr.	NAV ₹	1 year	2 year	3 year
SBI - ETF Nifty 50	87.61	0.61	7,625.01	87.92	5.3	--	--
SBI - ETF Sensex	297	1.66	2,210.55	296.71	3.6	6	15.2
GS CPSE ETF	22.94	0.61	2,136.27	22.91	-0.5	-2.6	--
GS Gold BeES	2,870.25	0.13	1,790.05	2,923.65	22.8	4.8	2.1
Kotak Banking ETF		--	1,430.43	192.76	5.1	--	--
R*Shares Gold ETF	2,730.15	0.03	1,410.93	2,827.74	22	3.7	1.7
GS Liquid BeES	1,000.00	0	1,072.29	1,000.00	--	--	--
GS Nifty BeES	880.64	0.68	1,045.14	884.21	4.7	6.3	15.3
SBI - ETF Gold	2,882.70	-1.02	1,011.24	2,999.68	22.8	4.7	2.1
GS Bank BeES	1,914.98	1.31	705.89	1,921.80	4.7	12.9	23.8
HDFC Gold Exchange Traded Fund	2,917.45	-0.23	637.97	2,975.11	22.2	4.5	1.9
Kotak Gold ETF	273.7	-0.33	515.31	291.62	22.6	4.6	1.9

Schemes	Latest price	Percen- tage change	Asset size ₹ cr.	NAV₹	1 year	2 year	3 year
UTI Gold Exchange Traded Fund	2,833.90	-0.26	483.12	2,929.04	22.9	4.7	2
R*Shares Banking ETF	2,063.10	1.36	349.87	2,069.05	5.1	13.6	24.8
Kotak Nifty ETF	870	0.81	345.96	875.3	3.7	5.7	14.7
Axis Gold ETF	2,843.95	0.14	235.67	2,977.54	22.6	4.6	2
UTI Nifty Exchange Traded Fund	880	1.31	226.76	880.71	--	--	--
Birla Sun Life Nifty ETF	88.87	0.7	191.02	91.27	5.4	7.2	16.2
ICICI Pru Gold iWIN ETF	92.51	1.44	125.72	302.11	-87.7	-66.9	-52.7
Kotak PSU Bank ETF	307.74	6.88	108	303.26	-10.8	-7.8	9.5
GS Junior BeES	225.2	-0.05	107.49	226.84	8.4	17.9	25.9
IDBI Gold Exchange Traded Fund	2,907.05	-0.35	101.29	3,058.25	22.8	4.8	2
Birla Sun Life Gold ETF (G)	2,980.00	0.85	85.01	3,060.49	22.8	4.8	1.8
Can Gold Exchange Traded Fund	2,955.00	0	79.67	2,955.03	20	3.7	0.7
SBI - ETF Nifty Bank	87.61	0.61	71.13	192.74	5.2	--	--

Schemes	Latest price	Percentage change	Asset size ₹ cr.	NAV ₹	1 year	2 year	3 year
LIC NOMURA G-Sec LTE Fund - RP (G)	16	0	70.86	15.87	12.5	--	--
Motilal MOSt Shares NASDAQ 100 ETF	306.99	-0.89	66.35	319.02	9.3	15.8	18.6
Quantum Gold Fund	1,407.80	-0.49	65.33	1,457.19	22.6	4.6	2
HDFC Nifty ETF	874.3	0.83	45.7	874.46	--	--	--
Motilal MOSt Shares Midcap 100 ETF	15	0	39.74	15.48	8.9	17.8	29.4
GS PSU Bank BeES	328.75	5.34	38.18	329.63	-10.8	-5.7	11.1
Motilal Oswal MOSt Shares Gold ETF	2,440.05	0	29.66	2,529.56	-6.1	-7.5	-4.2
ICICI Prudential CNX 100 iWIN ETF	92.51	1.44	27.62	92.31	5.4	8.5	21.1
R*Shares Nifty ETF	89.68	0.65	26.19	90.06	5.2	7.2	--
Motilal MOSt Shares M50 ETF	81.44	-0.07	22.5	83.67	4.3	3.8	16.6
GS Infra BeES	291.22	0.08	17.06	293.51	-8	-2.3	11.3

Schemes	Latest price	Percentage change	Asset size ₹ cr.	NAV ₹	1 year	2 year	3 year
R*shares Consumption ETF	40.27	1.46	16.2	40.15	10	14.8	--
UTI Sensex Exchange Traded Fund	284.3	0.41	15.04	285.12	--	--	--
R*Shares Dividend ETF		--	13.83	22.39	10.1	5.6	--
SBI - ETF Nifty Next 50	228.3	1.87	11.56	227.98	9.5	--	--
Edelweiss ETS - Nifty (Nifty EES)	6,800.00	0	11.11	8,857.63	5.3	--	--
Kotak Sensex ETF	288	1.03	11.11	288.64	3.4	4.2	14
R*shares CNX 100 ETF	90.02	0.75	7.99	90.3	4.8	8	17.1
GS Hang Seng BeES	2,021.59	-2.23	5.8	2,301.83	-0.1	2.4	6
ICICI Pru SPIcE Plan	289.1	0.94	5.29	289.71	3.6	5.4	11
HDFC Sensex ETF	2,831.70	0.77	2.14	2,850.36	--	--	--
GS Shariah BeES	199.94	0.47	2.02	198.99	3.5	7.2	13.6
IIFL Nifty ETF		--	1.5	891.36	10.7	21.5	20
SBI - ETF BSE 100	89	0	1.17	90.69	5.9	--	--

Source: Moneycontrol.com.

The table shows both the latest price and the NAV. The difference between them is the premium or discount. For example, the second largest ETF by assets under management (AUM) in India – SBI ETF Sensex – was trading at a premium since the market price exceeded the NAV. The column on asset size shows the size of aggregate assets in the fund. Going by asset size, Gold ETFs appear to be one of the most popular ETF sub-categories on Indian bourses. While Indians were already buying equities and mutual funds in 'dematerialised' or 'demat.' form, gold was generally confined to actual physical gold. This entails risks and costs, especially if the gold bought was a relatively small quantity as it is in most middle-class purchases.

In terms of sheer depth and diversity for ETFs – as in the case of many other financial instruments – the American market is unparalleled. Table 16.2 shows some leading American listed ETFs.

Table 16.2: Leading American-listed and traded ETFs (data as of August 2016; all ETFs have AUM greater than US$10B)

Symbol	Name	AUM
SPY	SPDR S&P 500 ETF	$199,078,733
IVV	iShares Core S&P 500 ETF	$78,848,730
VTI	Vanguard Total Stock Market ETF	$64,331,846
EFA	iShares MSCI EAFE ETF	$60,625,338
VOO	Vanguard S&P 500 ETF	$50,650,128
GLD	SPDR Gold Shares ETF	$42,263,875
VWO	Vanguard FTSE Emerging Markets ETF	$42,247,219
AGG	iShares Core U.S. Aggregate Bond ETF	$40,462,518
QQQ	PowerShares QQQ ETF	$39,819,856
VEA	Vanguard FTSE Developed Markets ETF	$36,054,093
VNQ	Vanguard REIT ETF	$35,748,349
LQD	iShares iBoxx $ Investment Grade Corporate Bond ETF	$32,175,395
BND	Total Bond Market ETF	$32,062,416

Symbol	Name	AUM
IWF	iShares Russell 1000 Growth ETF	$30,585,770
EEM	iShares MSCI Emerging Markets ETF	$30,506,950
IWD	iShares Russell 1000 Value ETF	$29,964,000
IJH	iShares Core S&P Mid-Cap ETF	$29,674,013
IWM	iShares Russell 2000 ETF	$29,372,266
VTV	Vanguard Value ETF	$22,713,427
VIG	Vanguard Dividend Appreciation ETF	$22,644,358
VUG	Vanguard Growth ETF	$21,605,198
IJR	iShares Core S&P Small-Cap ETF	$19,721,208
BSV	Short-Term Bond ETF	$18,245,990
TIP	iShares TIPS Bond ETF	$18,208,030
PFF	iShares U.S. Preferred Stock ETF	$17,530,434
MDY	SPDR S&P MIDCAP 400 ETF	$17,382,205
HYG	iShares iBoxx $ High Yield Corporate Bond ETF	$16,511,902
DVY	iShares Select Dividend ETF	$16,366,456
IWB	iShares Russell 1000 ETF	$16,304,662
IEMG	iShares Core MSCI Emerging Markets ETF	$15,736,560
XLF	Financial Select Sector SPDR Fund	$15,498,854
VYM	Vanguard High Dividend Yield ETF	$15,359,723
USMV	iShares MSCI USA Minimum Volatility ETF	$15,193,750
VO	Vanguard Mid-Cap ETF	$14,971,021
SDY	SPDR S&P Dividend ETF	$14,725,942
XLE	Energy Select Sector SPDR Fund	$14,088,528
EWJ	iShares MSCI Japan ETF	$14,041,405

Symbol	Name	AUM
VEU	Vanguard FTSE All-World ex-US ETF	$13,978,451
IVW	iShares S&P 500 Growth ETF	$13,948,014
VB	Vanguard Small-Cap ETF	$13,868,835
VCSH	Vanguard Short-Term Corporate Bond ETF	$13,541,048
XLV	Health Care Select Sector SPDR Fund	$13,226,073
IWR	iShares Russell Mid-Cap ETF	$13,052,762
XLK	Technology Select Sector SPDR Fund	$12,691,361
DIA	SPDR Dow Jones® Industrial Average ETF	$12,546,637
IEFA	iShares Core MSCI EAFE ETF	$12,354,174
JNK	SPDR Barclays Capital High Yield Bond ETF	$12,147,962
VGK	Vanguard FTSE Europe ETF	$11,809,001
CSJ	iShares 1-3 Year Credit Bond ETF	$11,189,394
GDX	VanEck Vectors Gold Miners ETF	$10,890,787
IVE	iShares S&P 500 Value ETF	$10,585,491
BIV	Intermediate-Term Bond ETF	$10,371,104
SHY	iShares 1-3 Year Treasury Bond ETF	$10,218,202
DBEF	Deutsche X-trackers MSCI EAFE Hedged Equity ETF	$10,174,016
RSP	Guggenheim S&P 500® Equal Weight ETF	$10,062,811

Source: Etfdb.com.

The annual expense ratios of these large ETFs are low (often below 0.25 per cent of the NAV), and the trading costs are also low because of the high liquidity. There are futures as well as call/put options with relatively thin bid-ask spreads often up to two years in the future on these ETFs. All this makes the execution of trade strategies very easy. A combination of all the above ETFs, and a few others (there are many non-US country-specific equity ETFs), can be used by investors to execute almost any strategic asset allocation plan.

Are ETFs derivatives?

Market commentators sometimes describe ETFs as derivatives. Going by the 'simple' definition in chapter 1 – that the price of the instrument is derived from the price of the underlying – it may appear that ETFs are indeed derivatives. However, whereas derivatives are 'side contracts' on some underlying security, many ETFs represent actual ownership. Hence, since they are actually collections of the underlying assets, they do not fulfil the second part of the definition in chapter 1 – of not being merely a collection of the underlying assets. Felix Salmon of Reuters summarised the position concisely:[1]

> The E-Mini is a derivative product by dint of being a derivative. It's a futures contract, a zero-sum game, an instrument whose value at expiry is a wholly transparent function of the value of some other financial instrument.
>
> The SPY, by contrast, is a derivative product only by dint of the fact that it's a product – a security, not a derivative – which is derived from aggregating 500 different stocks. You couldn't have the SPY without the S&P 500, so in that sense the SPY is derived from the S&P 500. But if you own shares of SPY, you have real wealth: real claims on real assets of 500 real companies in the real world.
>
> ... If all of the shares of SPY were to become vaporised tomorrow, then the S&P 500 itself would rise, since the total number of shares outstanding in the stock market would have fallen. Since the value of those 500 companies wouldn't have changed, the value per share would be higher.
>
> If all of the world's E-Mini contracts were to become vaporised tomorrow, by contrast, then the effect on the S&P 500 would be *de minimis*. E-Mini contracts are side bets on the S&P 500: they're not real-world claims on it

Therefore, for most ETFs, the answer to the question 'is it a derivative?', is 'no'. However, where the ETF is not a simple aggregation of certain shares, the answer could in some cases be 'yes'.

Cash-based ETFs

Cash-based ETFs (or 'cash ETFs') are simple aggregations of the underlying assets without gearing. They are not 'derivatives' and are a substitute for holding

---

1   http://blogs.reuters.com/felix-salmon/2010/10/01/etfs-arent-derivatives/.

the underlying. ETFs mimicking stock market indices and gold ETFs are examples. Cash ETFs themselves may fully replicate the exact combination of assets in the underlying index or may include only a representative sample of the components of the underlying index. If a representative sample is used, the ETF may not exactly match the movement of the underlying; the extent of non-matching is called the 'tracking error'.

Geared or leveraged ETFs

Geared or leveraged ETFs are ETFs which, through borrowing, promise a higher exposure (say two times or three times exposure, long or short) to the underlying, which may be a price index of shares or financial instruments or of one or more commodities. Thus, if a particular index moves up or down by 1 per cent, the ETF will move up or down by 2 per cent or 3 per cent. However, in a technical sense, these are still 'collections of assets' because the higher volatility is achieved by borrowing and then investing in the underlying; hence these are not derivatives in the strict sense.

Geared ETFs enable investors to gear up their portfolio without explicitly taking loans. Many investors prefer cash accounts to margin accounts because they do not want to entertain the possibility of any sort of 'margin call'. Moreover, in some jurisdictions and under certain circumstances, margin accounts may not be allowed to begin with. (For example, Indian residents are allowed margin accounts to trade in Indian markets, but not in foreign markets.)

Yet gearing can boost returns. One way of getting gearing without directly borrowing or running the risk of margin calls, would be to buy leveraged ETFs. For example, SSO (+2x ProShares Leveraged Long S&P 500) claims to offer just that. It has almost 2.5 billion dollars in assets, and seems to give '2x' returns (vis-a-vis the S&P 500) on a daily basis. But on a longer-term basis, the return from June 2006 to May 2017 was 83 per cent whereas the SPY ETF (a proxy for the S&P 500) returned 58 per cent over this period; in other words SSO did not yield twice the return of SPY.

Synthetic ETFs

Synthetic ETFs do not actually own the underlying asset. Instead the fund is invested in derivatives. Instead of actually holding components of an underlying index, synthetic ETFs use swaps and other derivatives to get an equivalent exposure. The holding of derivatives is such that the position is equivalent to holding the underlying index. Such ETFs often appear to have lower tracking error (that is, they follow the underlying index more accurately and with lower costs) than asset-holding ETFs. However, the disadvantage is the *additional counterparty risk* in relying on derivatives like swaps – which are mostly over-the-counter – to get the required exposure; if the parties to the swap contracts default on their obligations, the ETFs will lose heavily and fail to track the index.

Asia, Europe and North America all have synthetic ETFs but they are increasingly under regulatory scrutiny, and fund flows to 'physical' ETFs are growing. The exchange symbols of synthetic ETFs often start with the letter 'X'.

Structured ETFs

While, in a sense, all ETFs are 'structured', some bring together a combination of equity, debt and derivative exposure and these are known as 'structured ETFs' (see also structured products below). For example, the PowerShares S&P 500 Buy-Write Index (PBP) that has 218 million dollars assets under management is expected to underperform in bullish markets but over-perform in bearish markets. This is because, as the name suggests, such an ETF buys the SPY equivalent, but also sells OTM call options on it. This gives it regular premium, but it means PBP fails to participate fully on the upside in those periods when the underlying index performs well.

Exchanged-traded notes

Exchanged-traded notes (ETNs) are similar to structured ETFs, but they are 'notes' issued by a bank or a financial institution. As in the case of synthetic ETFs, the credit risk remains because the 'underlying' is not physically owned.

Inverse ETFs

Inverse ETFs are ETFs which take real or synthetic short positions in the underlying asset. By adding gearing, the ETF may be able to produce a '2x' or '3x' short position. (These are leveraged or geared inverse ETFs.) Examples at the time of writing[2] are SH (*-1x ProShares Short S&P500 Index*), TBF (*-1x*

---

2   The mention of any individual ETF or other fund is not entitled to imply any

ProShares Short 20+ Year Treasury), DGZ (*-1x PowerShares DB Short Gold ETN*) and REK (*-1x ProShares Short DJ Real Estate*) which are ETFs that can be used to take a simple short exposure to equities, treasuries, gold, and real estate in America, for instance. The TMV (*-3x Direxion Lev Short 20-Year Treasury*) provides a 'three times the index' short position on US Treasury bonds.

These ETFs can be used to get a short position on an account without actually short-selling any asset.

Volatility ETFs

Volatility ETFs are funds that allow the investor to 'buy' a volatility index. When the volatility index increases, the ETF rises in price and vice versa. As an example, the VXZ ETF (S&P 500 VIX mid-term futures) basically buys, as the name suggests, mid-term volatility futures on the S&P 500. There are also short-term volatility futures.

Structured products

Structured products are customised financial 'products' which are 'structured' (i.e., non-standard). They are usually created for large investors by combining the features of different kinds of financial instruments, often involving derivatives. They may offer the investor a combination of risk and return which cannot be easily obtained through any non-structured market instrument – for example, unlimited profit potential with guaranteed return of initial investment. The institution offering the product often breaks down the amount received from the investor into a combination of cash and one or more derivatives to be able to meet its obligation on the structured product and earn a return for itself.

Example 16.1

In 2014, a private bank offers a structured product that promises to give 60 per cent of the upside of the Indian Nifty 50 share index from July 2014 to June 2017 to investors, while guaranteeing that even if the index is lower on expiry, the initial amount invested would be returned. The Nifty is currently at 7,000. Because the initial investment is protected this is sometimes known as 'capital preservation', and many such products are named after this feature. How is the bank able to do this?

---

endorsement or criticism; the purpose is purely illustrative.

Solution:

Assume this investment product's minimum investment size is ₹ 10 lakhs. 60 per cent thereof is ₹ 6 lakhs. By buying call options equivalent in value to ₹ 6 lakhs, it is possible to get the benefit of appreciation in the Nifty. The bank would carry out the following transactions:

- *Buy ₹ 6 lakhs of call options on the NIFTY with an expiry date in June 2017 and the (ATM) strike price of 7,000. The number of options needed is 600,000/7,000 = 85.7 or 86. Say these options are available at ₹ 1,744 per contract. Therefore, ₹150,000 will be spent on buying these. (Readers should note that because the options are ATM, any increase in the Nifty will be reflected in an equal increase in the intrinsic value of the option.)*

- *(From the amount received, after spending ₹ 1.5 lakhs on option premium, ₹ 8.5 lakhs will be left.) Invest this in a fixed deposit at the three-year interest rate. Assume the annually compounded interest rate is 8 per cent*

Assume that in 2017, the Nifty has risen to 9,000. The return payable to the investor is:

[60 per cent x (9,000-7,000)/7,000] x 10,00,000 = ₹ 1,71,428. In addition, the initial capital of ₹ 10 lakhs has to be repaid.

The Nifty options with July 2017 maturity and 7,000 strike would (on maturity date) have an intrinsic value of:

(9,000-7,000) x 86= ₹ 1,72,000.

This will cover the return payable to the investor.

In addition, the fixed deposit would have matured. A three year deposit of ₹ 8.5 lakhs at 8 per cent compound interest would have appreciated to ₹ 10,70,755. This is more than the capital sum of ₹ 10 lakhs. The extra 70,755 rupees goes towards the bank's administrative and transaction costs along with their profit. (Note that, when designing the structured product, the extent of upside that can be given would vary based on interest rates, option prices etc.; the particular figures used here are hypothetical and only for illustration.)

There are medium to long term (three-five years) equity index options in India enabling this kind of transaction to be placed in this simple way. This may not always be the case: exactly corresponding options may not exist or may not have enough liquidity. In such cases, the intermediary bank may cover itself via various OTC derivatives, which may have higher transaction costs. In most cases, there are no exact hedges, and the intermediary's risk management is as much art as it is science, especially for the more 'bespoke' or customised products. It should be noted that there is credit risk in as much as the cash portion is invested by the intermediary. If the intermediary uses the cash internally and /or becomes insolvent, there is a risk of default.

The French government used a similar structured product to convince workers in a nationalised industry (Rhone-Poulenc) to take shares in the company when it was being privatised in the 1990s. The workers were given a guaranteed return and this persuaded them to accept part compensation in stock options instead of cash.[3] The structured product was offered through an investment bank.

Economic effects of ETFs and structured products

While ETFs offer many advantages to investors, it is not clear that their overall economic effect is positive. Israeli, Lee and Sreedharan have argued based on empirical studies that ETF ownership is associated with higher trading costs, a decline in analyst coverage and other negative effects.[4]

---

3 Raghuram G. Rajan and L. Zingales, *Saving Capitalism from the Capitalists*, Crown Books, 2003.

4 D. Israeli, C. M. C. Lee, S. A. Sridharan, 'Is there a Dark Side to Exchange Traded Funds: An Information Perspective', *Review of Accounting Studies*, forthcoming, available at https://papers.ssrn.com/sol3/papers.cfm?abstract_id=2625975, accessed on 14 May 2017.

Part – VI
Accounting, Taxation and Regulatory Framework

17

Accounting and Taxation

This chapter deals with the accounting and tax treatment of derivatives transactions. These are specialised topics in themselves and this chapter can only serve as an introduction to the subject.[1]

Accounting for derivatives

The increase in the range and complexity of derivative instruments, increased regulatory attention to accounting for derivatives after the global financial crisis, and differing accounting standards and rules in different countries, combine to make this subject exceptionally complicated. Indeed, derivatives accounting is probably the single most complicated topic in the field of accounting. This section presents a simplified summary intended to give the reader an exposure to the main concepts and issues.

Basic principles

The basic principles that govern accounting for derivatives can be summarised as follows:

a.   Derivatives must be shown in the balance sheet at 'fair value' (see below), and all changes in fair value must normally be recognised in the profit and loss account (also referred to in this chapter simply as 'P & L'). Thus, not only realised profits and losses, but also unrealised profits and losses must be recognised; not only must they be recognised but normally they should be recognised as part of current profits or losses. This is known as 'fair value accounting'. This is in contrast to the normal accounting convention of prudence or conservatism which would imply not recognising unrealised gains.

b.   *The general principle in (a) above will not apply if the derivative is a hedge.*

---

1   Readers should note that accounting and taxation standards and rules change from time to time and the material given here is based on the position at the time of writing. This chapter is intended to give a conceptual understanding of the important principles and issues and should not be taken as authoritative tax or accounting guidance.

To qualify as a hedge, a derivative transaction or position must meet certain criteria. The general principle for derivatives which are used as hedges is that their *accounting treatment must correspond to the treatment of the asset or liability being hedged.* This treatment is known as 'hedge accounting'.

Fair value

The term 'fair value' is important in relation to accounting for derivatives. Fair value is the *price that would be received to sell an asset/paid to transfer a liability in an orderly transaction between market participants.* It must be an 'arm's length' transaction where the parties are independent of each other, have no relationship to each other and where each is trying to protect his /its own interests. Where there is quoted market value established in a liquid and transparent market, fair value is the same as market value.

If the market for a financial instrument is not active, fair value may be established by using a valuation technique. Valuation techniques include:

- use of recent arm's length market transactions between knowledgeable, willing parties, if available;

- reference to the current fair value of another instrument that is substantially the same;

- discounted cash flow analysis;

- option pricing models; and

- techniques commonly used by market participants to price the instrument which have been demonstrated to provide reliable estimates of prices obtained in actual market transactions.

The chosen valuation technique should make maximum use of market inputs and rely as little as possible on inputs specific to the company concerned. It should incorporate all factors that market participants would consider in setting a price and be consistent with accepted economic methodologies for pricing financial instruments. The valuation technique should be 'calibrated' and periodically tested for validity, using prices from observable current market transactions or observable market data.[2]

---

2   This section draws on, but considerably simplifies, Ind-AS 109 and 113, Ministry of Corporate Affairs, Government of India. Available at: http://mca.gov.in/Ministry/pdf/INDAS113.pdf, accessed on 22 May 2017.

Mark-to-market

The term 'mark-to-market' (often abbreviated to MTM) is used to denote the practice of marking each instrument to its market value, i.e., valuing financial instruments at their market value at each reporting date. As the preceding discussion on fair value would have shown, where quoted market prices are available they represent the fair value. Hence, fair value accounting is also loosely referred to as mark-to-market accounting. A more precise view would be that mark-to-market accounting is a sub-set of fair value accounting.

Applicable standards

The accounting principles followed in the USA are known as US Generally Accepted Accounting Principles (US GAAP). These are derived mainly from accounting standards issued by the Financial Accounting Standards Board (FASB). Formerly known as Financial Accounting Standards (FAS), they have recently been codified into Accounting Standards Codifications (ASC).

Britain, continental Europe and many other countries follow International Financial Reporting Standards (IFRS) issued by the International Accounting Standards Board (IASB). Prior to the inception of IFRS, standards issued by the IASB were called International Accounting Standards (IAS) and several of them are still effective and have not been superseded by new IFRS. It is widely expected that India, and even the USA, will eventually converge with IFRS.

India follows its own accounting standards prescribed by the central government (in the Ministry of Corporate Affairs) after drafting by the Institute of Chartered Accountants of India and review by the National Advisory Committee on Accounting Standards. In 2013, a new Companies Act was passed which provides for a new National Financial Reporting Authority which would take the place of the earlier advisory committee. As part of a process of convergence with IFRS, the central government has notified 'Indian Accounting Standards' (Ind AS) which are gradually coming into force.

In 1998, FASB issued FAS 133 on 'Accounting for Derivative Instruments and Hedging Activities'. It applied to all types of derivatives and required them to be included on the balance sheet at fair values. For hedge accounting to be used, it required that the derivative being used for hedging must be 'highly effective' as a hedge and an assessment of this effectiveness must be recorded four times a year. This required appropriate disclosure and reduced company discretion. FAS 133 influenced accounting standards not only in the US, but also in Europe and it had a substantial influence on the IAS 39 issued by the IASB. Later FAS 133 was codified into ASC 815. Table 17.1 is a summary of the main accounting standards applicable to derivatives.

Table 17.1: Standards applicable to derivatives accounting

Country/Region	Framework of standards applicable	Specific standards/guidance applicable to derivatives accounting
USA	US GAAP	ASC 815, *Derivatives and Hedging*
Great Britain, Europe and many other countries	IFRS	IAS 39, *Financial Instruments: Recognition and Measurement* *Guidance on Implementing IAS 39* (IAS 39 IG) IFRIC* 9, *Reassessment of Embedded Derivatives* IFRIC* 16, *Hedges of a Net Investment in a Foreign Operation* IFRS 9, *Financial Instruments (effective after 2018)* *IFRIC denotes interpretations of IFRS by the IFRS Interpretation Committee.
India	Past: AS Current: Ind AS	AS 11, *The effects of changes in foreign exchange rates* AS 30, *Financial Instruments: Recognition and Measurement* Ind-AS 32, *Financial Instruments: Presentation* Ind-AS 107, *Financial instruments: Disclosures* Ind-AS 109, *Financial Instruments* Ind-AS 113, *Fair Value Measurement*

The discussion in this chapter is intended to give the reader a general conceptual overview, and so is not necessarily based on any one set of accounting standards.

As noted above, the basic accounting rule for derivatives which are not hedges, is that they should be:

- recorded at fair value in the balance sheet; and
- all changes in fair value should be shown in the profit and loss account as profits or losses.

Thus, the gains and losses on derivatives, whether realised or not, would affect the current reported profit of the entity using them. This treatment is often called 'fair value through profit and loss' and abbreviated to FVTPL or FVPL.

However, if a derivative is being used as a hedge, the accounting treatment may vary based on the specific circumstances and the general rule of FVTPL may or may not apply. In order to follow the accounting treatment in those cases, it is first necessary to understand some important concepts relating to *accounting for financial instruments in general* (of which derivatives are a sub-set).

Financial instruments

For the purposes of accounting standards, *financial instruments* are widely defined and would include cash, an ownership interest in an entity, or a contractual right to receive or obligation deliver cash or another financial instrument. Financial instruments may be assets or liabilities. According to IAS 39, any contract that gives rise to a financial asset of one entity and a financial liability or equity instrument of another entity is a financial instrument. (By this definition, not only investments in debt and equity securities, and bonds payable but even traditional assets and liabilities such as sundry debtors and creditors are technically financial instruments.) Equity issued by the entity itself are not financial instruments.

An instrument is treated as a *derivative financial instrument* if it fulfils the following criteria:

- The instrument has underlying asset(s) and a specific payment provision.
- The instrument requires relatively little investment at the beginning of the contract. For example, futures require no payment – except margin – and most call and put option premia are also small compared to the underlying exposure.

- The instrument permits netting, i.e., settlement of differences: Futures and options can be bought and sold without ever taking any delivery of the underlying, for example. That is, the instrument or contract must not be such that delivery is effectively mandated, because no secondary market is legal or liquid.

Intentions

Derivatives, like many other financial assets and liabilities, are classified for accounting purposes depending on the *intention* behind buying or selling the instrument. For instance when a financial instrument is purchased:

- It may be bought with the intention of reselling in the short-term, so as to earn a speculative profit (i.e., for *trading*).
- It may be bought with the intention of holding it till the maturity of the instrument (i.e., to be '*held to maturity*').
- It may be bought because the cash flows from the instrument or the changes in its value may act as a hedge against fluctuations in value of some other asset or liability (i.e., for *hedging*).
- It may be bought to be resold at some indefinite time in the future; thus there is no intention to hold to maturity but the timing of sale is indefinite and not necessarily in the near future (i.e., '*available for sale*').

The accounting treatment will vary depending on the intention.

There is a sound logic behind the basic principles outlined earlier. If a two-year government bond is purchased for short-term trading, it must be 'marked to market' i.e., must be valued at market value in the balance sheet and the unrealised gains/losses must be shown in the profit and loss account as profits or losses. Since the asset is held for short term trading, this accounting treatment enables readers of the accounts to better gauge the true financial position on the balance sheet date.

On the other hand, if the intention is to hold the bond for the next two years till its maturity, any short-term bond value changes will not affect the entity because it will not be selling the asset. Therefore, short term price fluctuations should not be reflected on the balance sheet or the profit and loss account. Since interest and principal payments are predictable, there is no benefit to readers of the accounts by adopting FVTPL; the FVTPL would result in the accounts exhibiting an artificial volatility because of market price changes between the present and the time of maturity. Rather than helping investors, they may be misled by FVTPL treatment. In such circumstances, common sense would indicate that the bond should be valued based on its final maturity value.

A company in the competitive marketplace should not change its stated accounting intentions frequently. For example, if a company changes the stated intention for a portion of a bond holding from 'held-to-maturity' to a 'for trading' just because interest rates have gone down and bonds prices have gone up, it could artificially boost its short-term profit. For this reason, accounting practice normally prohibits such companies from using the held-to-maturity provision for a period of time after such a change, effectively penalising such 'gaming' of the system; Ind AS 39 and IAS 39, for example, would then also require other held-to-maturity bonds in such a company to be reclassified as available-for-sale, whereby changes in the market value of the bonds are reflected in the balance sheet of the company (through changes in reserves or 'Other Comprehensive Income'), though not the profit and loss account. In the following discussion, the term 'P&L' is used as an abbreviation for 'Profit and Loss Account'.

Classification of financial assets

For accounting purposes, financial assets are classified as follows based on intention and corresponding accounting treatment:

a. Trading assets: Such assets should be accounted for at FVTPL.

b. Held to maturity (HTM) investments: These are carried at *amortised cost*. Amortisation is a process through which a cost or benefit incurred or received as a one-time lump sum though actually belonging to multiple periods, is apportioned to those periods. (For example, if a bond was purchased at a premium over the par value or a discount to the par value, that difference would be amortised over the remaining period until maturity; the transaction costs involved in buying the asset, like brokerage or transaction taxes would also be apportioned to different periods.) To qualify to be treated as HTM, there must be the intention and capacity to hold these instruments till their maturity/expiry. Equity investments cannot be treated as HTM because there is no maturity date.

c. Loans and receivables (this category is unlikely to involve derivatives): Long-term loans are treated as HTM assets as in two above and valued at amortised cost. Shorter-term receivables (e.g., sundry debtors or short term loans) can be simply recorded at the invoice amount. By definition, a derivative instrument cannot be a loan or receivable.

d. 'Available for sale' (AFS) financial assets: All assets not classified as one of the earlier three categories are classified within this category. For assets in this category a hybrid treatment is used: The fair value is reflected in the balance sheet, but unrealised gains/losses are not shown in the profit and loss account. Instead they are reflected as changes of reserves under the category of 'Other Comprehensive Income'. This treatment is called 'fair value through other comprehensive income' and abbreviated to FVTOCI or FVOCI. The main difference between FVTOCI and FVTPL is that unrealised gains and losses do not affect the periodic current profits reported by the entity (which is the figure most watched by the stock market). Except when used as hedges, derivatives would normally not be classified under AFS. This treatment is unlikely to be applicable to them except under 'hedge accounting'.

Accounting for trading assets on FVTPL basis

Assets requiring FVTPL are accounted for as follows:
- On acquisition, these are measured and recorded at fair value and the transaction costs are directly charged to P&L.
- On each subsequent reporting date, the investment will be measured at fair value and again the P&L will reflect incremental gains and losses.
- On disposal, the difference between the realised profit or loss and the profits/losses recognised earlier will be taken to P&L.
- Since there are regular and 'fair' updates on the books, no impairment tests are required for FVTPL assets.

For liquid securities, changes in fair value are basically the changes in market value. For less-liquid securities, some kind of formula may be needed (e.g., Black-Scholes).

Accounting for HTM assets

- On the date of purchase, they are recognised at purchase price excepting when used as hedges, derivatives would not normally be classified under this category plus transaction costs.

- On each subsequent reporting date, these HTM assets are amortised; in other words the total return expected to be earned till maturity is properly allocated to the different accounting periods, using the effective interest rates.

- Therefore, on maturity there will be zero profit and zero loss, assuming there is no *impairment* (see below).

- Impairment tests are required and any impairment loss shall be transferred to the P&L. Impairment means a loss of value arising from intrinsic causes as distinct from mere market value change due to change in market conditions. The impairment test is for the purpose of ensuring that the asset still meets the original assumptions. For instance if a five year bond is purchased, and the market value falls, this does not need to be shown as a loss normally so long as the repayment of the bond at the end of the period is assured; on the other hand if in year three, the issuer of the bond becomes insolvent, then the asset is impaired, and has to immediately be marked-to-market and the impairment loss has to be debited to P&L.

Accounting for loans and receivables

- Loans: Long-term loans are simply treated as HTM assets.

- Short term loans or receivables are initially recognised at the invoice amount.

- At the year end, if there is sufficient evidence that impairment has occurred, then the loss is transferred to P&L.

Accounting for AFS assets

- On the date of acquisition, such assets are recognised at purchase price plus transaction costs.

- On each reporting date, they are then measured at fair value and any difference is transferred to an 'investment revaluation reserve' (or a reserve with a similar name) which is part of other comprehensive income. On the selling of such assets, the reserve is transferred to the P&L.

- Meanwhile, if any impairment occurs, then also the investment revaluation reserve is transferred to P&L.

Financial liabilities

Trading liabilities are accounted for at FVTPL. All other liabilities (non-trading liabilities) are generally accounted for at amortised cost, though in certain circumstances an entity may decide to use FVTPL for them.

Embedded derivatives

Often an option or option-like derivative is embedded with a bond or some other security. Such securities are called *hybrid instruments* because they are created by a synthesis of non-derivative instrument(s) and derivative instrument(s). The former is often called the 'host' instrument in which the derivative has been 'embedded' (analogous to the term host used in the context of parasites!)

Accounting standards require that the host and the derivative be accounted for separately in many cases. The procedure for the separation of the carrying amount is:

- find the fair value of the host (non-derivative instrument); and
- deduct this from the total fair value of the hybrid to find the value of the embedded derivative.

Examples of such hybrid instruments could be convertible bonds (which have a conversion option for the holder) and mortgage pass-through securities (which have a call option for the issuer).

Hedge accounting

It was seen earlier that hedge accounting is the exception to the general rule that derivatives must be accounted for at FVTPL.

The specific accounting treatment to be used for a hedge depends on the nature of the hedge. Hedging, as explained earlier in this book, is a technique used to reduce uncertainty regarding an entity's cash flows or the values of its assets and/or liabilities. From an accounting point of view, there are three types of hedges:

- Fair value hedge: A fair value hedge is one used to protect against uncertainty in the value of assets which are being recognised at fair value. A more formal definition is that it is 'a hedge of the exposure to changes in fair value of a recognised asset or liability or an unrecognised firm commitment, or a component of any such item, that is attributable to a particular risk and could affect profit or loss'.[3]

- Cash flow hedge: A cash flow hedge is one which is used to avoid uncertainty in regard to an anticipated cash inflow or outflow. More formally, it is 'a hedge of the exposure to variability in cash flows that is attributable to a particular risk associated with a recognised asset or liability (such as all or some future interest payments on variable rate debt) or a highly probable forecast transaction; and could affect profit or loss.'[4]

- Hedging of (net) investment in foreign operations: This is the case of foreign investments. Analytically, this can be subsumed under one of the above two types of hedges.

Example 17.1

Q Ltd. holds ₹10 crore worth of long term bonds denominated in Japanese Yen which are accounted for at fair value (FVTOCI). To protect itself against volatility in exchange rates, it enters into Yen-Rupee forward contracts and then rolls them over periodically. The expectation is that the gains or losses on the swap will offset the losses or gains in the fair value of the bonds in rupee terms. This is a fair value hedge.

Example 17.2

R Ltd. sells textiles to Japan. It expects to sell ₹ 10 crore worth of goods in the coming half year. It enters into Yen-Rupee forward contracts to protect itself against any appreciation of the rupee. The expectation is that the gain or loss on the forward contract will offset the loss or gain on the export proceeds. This is a cash flow hedge.

Note that in both examples, the risk faced is the same, viz., yen-rupee exchange rate fluctuation, but the hedging purpose is different.

---

3   Ind-AS 109, Ministry of Corporate Affairs, Government of India, www.mca.gov.in, para 86, downloaded 26 May 2017.

4   Ind-AS 109, Ministry of Corporate Affairs, Government of India, www.mca.gov.in, para 86, downloaded 26 May 2017.

Prerequisites to apply hedge accounting

Because hedge accounting is the exception to the norm of FVTPL for derivatives, the entity seeking to use hedge accounting has to demonstrate to its auditors that the derivative transaction is in fact a proper hedge. All of the following prerequisites must be fulfilled:

a. Documentation: During the hedge initiation, there must be proper documentation of the anticipated hedging relationship between the hedge and the underlying. The risk management objective and the strategy undertaken should also be clearly mentioned. Without this, there are valid concerns that companies would try to use and abuse hedge accounting provisions retrospectively and asymmetrically. For instance, when the price falls, an organisation could try to pass off the derivative (which it really bought for speculative purposes) as a hedge so that the loss is not debited to current P&L.

b. Effectiveness: The negative correlation between the hedge and the underlying should both theoretically and empirically be high (the closer to 100 per cent in absolute terms, the better). Both at inception and on an ongoing basis, the hedging relationship should be effective in achieving offsetting changes in fair values or cash flows (whatever its specific purpose). Assessment and reassessment of effectiveness is required whenever accounts are prepared. If this criterion is not met, either at the beginning or mid-way, then the derivative should be treated as a free-standing one for accounting purposes. Therefore, there should be reliable measurements of effectiveness and a constant reassessing of the hedge on an ongoing basis.

Currently, under many standards, there is a requirement that the measured hedge effectiveness must be between 80 per cent and 125 per cent to qualify as a hedge; this measurement is performed *ex post facto* at each accounting date. This precise rule-based method of calculation has been criticised. For instance, if a hedge is 80 per cent effective it is treated as a hedge, but if it the effectiveness is 79.5 per cent it does not qualify. There could be instances where a hedge which was effective in an earlier period (say at 81 per cent) becomes ineffective in a future period (say, 78 per cent) and the resulting changes in accounting treatment can create confusion in the interpretation of accounts. Proposed changes under IFRS

9 will replace this with a different type of qualitative test on the basis of certain principles which will be applied *ex ante*.

c. Effect on reported earnings (or cash flows) of changes in fair values of relevant derivatives: To qualify as a hedge, a change in the fair value of a hedged item or variation in the cash flow of a hedged forecasted transaction must have the potential to change the amount recognised in reported earnings. If the underlying item or transaction would not affect profit or loss, then hedge accounting cannot be used.

Accounting for fair value hedges

In the case of a fair value hedge, any profits or losses from remeasuring the hedging instruments and the underlying asset being hedged will be transferred to P&L account. *In other words, both the item hedged and the hedging instrument would be treated as FVTPL. This would be the case even if the underlying asset being hedged is not a FVTPL one*, because if both the underlying and hedge are not accounted for in a similar manner, the whole purpose of hedge accounting would be defeated.

Therefore, if a derivative has been stated to be a hedge for an AFS (available-for-sale) security, then (along with the derivative fair value changes) the fair value change of the AFS security would also be reported in the P&L (not under other comprehensive income through reserves, as is the case usually) until the derivative expires. If the derivative expires while the AFS has still not matured, then the accounting would revert to 'normal' AFS accounting (FVTOCI) subsequently.

Accounting for cash flow hedges

In this case, the portion of profit or loss on the hedging instrument determined to be an effective hedge is transferred to an equity account under the name of 'hedging reserve'. The rest of the gains or losses go directly to P&L. When the underlying transaction is recorded in the books (e.g., when the anticipated cash flow happens), the corresponding amount in the reserves is transferred to P&L in a manner that corresponds to the accounting for the underlying transaction.

Accounting disclosure requirements with respect to derivatives

The major requirements for disclosures related to financial instruments are as follows:

- The entity should disclose the fair or carrying value of its various instruments in its financial statements – in the body, in a separate note, in a table, or any other clear and understandable format.

- Motives for holding specific derivatives must be mentioned – for trading, for hedging etc. Also the hedging context, if applicable, should be mentioned (fair value or cash flow).

- The company should not combine or aggregate or 'net out' its various derivative exposures.

Accounting for employee stock options (ESOPs)

Until 1995, the stock option cost charged to the profit and loss statement for an ESOP in many countries was just its 'intrinsic value'. Because most ESOPs are ATM or OTM, the intrinsic value would be nil.

Then FAS 123 was issued. This encouraged, but did not mandate, companies to account for the fair value of the ESOPs on their income statements. If the fair value was not reported there, then it had to be a footnote to the company's accounts.

In 2004, IAS 2 and an updated FAS 123 were issued requiring companies to account for stock options in their P&L. This made stock options less popular compared to earlier because companies had to record an expense against profits whereas earlier the ESOPs involved no charge to current profits. Typically, some version of the Black-Scholes' formula is used to account for ESOPs. However, one must remember that these tend to be exercised earlier than other options because the employee is not allowed to sell them. Capturing this would require an additional model of early-exercise behaviour and incentives.

Challenges in derivatives accounting

The field of accounting for derivatives is in a flux globally because of the complexity of the instruments, the complexity of the accounting treatment and the differing opinions on the best ways of handling that complexity. There are arguments for/against a rule-based approach or a principles-based approach as seen briefly in respect of the 80 per cent to 125 per cent effectiveness rule.

The application of fair value accounting for financial instruments is itself not without critics. One of the drawbacks of fair value accounting, or more particularly MTM accounting, is that it tends to be 'pro-cyclical'. When an economy is booming, asset values rise. These rising values get reflected in the market valuation of securities. In an earlier era, unrealised gains would not be reflected in profit and loss or the balance sheet. Since they would not be in the reported figures, the banks or other institutions owning them would not report higher profits or asset valuations. But with MTM accounting, the current reported profits and asset values of banks would be boosted by MTM gains; this in turn would enable the banks to look better in terms of their solvency and capital adequacy and help them to lend more. Thus, the more the market rises, the more they could lend. On the other hand, in a slump the market values of securities would fall. This would generate reduced profits or increased losses and reduced asset values for financial institutions holding them. Since their solvency and capital adequacy would be reduced, the institutions would have to reduce their lending, thereby worsening an already pessimistic economic outlook. In other words, the effects of MTM accounting are to exacerbate both upturns and downturns in the economy. For this reason, many experts question whether fair value accounting is really the right way to account for financial instruments and derivatives.

These challenges are global. In addition, derivatives accounting in India faces additional complications. Firstly, derivatives are relatively new entrants to the Indian corporate financial scene and accountants are gradually gaining experience in handling them. Secondly, before Ind-AS, there were some ambiguities in what constituted 'generally accepted accounting practice'. AS-11 – *The Effects of Changes in Foreign Exchange Rates* was mandatory. On the other hand AS-30 – *Financial Instruments: Recognition and Measurement*, was only advisory in nature.

In the case of currency futures and forwards, AS-11 has been applied so far. The exact details depend on whether the company is using these instruments for hedging, trading or speculating. For the latter two, as expected, MTM accounting is done. For non-monetary items under AS-11, historical cost is recorded while the hedging derivatives' losses or gains are recorded as profit or loss – creating an imbalance. For example, an Indian company having a

European subsidiary will, under AS-11, record its Euro investment as a fixed cost, while being short Euro futures to hedge currency risks (this can be rolled forward periodically). If the Euro rises, this may be shown as a loss while not accounting for gains in the value of the subsidiary. Thirdly, Indian accounting practice is going through a major process of change as the country proceeds to converge its accounting procedures with that of other countries. This is like one stream (which is changing course frequently) attempting at converging with another larger stream (IFRS) which is itself constantly changing course. Also, some companies are under Ind-AS while others are not, and this can make comparisons between them quite difficult. Finally, not all derivatives accounting guidelines are issued by the Ministry of Corporate Affairs. In the case of interest rate swaps, to take an example, such guidelines are issued by the Reserve Bank of India.

Tax treatment of derivatives

The tax treatment of derivatives in India is drawn primarily from Section 43, sub-section five – hereinafter called Section 43(5) – of the Income Tax Act 1961. There is a basic difference between the treatment of hedges and the treatment of transactions which are not hedges. There is of course, sound economic reasoning behind this differentiation. The tax treatment of transactions which are not hedges is complex.

Set off general rules

Before coming to the specific issues regarding tax treatment of derivatives, it is important to note the general scheme of the Act regarding set off of incomes and losses. Under the Act, different types of income are grouped under what are called 'heads' of income. The three possible *heads* of income relevant to derivatives transactions are business income, capital gains and income from other sources. Within each head, there could be different *sources* of income. (For example under the business income head, a person may have two different businesses, say one dealing in textiles and another of dealing in shares.) The general rule under Section 70 (with some exceptions, particularly regarding capital gains) is that *within a particular head of income, gains or losses from one source can be offset against losses or gains from another.* Under Section 71, again with some exceptions, it may also be possible to offset losses under one head of income against income from another head. In either case, the income would be taxed at the rate applicable to the assessee after offset of other gains and losses under the same head. Income from a 'speculation business' is an exception to this general rule.

Transactions used as hedges

When a derivatives transaction is used as a hedge as defined in Section 43(5) clauses (a), (b), or (c), then regardless of whether or not it was done through a recognised stock exchange or recognised association, it will be taxed on the same basis and under the same head as the underlying item being hedged; the gains or losses on the derivatives contract will be set off against the corresponding losses or gains on the underlying and can also be set off against other losses or gains as per the general rule described above.

Transactions which are not hedges

Till 2005, all futures and options trades other than those eligible to be treated as hedges under Section 43(5) (a), (b) or (c), would in most circumstances be treated as 'speculative transactions' forming a 'speculation business' within the meaning of Section 28 of the Act. The income from such transactions would be taxed under the head of business income at the normal rates applicable to each person but *because it was speculative in nature, any loss on futures or options could not be set off against any other business income or non-business income and other business losses could not be set off against futures or options income.* If a loss was incurred on a speculative trade, it could only be carried forward for four years, and then set-off in the future against a future speculative income as and when it materialised (subject to the four year time limit).

In some cases – for instance, when the transaction was rare or infrequent or exceptional – the gain or loss might not be treated as a speculation business and then would be taxed under income from other sources.

In 2005, this regime underwent an important change. 'Eligible transactions' carried out through screen-based trading in approved stock exchanges are no longer treated as speculative for tax purposes even though they may be speculative in economic intent. From 2014, and following the introduction of commodity transactions tax, this treatment has been extended to commodity derivatives traded through screen-based trading on recognised associations. Commodity derivatives are specifically defined under the Finance Act 2013. Appendix XX.1 reproduces Section 43(5) and Section 70 relating to 'speculation business' from the Income Tax Act and the legal definition of commodity derivatives from the Finance Act 2013.

After these changes, derivatives transactions are of two types:

- eligible transactions; and

- other transactions.

If a derivatives transaction (though not a hedge) is an *eligible transaction*, then it

- will not be treated as a speculative transaction and hence not part of 'speculation business'; and

- may be treated as (non-speculative) business income, or as income from other sources or as capital gain, *depending on the type of derivative instrument and other circumstances.*

Other transactions would ordinarily be treated as speculation business, though in some circumstances this may not be the case. This is discussed further below.

Futures contracts which are not hedges

Futures contracts (unless they are actually settled by delivery) do not involve transfer or delivery of the underlying asset. Therefore, the gain or loss from them cannot be taxed under the head of capital gains and can only come under either business income or income from other sources. The first point is whether the futures contract is an eligible transaction or not.

Eligible transactions

If the futures contract is an eligible transaction, then it may be either a non-speculative business income or an income from other sources. If the person involved is a regular trader in futures, then the gains and losses would be taxed under the head of business income. If the person involved is an investor, it would be accounted for under income from other sources.

The line between trading and investing is very blurred and there are no hard and fast rules. This is further discussed below.

If actual physical delivery is taken, the futures contract will be treated as though it were a normal contract for purchase or sale.

Transactions which are not 'eligible transactions'

If the transaction is not an 'eligible transaction', and the next step is to determine whether the transaction constitutes a speculation business or not. Explanation one to Section 28 of the Income Tax Act, dealing with speculation business, provides that:

> Where speculative transactions carried on by an assessee are of such a nature as to constitute a business, the business (hereinafter referred to as 'speculation business') shall be deemed to be distinct and separate from any other business.

Thus, the test is whether the transactions 'are of such a nature as to constitute a business'. The extent, frequency and nature of the transactions would influence the legal determination. When in doubt, the conservative approach would be to err on the side of caution and consider short term trading transactions in derivatives to be a 'business'.

If the futures contracts are of such nature, frequency, etc. as to constitute a business, then the gains and losses will form part of 'speculation business'. Losses from speculation business:

- can not be set off against any other business income; and
- can only be:
  a. set off against gains from a speculation business of the current year, or
  b. carried forward to be set off against gains from future speculation business for up to four years.

Speculative losses cannot be offset against any other business income.

Options which are not hedges

Gains or losses from trading in options (i.e., buying and reselling the same option before it expires) will be treated in the same way as futures contracts, depending on whether they are 'eligible transactions' or not. Thus, they may be either business income (if the transaction is eligible and the person is doing options trading as a business) or as income from other sources (if the transaction is eligible and/or the person is an investor) or as income from speculation business (if the transaction is not eligible and it is in the nature of a business).

Where there is no trading but an option is bought and then expires unexercised, the option premium paid is an expense while option premium received is an income. This may either be under the business income head (if the person is in the business of trading options) or income from other sources (if the person is an investor, not in the business of trading them).

Gains arising from *exercising* an option will be treated as business income for a trader. For an investor, gains from exercising an option will be treated as a capital gain rather than as income from other sources because there is (legally) an 'extinguishment of a right' when the option is exercised. Generally an out-of-the-money option will not be exercised so the question of a loss from exercising an option would not arise.

Figure 17.1: Tax treatment of derivative transactions

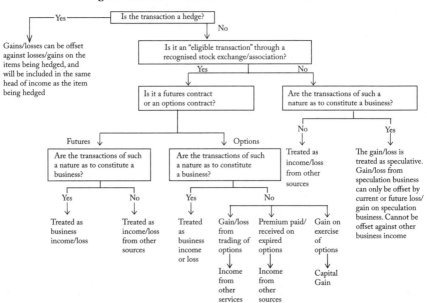

Swaps and other derivatives

In India, swaps and other derivatives are used mainly as hedges, and speculation through swaps etc., is generally not permitted by the RBI. Since they are hedges, their treatment will correspond to that already discussed earlier in the paragraph on taxation of transactions used as hedges.

Constructive sale provisions in the USA

Box 13.1 illustrated the way derivatives can be used to defer and possibly avoid taxes. In the United States, the tax laws now have provisions to regard certain derivative transactions as 'constructive sales' of another asset in cases where derivatives are used as an indirect way of to effectively closing out a position in the cash market, e.g., in equities or commodities or bonds. Box 13.1 mentioned the use of equity collars (selling a call with a strike price above the current price, and buying a put with a strike price below the current price) where the strike prices are close to the current price effectively 'locks in' the current price and a small range around it. (This then greatly reduces the margin requirements set by most brokers, and the investor can substantially withdraw a big part of the current market value of his equity holdings without selling them.) Another method is the use of equity swaps by company insiders to offset their exposure to the firm and lock in a certain appreciation. Because the cash market asset has not been sold, capital gains tax is deferred or avoided. Thus, derivatives are sometimes used as tax avoidance tools rather than risk management tools.

The Internal Revenue Service (IRS) of the United States has been treating such transactions as a 'constructive sale' for tax purposes (that is, they are deemed to be sales and taxed accordingly). In less developed markets like India, the tax authorities have not yet started paying a lot of attention to such constructive sales of financial assets through the 'creative' use of derivatives.

Appendix 17.1

Extracts From Legal Provisions Relating to Taxation of Derivatives
Section 43

'Speculative transaction' means a transaction in which a contract for the purchase or sale of any commodity, including stocks and shares, is periodically or ultimately settled otherwise than by the actual delivery or transfer of the commodity or scripts:

Provided that for the purposes of this clause –

a.   a contract in respect of raw materials or merchandise entered into by a person in the course of his manufacturing or merchanting business to guard against loss through future price fluctuations in respect of his contracts for actual delivery of goods manufactured by him or merchandise sold by him; or

b.   a contract in respect of stocks and shares entered into by a dealer or investor therein to guard against loss in his holdings of stocks and shares through price fluctuations; or

c.   a contract entered into by a member of a forward market or a stock exchange in the course of any transaction in the nature of jobbing or arbitrage to guard against loss which may arise in the ordinary course of his business as such member; [or]

d.   an eligible transaction in respect of trading in derivatives referred to in clause [(ac)] of section 2 of the Securities Contracts (Regulation) Act, 1956 (42 of 1956) carried out in a recognised stock exchange; [or]

e.   an eligible transaction in respect of trading in commodity derivatives carried out in a recognised association, shall not be deemed to be a speculative transaction.

Explanation 1: For the purposes of clause (d), the expressions

a.   'eligible transaction' means any transaction,

   i.   carried out electronically on screen-based systems through a stock broker or sub-broker or such other intermediary registered under section 12 of the Securities and Exchange Board of India Act, 1992 (15 of 1992) in accordance with the provisions of the Securities Contracts (Regulation) Act, 1956 (42 of 1956) or the Securities and Exchange Board of India Act, 1992 (15 of 1992) or the Depositories Act, 1996 (22 of 1996) and the rules, regulations or bye-laws made or directions issued under those Acts or by banks or mutual funds on a recognised stock exchange; and

ii. which is supported by a time stamped contract note issued by such stock broker or sub-broker or such other intermediary to every client indicating in the contract note the unique client identity number allotted under any Act referred to in sub-clause (A) and permanent account number allotted under this Act;

b. recognised stock exchange' means a recognised stock exchange as referred to in clause (f) of section 2 of the Securities Contracts (Regulation) Act, 1956 (42 of 1956) and which fulfils such conditions as may be prescribed and notified by the Central Government for this purpose;]

Explanation 2 – For the purposes of clause (e), the expressions

a. 'commodity derivative' shall have the meaning as assigned to it in Chapter VII of the Finance Act, 2013;

b. 'eligible transaction' means any transaction,

i. carried out electronically on screen-based systems through member or an intermediary, registered under the bye-laws, rules and regulations of the recognised association for trading in commodity derivative in accordance with the provisions of the Forward Contracts (Regulation) Act, 1952 (74 of 1952) and the rules, regulations or bye-laws made or directions issued under that Act on a recognised association; and

ii. which is supported by a time stamped contract note issued by such member or intermediary to every client indicating in the contract note, the unique client identity number allotted under the Act, rules, regulations or bye-laws referred to in sub-clause (A), unique trade number and permanent account number allotted under this Act;

c.   'recognised association' means a recognised association as referred to in clause (j) of section 2 of the Forward Contracts (Regulation) Act, 1952 (74 of 1952) and which fulfils such conditions as may be prescribed and is notified by the central government for this purpose.

Under Section 106 (5) of Finance Act 2013, 'commodity derivative' means

a.   a contract for delivery of goods which is not a ready delivery contract; or

b.   a contract for differences which derives its value from prices or indices of prices –

  i.   of such underlying goods; or

  ii.   of related services and rights, such as warehousing and freight; or

  iii.   with reference to weather and similar events and activities, having a bearing on the commodity sector.

Explanation 1 to Section 28

Where speculative transactions carried on by an assessee are of such a nature as to constitute a business, the business (hereinafter referred to as 'speculation business') shall be deemed to be distinct and separate from any other business.

Section 73 regarding losses in speculation business

a.   Any loss, computed in respect of a speculation business carried on by the assessee, shall not be set off except against profits and gains, if any, of another speculation business.

b.   Where for any assessment year any loss computed in respect of a speculation business has not been wholly set off under sub-section (1), so much of the loss as is not so set off or the whole loss where the assessee had no income from any other speculation business, shall, subject to the other provisions of this chapter, be carried forward to the following assessment year, and:

  i.   it shall be set off against the profits and gains, if any, of any speculation business carried on by him assessable for that assessment year; and

ii. if the loss cannot be wholly so set off, the amount of loss not so set off shall be carried forward to the following assessment year and so on.

c. In respect of allowance on account of depreciation or capital expenditure on scientific research, the provisions of sub-section (2) of section 72 shall apply in relation to speculation business as they apply in relation to any other business.

d. No loss shall be carried forward under this section for more than [four] assessment years immediately succeeding the assessment year for which the loss was first computed.

Explanation: Where any part of the business of a company ([other than a company whose gross total income consists mainly of income which is chargeable under the heads 'interest on securities', 'income from house property', 'capital gains' and 'income from other sources'], or a company [the principal business of which is the business of banking] or the granting of loans and advances) consists in the purchase and sale of shares of other companies, such company shall, for the purposes of this section, be deemed to be carrying on a speculation business to the extent to which the business consists of the purchase and sale of such shares.

18

Infrastructure for Derivatives Trading

Derivatives can be traded on exchanges, or OTC. In principle, not much infrastructure is required for OTC trading – all it requires is for two parties to agree. Exchanges originated as informal below-the-tree marketplaces for hedging and speculating. In earlier days, an exchange was often merely a known marketplace in contrast to isolated one-on-one transactions, and did not afford one the counterparty protections of a modern clearing house. Nonetheless, the public and open nature of the transactions meant that the credibility and reputation of both parties were involved and this offered some protection against default.

Exchanges are essentially the first layer of regulation for exchange-traded derivatives. Modern exchange trading generally reduces counter-party risks because the two parties are shielded from each other by the exchange's clearing houses, their margin requirements and regulatory safeguards. For example, A and B can decide on a wheat transaction for next year directly with each other (that would be a forward contract) or through an exchange (a 'futures' contract). In India, forward contracts in commodities outside an exchange are, unless intended for and closed by delivery, generally illegal. Since the financial crisis of 2008-09 there has been a global push towards promoting exchange-based trading above OTC trading (bringing it closer to the long-standing Indian position). The infrastructure requirements of an exchange and its various stakeholders are acquiring greater significance.

Yet, non-exchange contracts will always remain, primarily because the standardised terms of exchange traded derivatives may not match the specific needs of certain hedgers. The biggest advantage of OTC markets for participants is that terms can be customised.

Apart from this 'genuine' reason for using OTC contracts, another motivation for treating contracts as OTC (even when customisation is not needed) is regulation. OTC contracts may be legal but exempted from the regulatory requirements applicable to exchange-traded transactions, in many countries. Therefore, large but semi-standardised 'OTC' markets have grown in certain countries and for certain instruments. Many of them use a large number of standardised terms agreed upon by industry participants. Such contracts, though nominally are over the counter, have exchange-like characteristics: they are OTCs for the purpose of avoiding government regulation, but in practice an informal 'exchange' or association works.

The swaps market under the International Swaps and Derivatives Association is a prime example. In this case, phone conversations on OTC desks are properly recorded. Since these OTC contracts can be customised, they often require strong technology and back office support too. The main differences between these 'organised' OTC markets and recognised exchanges is the lack of transparency on open positions and the extent of customisation.

The regulatory push away from OTC markets after 2008 happened because, during the crisis, it became impossible to know precisely which banks and insurance companies had how much mortgage CDS exposure. Had there been an exchange, not only would there have been better information but the crisis could possibly have been ameliorated because the appropriate margin requirements would already have been posted and opposite positions could have been netted out. In the absence of information, risks were often gauged by the level of gross rather than net exposure.

Till about two decades ago, many exchanges were 'mutual' (see under *Ownership and membership* below) and had an 'open outcry' system which involved traders actually meeting each other on the 'floor', shouting and gesticulating to buy and sell (see below under *Market microstructure*). Currently most exchanges are for-profit and have electronic trading. Thus, the trend in stock, commodity and other exchanges is towards *demutualised and electronic* exchanges. The new demutualised (for-profit) exchanges have also witnessed several mergers and acquisition.

Institutional infrastructure: Depositories

Technology and policy liberalisation have revolutionised the Indian stock, and to a lesser extent, commodity exchanges in the last two decades. Regulatory relaxations, competition amongst old and new exchanges, changes in trading systems and rising awareness have all contributed to rising volumes and liquidity. The traditional settlement and clearing systems have also been overhauled in many cases.

In the equity markets, a 'depository system' was created. Depository simply means a place where something is deposited for safety. A depository in finance is an organisation or a custodian which hold securities in electronic form and facilitates the transfer of ownership of securities on the settlement dates. This system is similar to the opening of an account in a bank wherein a bank will hold money on behalf of the investor.

Some of the benefits of a depository system for securities are:

● Immediate allotment, transfer and registration of securities.

● Elimination of risks associated with physical securities.

● Reduction in paperwork and transaction costs.

● Decrease in fraud.

The National Securities Depository Limited (NSDL), a public limited company promoted by the NSE, Industrial Development Bank of India, the Unit Trust of India and State Bank of India was registered in June 1996 with SEBI. Central Depository Services Ltd (CDSL) is the other Indian depository, promoted by the Bombay Stock Exchange with banks such as State Bank of India, Bank of India, Bank of Baroda, HDFC Bank, Standard Chartered Bank and Union Bank of India and it commenced operations in 1999.

The depository interacts with investors and clearing members through intermediaries called depository participants (DPs) and performs a wide range of functions through these DPs. These services are both 'core' and 'special'. The core services are acting as depository of securities and trade settlement. The 'special' services include dematerialisation and rematerialisation, account transfers, allotments during IPOs, distribution of both dividends and bonus/ rights, locking/unlocking accounts, and various internet-based services.

It should be noted that the position of commodity markets is different because physical stocks of commodities are involved, not just dematerialised paper assets. In such markets, custodians or clearing houses also have to operate warehouses.

Organisational links for the derivatives market with spot market

Several derivatives markets are run as part of the same organisation as the spot market. For instance, stock options and index futures on the Nikkei index are traded on a separate floor of the Tokyo Stock Exchange. Similar is the case with equity derivatives in India. Other derivative markets are not organically linked to any spot market. The Chicago Mercantile Exchange and the London

International Financial Futures and Options exchange are examples. This is known in market jargon as the 'location' issue. Location is often linked to regulatory jurisdiction – if the regulators for spot and futures trading are different (as in the case of financial futures in the USA), the markets are usually separate.

Ownership and membership

Various ownership structures exist for futures and options markets globally. Some markets are profit-seeking joint stock companies, while others are associations or companies of a non-profit nature. Both these structures are found in India also.

In essence, exchanges can be *mutualised* or *demutualised*. Mutual exchanges were formed as non-profit associations or non-profit companies by brokers who felt the need for a clearing house etc. Ownership was restricted to members (hence the term mutual obligations were always to fellow members of the exchange) and the association functioned like a cooperative. Often consent of existing members was needed to admit new members.

Demutualised exchanges are limited companies, generally with a for-profit orientation, which own and run an exchange. The management and ownership of the exchange is not necessarily in the hands of major brokers who are members of the exchange and non-brokers can own equity. Membership is distinct from ownership (membership refers to the right to trade on the floor of the exchange). The by-laws of each exchange normally establish the membership criteria, the most important of which is usually financial solvency of a prescribed level. Often there are different categories of membership, with different membership rights. In most Western markets, membership is freely transferable, subject to meeting the exchange requirements.

Both types of exchanges have advantages and disadvantages. Profit seeking exchanges tend to be more efficient and user-oriented and can attract equity capital. However, they may often not start trading in instruments where trading volume is just at break-even level and may possibly have a greater motivation to 'cut corners' in regulatory matters in order to attract business because their own revenue is directly linked to trading volume.

Intermediaries and brokers

In all derivative exchanges, there are numerous intermediaries who bring together buyers and sellers. These intermediaries may or may not be members. Often, each type of intermediary has a distinct specialisation. Member-brokers in developed country markets are generally (but not always) large corporate entities while in Indian exchanges many of them are individuals or partnership firms. Member-brokers may employ sub-brokers to procure business. Some brokers may act as 'market-makers' (i.e., hold a minimum quantity of positions and provide liquidity) while others may only execute trades. The terms 'floor-broker' or 'pit-broker' or 'pit-trader' refer to the persons (usually from a member firm) who actually carry out trades on the exchange floor. Trading staff and non-trading staff may wear distinctly coloured clothing for easy identification on the exchange floor. There are 'scalpers' who are floor traders who try to profit from very small price changes and carry out a number of trades, each of which is only held for a short while; they rarely carry over any position beyond the trading day. Scalpers add considerable liquidity to a market and facilitate smooth trading. 'Day-traders' hold positions for longer than scalpers but still liquidate them each day so that they are not exposed to overnight risks. Scalpers and day-traders together are also called 'locals'. 'Futures commission merchants' are those who only execute orders for clients and do not trade on their own account. Many of these terms are peculiar to particular markets and should not be taken as standard.

Initial and variation margin

It was noted in chapter 2 that only a small deposit or 'margin money' is needed to trade in futures. When entering into a futures transaction, an amount known as the 'initial margin' is to be paid, generally determined as a percentage of contract value and fixed by the exchange and/or the regulatory authority. Normally this ranges from 5 to 10 per cent but is often lower for financial futures. Provisions for margin may distinguish between hedgers and speculators, with the former often being allowed to pay margin on net exposures or at a lower percentage. The holder of an open position is required to maintain this overall level of margin with reference to his opening price, usually with a permissible 'grace' level of fluctuation. The purpose of margin money is to guard against default. When the price of the futures contract changes in an adverse manner (exceeding the permissible 'grace' band of fluctuation if any), the holder of the open position will get a 'margin call', i.e., a requirement to deposit additional funds with the exchange. If he fails to meet the margin call, his position will be closed out. On the other hand, if the price moves favourably, the holder of an open position can withdraw cash to that extent.

Example 18.1

S, a speculator, buys 5,000 oz. of November silver futures at $25/oz. The prescribed rate of margin is 10 per cent. The initial margin is thus $12,500. Two weeks later, the price falls to $24.5/oz. S now has an open (i.e., unrealised) loss of (5,000 oz x $0.5) = $2,500 and her net margin available is $12,500 – 2,500 = $10,000. She gets a margin call requiring her to pay $2,500 immediately, which she does.

Example 18.2

Another two weeks later the price is $25.5. The margin required is $12,500 since her opening price was $25. She has paid initial margin of $12,500 plus variation margin of $2,500. In addition she has an open profit of $2,500. Her position is worth $12,500 + 2,500 + 2,500 = 17,500. He has excess margin of $17,500– $12,500 = $5,000, which he can withdraw.

Options markets usually do not require margins from option buyers, who have no obligations beyond payment of premium. Option writers are always subject to margins as in futures markets.

Tick and tick size

Each exchange usually prescribes the minimum unit of price variation, known as the 'tick size'. Thus, it may be specified that gold prices shall be quoted in 25 cents multiples. If the price of gold is $1,301.50, the next price can be $1,301.25 or $1,301.75 but not $1,301.51. Traders often compute profits or losses by counting the number of ticks and multiplying by the contract value.

Contract size and delivery months

The exchange, often in consultation with the regulator, determines the minimum contract size and the futures or options contract months to be traded. Depending on demand, there may be a contract for each month or one for every two or three months.

Settlement frequency

Settlement is the process by which changes in position are recorded and each participant is credited (debited) with open gains and losses, so that margin calls can be assessed and collected. In international markets, settlement is usually done daily on the basis of the 'settlement price', usually the closing price. In some Indian futures markets, settlement is done only weekly on the basis of the weekly settlement price. In principle, daily settlement is obviously preferable; however transaction costs of conducting daily settlement may be higher. Weekly settlement is only appropriate when volumes and volatilities are low.

Delivery mechanism

In commodity futures markets, delivery means physical delivery of the commodity by the buyer to the clearing house. In financial futures markets, delivery may mean actual delivery of the concerned security (for instance Treasury Bonds) or financial settlement (i.e., settlement of money value of the contract without actual delivery of anything), usually in the case of index futures.

Physical delivery of commodities can only be made at one or more delivery points specified by the exchange or clearing house. Sometimes, a price adjustment may be made if delivery is made in one place instead of another, to reflect transport costs. Physical delivery can be made not only on the basis variety or contract grade, but of other 'tenderable varieties' or 'deliverable grades'. In such cases a price adjustment is made to reflect the quality difference between the basis variety and the tendered variety. The extent of the price difference is known as the 'tendering difference' (i.e., difference between the variety tendered and the basis variety) in Indian commodity futures markets and by similar terminology elsewhere. Ideally, the tendering difference should reflect the price difference between the varieties in the spot market (adjusted for any transport costs arising from differences in place of delivery).

Clearing houses

All well-developed futures and options markets use a clearing house system. In this system, the exchange has an arrangement with a 'clearing house' or 'clearing corporation' (usually a separate legal entity), whereby the latter becomes the counterparty to every trade in the exchange. Suppose A buys copper from B. Without a clearing house – the transaction would be as in Figure 18.1.

Figure 18.1: Transaction without clearing house

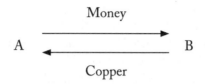

Figure 18.2: Transaction with clearing house

In the latter case, legally, A and B have no *contract with each other – their contracts are with the clearing house.* The clearing house acts as the seller to every buyer and buyer to every seller. The regulatory significance of this is that *if A defaults, B is not affected: the clearing house will still perform its obligation to B.* The clearing house mechanism *insulates participants from default risk.* To do this effectively, the clearing house has to be a highly capitalised and well run institution which has sufficient liquid funds and physical stocks to withstand individual defaults. Clearing houses are usually owned by banks, financial institutions and major brokers. The clearing house can earn profits by means of deploying the cash margins deposited with it by both buyers and sellers. Many Indian futures markets do not have full-fledged clearing houses at present. What is called 'clearing house' in many Indian markets is usually more of an accounts section which matches sales and purchases, accounts for margins, etc.

Trading systems ('market microstructure')

There are many ways of classifying trading systems – based on methodology (open outcry, screen based), price discovery (continuous auctions, batch auctions, crossing networks, quote-driven, hybrid) and intermediaries (dealers, brokers, hybrid).

Physically crying out bids (open outcry) is increasingly rare and public trading is now gravitating towards screen-based models.

In an open outcry system, there is a physical trading floor where traders shout out their trades. A trader is usually required to keep shouting till his trade is executed, unless he no longer wishes to carry out the trade. Since many people will be shouting at the same time, there is a lot of noise and to make trading intentions clearer, designated hand signals are used to supplement what is shouted out. In multi-contract exchanges, there are different 'pits' for each contract and a trader must stand in the designated pit for a given contract in order to trade in it. (The pit is often a hexagonally shaped enclosure with two or three steps leading down to the centre.) Open outcry in one sense was similar to a 'continuous auction'.

Auctions are often used in price discovery for commodity and currency market trading and for secondary trading in equity markets; there may be batch auctions for the day's opening and ending prices, and continuous auctions for intra-day trading.

Quote-driven or dealer-driven markets

Quote-driven or dealer-driven markets are those where traders generally go to a dealer to buy or sell a certain security instead of trying to directly (or through a broker) connect to another investor, speculator or hedger. The dealer often keeps an inventory of securities and has bid-ask prices for them and is ready to trade on them immediately. While the dealer may continuously try to hedge as effectively and inexpensively, these hedges are imperfect and the dealer bears the risk of the ticker going against him or liquidity falling before he 'resets' his inventory. Hence, the more volatile or illiquid a market and the greater the credit risk (e.g., in OTC markets), the greater the bid-ask spread. Sometimes dealers are even rewarded financial incentives by exchanges or bourses for being 'market makers'.

A broker does not generally keep an inventory and bid-ask quotes for a variety of securities. At the risk of over-simplifying, brokers are market-takers not makers. Brokers represent their clients and help them find liquidity for their trades (but do not generally provide it themselves). Dealers – who stand alone and represent no one – will seek to understand the information arising from any trade. For instance, a dealer when given a large order may like to understand why a particular person wants to buy share X (especially in a large quantity, say) when others do not, because the dealer himself has a stake in the share.

Of course, even dealers or quote-givers must regularly balance or reset their books – and since this mostly happens amongst themselves in such markets, they may use various other ways of dealing with each other – auctions and/or other methods like electronic crossing networks (where various trades are cleared at once at frequent but discrete intervals). With the coming of electronic or screen-based trading, hybrid methods are increasingly more popular – markets generally run on the auction or order-driven method, but leading brokers and traders can double up as dealers (officially or unofficially) and hence becoming a quote-driven market too.

The degree of automation on order-driven markets can vary significantly:

- Order routing: Orders are automatically routed to exchange floor, but actual execution is manual.

- Order routing and matching: The computer acts like an automated broker and matches the trades, but clearing and settlement is done separately.

- Order routing, matching, clearing and settlement: The computer not only matches trades but automatically does the clearing and settles brokers accounts also.

Each of these systems has both advantages and disadvantages. Some of the advantages of open outcry systems are that traders can see and hear many markets at once, enabling rapid response to new information and new traders can gain knowledge and experience by observing experienced traders and competitors – something which they cannot do over a computer. Open-outcry seems to attract more individual traders. However, it has a higher chance of errors and, in the developed country context, entails higher costs of expensive skilled manpower. Screen-based trading is operated by traders sitting in their offices who do not need to actually meet. Advantages are wider geographical reach, better audit trails and more transparency.

Automation has brought in its wake High Frequency Trading (HFT) that has been worrying some market participants and regulators. In this case, through various Direct Market Access (DMA) software platforms along with ultra-fast connections to the bourses, some big institutional traders and investors get what some feel is an 'unfair' advantage. More pertinently, some feel that volatility has been increased significantly because of HFT. Algorithmic trading is an approach where buy and sell signals are generated based on calculations coming from a pre-set mathematical algorithm.

In some cases, nanoseconds make a difference, and hence, some market participants prefer to have their servers near to the server of the exchange. While this may, *ceteris paribus*, make the markets even more liquid, collective algorithmic meltdowns are likely to occur more frequently a and cause 'flash crashes'. Automated portfolio insurance and momentum following indicators of all sorts get triggered much more quickly now. These may even be triggered by a simple faulty order entry. Regulators face the challenge of maintaining a fair marketplace while also adapting to modern technology.

19

Regulation of Derivatives Trading
An Introduction

W. R. Natu, a former Chairman of the Forward Markets Commission and one of the pioneer futures regulators in India summarised the need for regulation in the following words:

> The private interest of an operator can ... be at considerable variance with the interest of the trade and public interest. It is because of this divergence that the need for regulation arises.

While this was in relation to futures markets, it is applicable to derivatives generally. In addition to the need for regulation in order to secure the public interest, there is also another justification, at a more practical and down-to-earth level, for regulating derivatives. This arises in connection with such matters as which varieties of a particular commodity or financial instrument may be delivered against the futures market, where delivery can be given or taken, how price differences are to be fixed between one variety and another, etc. Generally, regulations on such matters are framed by the exchanges which operate futures markets, and the national regulatory authority does not come into the picture except in abnormal circumstances.

Regulatory instruments

The main instruments of regulation used by the regulatory authorities and/or governing bodies of individual markets for ensuring orderly trading, are the following:

a. Margin variation: As explained earlier in this book, margin is a proportion of the contract value which a buyer or seller in the futures market is required to put up against his transaction. The purpose of margin is to prevent defaults. The higher the margin the greater the amount of capital which is locked up against a particular transaction and, therefore, the higher the cost of the contract. Increase in margins is an inducement to reduce the volume of trading, and vice-versa. Increase in margin is generally resorted to when the regulatory authorities feel that there is an excess of speculative activity. On the other hand, decrease in margins is prescribed when it is felt that there is inadequate trading activity thus impairing liquidity of the market.

b. Imposition of special margins: Special margins, which are over and above the ordinary margins referred to in (i) above, are generally imposed on only one side of the market-place. For example, when it is felt that there is an excessive amount of speculative buying in the market, it may be decided to impose a special margin on buyers alone. Whereas variation of margins is an instrument designed to affect trading volume in the market as a whole, special margin is an instrument intended to affect trading volume on one side only. Special margins are generally imposed with 'threshold' prices, so that they are levied only when prices are above or below certain limits.

c. Daily or weekly limits on price changes: It is generally provided that prices may not change by more than a certain limit on any one day of trading. This is sometimes extended, in India, by a similar provision for weekly limits on price changes. The idea behind temporary limits on price fluctuation is that there are times (generally after an unexpected major event) when markets can get into a frenzy of unthinking or blind price movements. At such times, by calling a halt to trading when price change exceeds a certain amount, market participants are given more time to think over the price situation in a sober and well-informed manner. On the resumption of trading, they are then able to trade (hopefully!) in a more orderly fashion.

d. Limits on open position: To avoid manipulation or excessive speculation by large operators, limits are imposed on the maximum open position which can be held by any one operator. The limit is generally only applicable to speculative open position, but in practice it is often difficult to draw a precise line between hedging and speculation.

e. Temporary suspension of trading: This measure is resorted to when it is felt that there has been an over-dose of speculative manipulation which has rendered the futures market completely out of tune with reality. Existing futures contracts may even be closed out compulsorily at a rate, fixed by the authorities, which does not give the 'offending' parties the speculative gain for which they have aimed. A somewhat similar measure is refusal of permission to commence trading in a particular contract.

f. Change in number and/or timing of contracts traded: Sometimes, regulatory authorities may feel that the number and/or timing of the futures contracts being traded is not well suited to the seasonality of supply or demand in the commodity. In such cases, they may change the number of contracts traded or change the delivery dates. (For instance, instead of trading the February, April, June and November contracts, it may be decided to trade March, June, August and November contracts). Since the patterns of seasonal supply and demand in a commodity change only very slowly, this is obviously a rare measure.

g. Fixation of price limits: This is a measure whereby a maximum price and/ or minimum price is fixed beyond which the futures market is not allowed to go. Once the limits are reached, all transactions can only be undertaken at that price or within the acceptable price range. This is a measure which had been frequently resorted to in India in the pre-liberalisation era, in times of shortage or glut.

h. Indefinite suspension or banning of trading: This measure, which needs no explanation, is an extreme step which has been undertaken in India many times by the Forward Markets Commission.

Regulation of derivatives trading in India

Regulation of derivatives in India falls under two agencies, both of which are headquartered in Mumbai.

RBI

The RBI regulates interest rate derivatives, foreign currency derivatives and credit derivatives. The RBI issued comprehensive guidelines on derivatives in April 2007 and amended them in November 2011[1]. 'Comprehensive Guidelines

---

1 'Comprehensive Guidelines on Derivatives', RBI Document, available at: http://rbidocs. rbi.org.in/rdocs/notification/PDFs/76926.pdf.

on Over the Counter (OTC) Foreign Exchange Derivatives and Overseas Hedging of Commodity Price and Freight Risks' were issued in December 2010.[2]

SEBI

Equity derivatives are regulated by SEBI. Equity derivatives include single stock futures and options and index futures and options. India has derivatives on sub-indices or sector indices too. The Securities Laws (Second Amendment) Act 1999 included derivatives in the definition of Securities.

Initially futures and options were permitted only on S&P Nifty and BSE Sensex indices. Subsequently, derivatives on sector indices were also permitted. Derivative contracts are permitted on an index, if 80 per cent of the index constituents are individually eligible for derivatives trading.

Derivative products on equities, equity indices (broad and sector indices) have been introduced in India in a phased manner starting with Index Futures Contracts in June 2000. Index options and stock options were introduced in June 2001 and in July 2001 followed by stock futures in November 2001. Sector indices were permitted for derivatives trading in December 2002. In 2008, contracts on longer tenor index options, volatility index and bond index was introduced. In 2008, SEBI also permitted exchange traded currency derivatives.

In recent years, SEBI has permitted the trading of 'mini derivatives'. At the time of the introduction of mini derivatives, the minimum contract size was fixed at rupees one lakh (one hundred thousand). While the ostensible purpose of the mini derivatives contracts were to allow small investors to hedge, in reality, based on evidence from around the world, it appears to have simply drawn the small investor into speculating on stocks and stock indices.

Turnover in equity derivatives in India is now one of the largest in the world. It exceeds the turnover in the underlying stocks. The derivatives turnover on the NSE has surpassed the equity market turnover.[3] In India, as in many other countries, financial derivatives are primarily speculative instruments.

Because of the multiplicity of regulators, many commentaries on the derivatives markets in India concentrate on one or other segment and few take a comprehensive view. The Financial Sector Legislative Reforms Commission

---

2   http://rbidocs.rbi.org.in/rdocs/notification/PDFs/APR32281210.pdf.

3   *Indian Securities Market Review 2011*, chapter 6, National Stock Exchange of India, 150.

of the Government of India in 2013 recommended a closer integration of the different regulators.

In accordance with these recommendations, the Forward Markets Commission (FMC) which used to be the regulator for commodity futures and forward trading in India, was merged with SEBI in 2015. Since then, SEBI has taken over regulatory powers in respect of commodity derivatives. The erstwhile FMC was the first derivatives regulator, having been set up under the Forward Contracts (Regulation) Act of 1952. It functioned under Food Ministry due to the fact that, in the early years, most of the forward markets were in food and other essential commodities and the mandate for regulating prices of essential commodities fell under this ministry.

Part – VII

Portfolio Management and Management of Derivative Risks

20

Portfolio Management and Derivatives

Derivatives create new investment opportunities. This chapter examines techniques which are used in portfolio management with particular reference to derivatives.

Readers are likely to have heard of Lehman Brothers, the once-famous and now-notorious American investment bank which became bankrupt in 2008. Figure 20.1 below shows the price of the shares of Lehman Brothers from 2004 to 2008. It was difficult to predict that Lehman Brothers would go bankrupt when it was hitting all-time highs in early 2007. Even in early 2008 its share price was higher than in 2004. Within a few months, it collapsed. Clearly the market valuation did not reflect the company's inherent position and the stock market did not have the right information as would have been expected under textbook finance theory.

Consider the hypothetical case of a person whose entire portfolio of investments consisted of only the shares of Lehman Brothers. He would have lost all his money. And if he was leveraged through futures, margin loans etc., then there would have been large margin calls as well in which extra payments over and above the initial equity had to be paid to the broker.

Figure 20.1: Lehman Brothers Share Price 2004–08

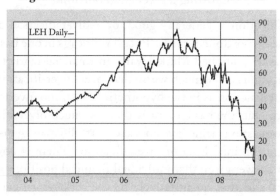

Source: http://ktcatspost.blogspot.in/2008/09/meet-lehmans-board-of-directors.html, last accessed 3 January 2017.

The conventional answer would be that the investor should have diversified into other shares. And indeed, compared to a portfolio invested entirely in Lehman Brothers, a diversified portfolio of equities would have done better. But almost all broad-based equity indices lost half, if not more, of their net worth during the period from late 2007 to early 2009 which marked the global financial crisis. Thus, diversification into other equities would have provided only limited protection. This illustrates that true diversification does not mean just different equities; it entails diversification across asset classes as well, with equities constituting just one asset class. Government bonds, corporate bonds, convertible debentures, preferred shares, precious metals, other commodities and cash or short-term bank deposits/money market investments, real estate etc. are other asset classes. Having some exposure to them in one's portfolio in 2008 would have cushioned the fall more than a pure equity portfolio.

Derivatives as a portfolio management tool

Prudent use of derivatives can offer benefits in improving the risk/reward balance of a portfolio by *creating new ways of diversifying and controlling risk, especially in terms of creating combinations of long and short positions.* The examples in earlier chapters illustrated the way derivatives can be used to control exposures in ways that would not be possible using only the cash markets.

Creating a diversified portfolio

While diversification is generally good, over-diversification can be a bad thing by reducing portfolio returns. 'Put all your eggs in one basket and then watch that basket', quipped Mark Twain. In financial markets, no or very little diversification can be much worse than over-diversification since it can lead to total destruction as in the hypothetical portfolio invested entirely in Lehman shares, but the basic point is that too much diversification is not desirable. The question facing investors and portfolio manager is thus: 'What is the "right" or optimal level of diversification?' There is obviously is no single correct answer given that individual financial positions and attitudes to risk differs, and that quantitatively precise risk/return calculations are never accurate in hindsight.

According to Ray Dalio, founder of Bridgewater Associates (a large hedge fund) the 'holy grail' of investing is finding around fifteen diversified (mostly uncorrelated) good 'bets' (i.e., positions which pay off in different circumstances).

While the number fifteen is approximate and not written in stone, if one adds many more positions (say fifty or more), he or she risks losing focus and the ability to monitor the portfolio. No doubt, some strategies based on statistical or volatility arbitrage may require holding many different assets in the portfolio to derive the benefit of the 'law of large numbers'. On the other hand, if there are too few positions, the risk of too much concentration and idiosyncratic or company-specific risk increases.

However, portfolio diversification has limits. There are few truly uncorrelated bets in this world and correlations have an uncanny way of rising just when markets crash.

Other means of reducing risk: Long-short combinations and market-neutrality

Risk (per given unit of expected return) can be reduced by diversification, as discussed above. But it can also be reduced by adding some short positions to a portfolio of long positions. Since the risk per unit of return has diminished, one can preserve the same overall level of return by adding some leverage. This is the essence of the strategy employed by most so-called 'hedge funds'.

Alfred Winslow Jones is crediting with creating the first hedge fund – 'hedging' a long portfolio with some shorts. Then, when the general market went up, his long positions were expected to go up faster than the market (since under-valued stocks would be bought) and his short positions would either not rise as much as the general market, or might even fall in price (again, since over-valued stocks were shorted).

Conversely, when the market went down, the expectation was that the long positions would fall by a smaller amount (or perhaps even rise a bit in absolute terms) and his short positions would fall by an even bigger margin than the market. In this way, the long-short investor does not concentrate on beating an index but tries to make money in every period. This is in contrast to the general practice of comparing returns with a market benchmark; after all what good is it to an investor if a portfolio manager beats the Nifty index by losing 'just' 12 per cent when the Nifty index fell 15 per cent?

When the positions are structured such that the size of the long positions and short positions are almost equal (adjusted for betas, or the individual volatility of stocks), then that is specifically called a 'market-neutral' strategy. In practice, most so-called market-neutral portfolios have a slight excess of long positions over short positions. Since shorts hedge the longs, the term 'hedge fund' came into existence. The managers of these funds claimed to deliver absolute returns – that is gains on the invested capital, no matter what the direction of the general market. Many of the world's hedge funds invest across regions and asset classes, and simultaneously take at least some short positions. This helps them both diversify and hedge their portfolios. Hopefully, it helps them beat the market on a risk-adjusted basis, at least gross of fees.

Alpha-beta separation

To succeed in investing one must be able to accurately spot value where others see rot, and accurately identify rot where others see value (relatively speaking). Once this is done, the power of derivatives, if carefully used, could further propel returns. The key skill is to be accurate in finding value; derivatives – for all their glory or villainy – remain mere tools which can amplify the returns (positive or negative) to the correct or incorrect identification of opportunities.

An 'ideal' portfolio would combine a well-designed asset allocation strategy (which would determine an acceptable targeted level of market risk or beta), and within each asset strive to out-perform the relevant index (by generating idiosyncratic return or alpha). This combination of strategies can be called alpha creation on top of beta overlay. These two different skills – asset allocation requires a strategic understanding of geo-economics and global macro forces, along with potential tactical adjustments according to the latest news and expectations. Alpha generation on the other hand is less about macro-economics, and instead more about accurate company-level and industry-level valuation and analysis. Beta mainly requires top-down analysis, while alpha requires mainly bottom-up analysis.

The broad macro-economic scenarios and the general advice given in each circumstance are as follows:

- Increasing growth with falling inflation: broadly bullish for equities and corporate/emerging market bonds

- Increasing growth with increasing inflation: bullish for commodities and short-term or inflation-linked bonds

- Decreasing growth with increasing inflation: bullish for precious metals and other real assets

- Decreasing growth with decreasing inflation: desirable to hold cash or cash equivalents

Harry Browne, an American politician and investment advisor, first described these broad scenarios and suggested the holding of a portfolio that would combine all of the above asset classes so that it would be diversified across all the above scenarios. He called it the *permanent portfolio*. Ray Dalio has a modified version of the same broad concept in Bridgewater's All Weather portfolio product for institutional clients and the US-based Oxford Club investment newsletter has a 'Gone Fishing portfolio' of a similar type.

Risk parity and the application of derivatives

While some analysts advocate allocating about a quarter of the portfolio to each scenario, others advocate allocating a quarter of the *risk* to each scenario. For example, short term inflation-adjusted bonds of a developed country's government are the lowest risk asset category; there is very low sovereign risk with regard to default, inflation protection is present and with short term bonds the price risk is lower because of the reduced duration. Since this asset is low risk, if these bonds are part of a portfolio having four equal classes, it should arguably have a weight of more than 25 per cent of the portfolio, so that it would then carry 25 per cent of the portfolio risk.

This concept is called *risk parity*. For example, a portfolio that is half stocks and half medium-term government bonds will not have half of the risk in each asset class as well. Rather it is likely that 80-90 per cent of the volatility of the total portfolio comes from stocks even though they account for half the value.

Risk parity, therefore, is not the equal allocation to various assets in a portfolio but equal risk exposure to various assets. In the 50-50 stocks-bonds portfolio example, if one wants higher risk-adjusted returns then it might be worthwhile to buy 30-40 per cent stocks and 60-70 per cent bonds, and then lever up moderately depending on the target return. This would produce lower risk per unit of return.

International diversification

Indian investors now have the ability to invest in other countries. Investing in various regions can potentially give them an edge, in terms of risk reduction, beyond diversifying in various asset classes within India such as equity, debt, real estate, precious metals etc. The benefits of global diversification are likely to be higher for those economies which are small compared to the global economy and not fully integrated. Empirical data substantiates this.[1] The Indian economy, despite growing briskly and integrating with the world, still fulfils these criteria and hence it may make even more sense for an Indian investor to globally diversify than say, an American one. Already, resident Indians can trade in Hang Seng futures and S&P 500 futures (as well as options) through the NSE in Mumbai. Indian investors can also use the RBI's Liberalised Remittance Scheme, to directly invest in foreign securities, ETFs etc., up to specified limits (currently $200,000 per year per individual). The RBI allows only cash accounts for foreign investing, and buying and selling on margins is not permitted. However, using options it is possible to be both long and short using options strategies.

---

1 Peter Stanyer, 'Guide to Investment Strategy: How to Understand Markets, Risk, Rewards and Behaviour', *The Economist*.

21

Management of Derivative Risks

There can be no doubt that derivatives are powerful tools for risk management. If used improperly, however, derivatives can produce disastrous results. With derivatives becoming increasingly important, it has become crucial for banks, financial institutions and indeed non-financial companies to properly assess, manage and account for risks arising from derivatives transactions. While many earlier chapters have dealt with the use of derivatives in the management of risk, this chapter deals with the *management of risks arising from the use of derivatives.*

Enterprise risk management – covering not only financial but many other kinds of risk – is a rapidly expanding subject by itself. This chapter is a brief and introductory overview of the main principles and practices relating to a subset of those risks – the risks arising from derivatives.

An enterprise is subject to many kinds of risk and derivatives are just one and not necessarily the most important. Nevertheless, several characteristics of derivatives make them 'special' and different from management of many other types of financial risk. First and foremost, derivative instruments are highly 'geared'. Because of this, it is possible in certain kinds of derivative transactions to lose far more than the original capital deployed in the transaction. In a normal business deal, with an investment of ₹ 10 million the maximum loss that can be suffered is ₹ 10 million or thereabouts. However, if ₹ 10 million is deployed in a derivative transaction as margin through writing of options or a speculative futures contract, it is quite possible to lose ₹ 100 million, that is, ten times the value of the capital put in. This is the single most important reason why derivative transactions require a much tighter supervision and control mechanism.

Secondly, derivative markets move at great speed. The markets are open virtually on a twenty four-hour basis, due to the integration of various exchanges across the world. Big price movements can occur overnight. (This is a feature they share with stock and spot foreign exchange markets.)

Thirdly, several derivative transactions fall into a grey area between hedging and speculation. Derivative securities used as hedges are a risk-reducing device, but derivatives used for speculation become a risk-enhancing device.

The fourth problem with some derivatives, especially the increasing tribe of complex and synthetic derivatives, is their sheer complexity. The precise financial implications of market price movements on the derivative transaction are often not obvious and not easy to comprehend.

Derivatives are very powerful instruments; just as a surgeon's scalpel used to perform intricate surgery can be misused to commit murder, so too can derivatives be used and misused. Every firm that uses derivatives must therefore exercise due caution and care in handling its derivative exposures.

Types of risks

Risks involved in derivatives trading can be of the following kinds:

- Credit risk or default risk: The risk that a counterparty will default on its obligations. This is generally negligible for exchange-traded derivatives but needs careful attention in the case of OTC derivatives.

- Operational risk: The risk that errors (or fraud) may occur in carrying out trades, in placing orders, making payments, or accounting for them etc.

- Model risk or formula risk: Options and many synthetic derivatives are priced using complicated mathematical formulae which make numerous assumptions. There can be occasions when the models fail to give accurate price data because the assumptions no longer hold (e.g., actual volatility far exceeds historically-based estimates) or because of undetected flaws in the models. Many traders, especially the less-experienced ones, take the models as infallible gospel, especially as most of the models work well most of the time. This risk is increasing with the increased use of computerised pricing models based on elaborate mathematics which the trader may not understand. A trade which fully complies with all pricing policies may thus still end up with unexpected – and disastrous – results.

Example 21.1

The Thai baht had been pegged to the US Dollar for many years. Historical levels of currency risk were thus low. Similarly, the economy of Thailand had enjoyed many years of steady growth. Suddenly in 1997, there was a major currency crisis, the stock market plunged and the entire Thai economy was thrown into turmoil. Numerous sophisticated computer models which had been used to estimate risks and prices for Thai assets proved completely erroneous as a result, causing heavy and unexpected losses to those who had relied on them.

- Liquidity risk: The risk that a derivative cannot be purchased or sold quickly enough at a fair price, due to lack of sufficient trading volume (liquidity) in the market. Liquidity risk is greater for OTC derivatives.

- Legal risk: The risk that the law or a regulatory rule may be changed or reinterpreted causing an adverse financial impact on a derivative transaction.

- Market risk: The risk of adverse changes in the market price of a derivative.

The focus of the discussion that follows will be mainly on market risk and operational risk. The discussion will emphasise the perspective of a hedger, *but the same principles can be applied by an entity using derivatives for trading.*

Using and managing derivatives

Successfully using derivatives requires a well thought-out and planned approach from the start. For successful use of derivatives, a company must:

a. evolve a clear policy;

b. establish a system of controls to monitor adherence to the policy; and

c. enforce adherence to the system of controls.

These three aspects are elaborated below.

Policy on derivatives

Any firm that uses derivatives for hedging needs to evolve a clear set of policy guidelines. These guidelines should cover the following:

- What types of risks can potentially be hedged given the available hedging instruments?

- Of the risks which are potentially 'hedgeable', which risks does the company want to hedge?

- For those risks which the company decides to hedge, should the hedging be universal (i.e., at all times) or selective (i.e., confined to periods when adverse price risks are expected)?

- Should hedges be for the full value of the expected exposure or can they be for only part of the exposure?

- Who is empowered to take the decision on when to hedge and how much to hedge?

- Does the company envisage only straightforward hedges (i.e., in the same or very similar items) or does it permit more complex and involved or synthetic hedges?

In deciding this hedge policy, the company has to keep in mind legal, accounting and taxation implications. If the entity happens to be a financial intermediary like a bank or broker, this policy should also make a clear distinction between trading for a client (which does not expose the unit to market risks) and proprietary trading, i.e., trading for its own account. It is the latter which requires very careful control, but accounting and control systems for the former must be strong enough to isolate client transactions correctly.

Control system

Having established a derivatives management policy, it is necessary to have a system of controls to ensure that the policy is followed. The control systems would normally encompass the following:

- Which levels of staff are authorised to enter into which types of transactions.

- Restrictions on counter parties with whom dealings should/should not be made.

- Limits for derivative exposure in terms of absolute value and/or a proportion of spot exposure or any other variable.

- Separation of trading (front office) and book-keeping (back office) functions. (This is absolutely vital.)

- Internal audit procedures to ensure that figures reported correspond with actual contract status.

- Comprehensive reporting system (including reports to the highest level of management on a prescribed periodic basis) to cover (*inter alia*) the extent of risk exposure through derivatives, the present loss or profit on open positions, a sensitivity analysis to price changes, etc.

- In the case of intermediaries and financial institutions: (i) proper review of incentive bonuses (if any) for trading staff to ensure that they do not have an incentive to take undue risks in search of bonuses, but at the expense of the institution; (ii) separation of proprietary trading responsibility from exposure monitoring responsibility, so that those in charge of monitoring have no responsibility for, or vested interest in, trading profits.

Given the complexity of many derivatives transactions, there is often a tendency to feel that control of exposures is a 'high-tech' activity not susceptible to normal financial control methods. This is not true. Derivative transactions may be complicated, but to ensure adherence to laid down policy, it is conventional financial and management accounting procedures that are crucial.

Enforcing the control system

Any control system is only as effective as its enforcement. The Barings disaster (where a single rogue trader caused the bankruptcy of an old and established institution) was largely (though not entirely) a case where a company had sound policy and reasonably adequate control systems, but failed to stick to its own controls.

Some of the elements that need careful supervision and enforcement are:

- A system of review of the reports received (including internal audit reports) by a sufficiently high level of management, and if necessary by external technical experts.

- A firm adherence to position limits etc., once these have been set. (Any change in limits must come as a change of policy by the authority empowered to make policy and after a careful review – not at operational level or in response to an 'urgent' request from those in charge of executing transactions.)

- Rotation/transfer of key traders (including very successful ones) from one portfolio to another (this would be feasible only for large scale trading organisations).

- Ensuring that trading staff (howsoever senior) have no repeat, no control, whether administrative or financial, over back-office operations.

- Careful watching of exceptionally successful trading staff – big winners are often those who take big risks; the same big risks can turn them into big losers later. Today's rising star is often tomorrow's falling meteor!

One point which cannot be over-emphasised is that the involvement of top management, including, wherever appropriate, the Board of Directors, is essential. The magnitude of potential derivative losses is so large that this is one area which cannot be delegated much. Management must not only obtain regular reports and review them, but must always be aware of the potential 'worst case scenario'.

When entering into a new or complicated type of derivative transaction, it is necessary to insist on sensitivity analysis and depiction of the worst case scenario. It is always advisable to ascertain (and obtain a written commitment on) the costs of unwinding a position: often 'zero-cost' derivatives cannot be unwound (closed out) without a cost. Bankers and brokers earn fat commissions from over-the-counter and synthetic derivative transactions (the more complicated, the better) and therefore the 'worst-case scenario' is often the 'least-explained scenario'. To quote one well-known case, the Bankers Trust (one of America's biggest banks and one of the leaders in the derivatives field) actively promoted and sold its clients complex derivatives which ultimately ended up producing large losses. The Federal Reserve Bank of New York had to step in with regulatory restrictions on the bank's derivatives business including strict supervision, as it felt the bank had not acted properly and that the clients had not understood the risks they were taking.[4] Textile exporters in Tiruppur, Tamil Nadu are engaged in litigation with banks for allegedly selling derivatives on the basis of misleading information. Some derivatives users (in India and abroad) are going in for independent risk management advice through consultants, because of the feeling that banks are guided more by their own commissions than by the clients' interests. However, appointment of a consultant – howsoever competent – is no substitute for supervision on a fully-informed basis, by a company's own management.

Value-at-Risk (VAR or VaR)

In the preceding section on managing risk, there was reference to 'limits for derivative exposure', and sensitivity analysis of the effects of price changes. For companies with limited derivatives transactions, these are relatively simple to assess. However, for financial institutions and companies with a large volume of derivatives transactions, the task of measuring the risk inherent in the overall derivatives position is very complex. One of the main and widely accepted methods for doing this is the VAR

VAR is a statistical concept. It is an attempt to answer the question: 'What is the maximum amount I can lose from this particular set of holdings, within the next day (or week, or month, or quarter)?' More precisely, it is an estimate, with a predetermined confidence interval, of how much an entity can lose from holding a position over a set time horizon. The confidence interval can be 95 per cent, 98 per cent, 99 per cent etc., (but never 100 per cent). The time horizon could range from a single day (for trading operations) to a month or longer for portfolio management. The estimate is based on historical data of volatilities of individual prices and of the correlation between prices. (If the prices of two derivatives are closely correlated, then the risk during an adverse move is more than if they are poorly correlated.) The VAR figure (for the defined confidence interval and time horizon) is then computed and reported regularly. Exposure limits are also set in terms of VAR.

Example 21.2

A company holds a long futures position worth ₹ 5 crores which is known to have a daily volatility (based on historical data for the last six months) of 1 per cent. What is the value at risk over a one day horizon, using a 98 per cent confidence interval and assuming the risks are normally distributed?

Solution:

From the standard normal distribution tables, it can be found that 98 per cent of the distribution falls within 2.05 standard deviations of the mean. (i.e., leaving only 2 per cent in the left hand 'tail' of the distribution). The mean in this case is the volatility of 1 per cent. The VAR is:

₹ 5 crore '1 per cent' 2.05 = ₹ 10,25,000

In this case correlation data was not needed as there was only one instrument.

A simple way of looking at the VAR in the above example, is that 'one can be 98 per cent sure that the loss from the futures position over the next one day will not exceed ₹ 10,25,000'.

Though VAR has been explained in very simple terms above (to convey the essence of the concept to the reader) the actual computation for a large real-life portfolio is a complicated business. Historical data on volatility and correlation for each item are necessary and need to be constantly updated. Various mathematical models are necessary to compute the volatility of a portfolio, based on the interplay of innumerable factors affecting each instrument. Different

313

analysts may use different methods – some may use 30-day historical data to estimate the volatility, others the 60-day data and yet others the six-month data.

Some may use a 95 per cent interval while others use a 99 per cent interval. For the same circumstance, some may calculate a 'one-day' VAR, others a one-month VAR (the latter will always be higher). This can create problems for management, accountants, auditors and regulators.

VAR can be applied at the portfolio level or at an institutional (entity-wide) level. VAR, when employed at an institutional level can provide the senior management with a regular one-number summary and trend of the risks facing the firm. (However, this 'one number' dependency is can be a major weakness because the calculation of the single number may ignore unexpected correlations and extreme events – see below.)

The process of measuring risks involves several components:

a.   enumerating the portfolio positions;

b.   from market data, constructing the distribution of risk factors (normal, empirical or other);

c.   mapping (i.e., linking) the various positions to the different risk factors;

d.   constructing the distribution of portfolio returns using probability distributions (which may be parametric, historical, Monte Carlo etc.); and

e.   summarising the downside risks and calculating the VAR.

Various proprietary systems developed by investment banks and others exist to help companies measure and manage their risk exposures and calculate measures like VAR and Risk Adjusted Return on Capital (RAROC).

Limitations and weaknesses of VAR

The limitations and weaknesses of VAR are of two kinds – fundamental (inherent) weaknesses and purely practical limitations. On the practical side, there are high costs of maintaining and operating a VAR-based system – computer hardware and software, obtaining price data, keeping skilled specialist staff or paying outside experts etc. Even with all the costs, data may still be insufficient in several cases.

Coming to the more fundamental weaknesses, it should never be forgotten that VAR is a probabilistic estimate. Even if the data is perfect and all the assumptions in the model hold perfectly, the loss can exceed VAR once in

20 occasions (for a 95 per cent interval) or once in 100 occasions (for a 99 per cent interval). This is not a small risk: even at a 99 per cent level, two or three days a year can routinely fall beyond the VAR figure! Secondly, there are a number of assumptions made in the VAR calculation process. Generally, historical data on volatility and correlation is taken to represent future volatility and correlation. Price changes are assumed to follow a 'normal distribution'. Both these assumptions may not hold in practice. Volatilities do change, and they tend to change most in times of turmoil – assumed historical volatilities can then be highly misleading (see Example 21.1). Similarly, the 'tails' of price distributions for financial markets may be (and often are) 'fatter' than those of the normal distribution. i.e., the probability of occurrence of extreme events which fall in the 'tail' of the distribution may be larger than that indicated in a normal curve (hence, the description of the tail is 'fatter' than shown in a normal curve). When the assumptions fail to hold, losses can greatly exceed VAR estimates. In the *Mahabharata*, Karna was cursed to lose his formidable military prowess when he needed it most – VAR potentially has the same problem of failing when needed most!

There are other measures of risk too. A variant of VAR is the liquidity-adjusted VAR. This takes into account the decrease in liquidity which may occur during steep market falls. Another variant uses the semi-standard-deviation and focuses only on unfavourable risk; it considers the variability of returns only on the downside without offsetting it with the probability of favourable risk. Similarly, there is the maximum drawdown VAR measure which (in simplified terms) estimates the worst possible loss based on the maximum variation from maximum to minimum in the past.

Stress-testing

Because of the deficiencies of VAR, it is essential that all derivatives users do 'stress-testing'. Stress tests involve moving key variables one at a time (and occasionally all of them together) along with using historical and prospective scenarios. The events to be guarded against include dramatic changes in government policies, coups, wars, currency devaluations, sovereign defaults etc. Essentially, stress testing is just another term for sensitivity analysis. It involves asking questions like; 'What will happen to my portfolio if the rupee is devalued by 40 per cent within 30 days' or 'what if the oil price rises 100 per cent in 30 days at the same time that the rupee is devalued by 40 per cent', though historical data may show these contingencies to have an insignificant probability. 'Extreme values' and fat tails can and do happen in the real world, and one must be prepared for these 'worst cases'.

A technique that is becoming more common in financial risk management is the Extreme Value Analysis (EVA). Given a sample of data, the attempt is to understand what could be the probability of an event (generally a negative event) more extreme than any in the sample.

VAR – an evaluation

Despite its flaws, VAR is one of the best available techniques for measuring the risk of a large and complicated portfolio. It must however be used with caution and in conjunction with stress tests. There is (what the authors would call) a 'sophistication risk' in VAR: because of its highly mathematical methodology with a plethora of Greek symbols, equations and derivatives (the word being used here in its old-fashioned mathematical sense!), non-specialists can easily get the impression that it is a very precise or accurate measure of risk. Users of VAR must make clear to senior management, its precise scope (as a probabilistic measure) and the fact that no measure is perfect, even in terms of measuring market risk. It also provides no protection against operational risk. Derivatives are like a powerful engine in a car, which allows one to drive faster in the markets. In an eloquent comment on VAR, using this simile, Jorion stated:

> ... VAR is like a wobbly speedometer which gives us a rough indication of speed. Derivatives disasters have occurred because drivers or passengers did not worry about their speed. Of course there can be other sources of crashes (such as blown tires). Such accidents can be compared to operational risks, against which VAR provides no direct protection.[1]

For entities who use derivatives sparingly or use only one or two types of derivatives, the costs of a full-fledged VAR system are unlikely to be justified. These entities can obtain a fairly good understanding of their risk by scenario and sensitivity analyses on a 'what if' basis, always keeping the 'worst case' in mind.

---

1   P. Jorion, 'In Defence of VAR', *Derivatives Strategy*, Volume 2, No. 4, April 1997.

The need for sound judgement

It was mentioned in the previous section that there is no substitute for management judgement in such matters. This point is worth repeating. J. P. Morgan, the bank which is a world leader in VAR, candidly states:

> ... no amount of sophisticated analytics will replace experience and professional judgement in managing risks.[2]

One could go even further and say that professional judgment (of derivative professionals alone) may not be sufficient. When a derivative strategy is being decided upon, the advisability of the strategy and its risks must be clearly and intelligibly communicated in a form understandable by non-specialist top managers and those responsible for the decision must ultimately take the decision not just on the basis of models and mathematics, but also on the basis of sound common sense.[3]

Last but not the least, and often the most overlooked aspect of risk management, is the need for *admission of ignorance* by derivative users. If they do not understand a product, they must ask for repeated explanations until they actually understand all the risks, even if this makes them appear unsophisticated or less knowledgeable. If they still do not understand the working of the structure, they should avoid the transaction. As mentioned in chapter 1, the worst risk of all is ignorance.

---

2   Introduction to Risk Metrics, third edition, J. P. Morgan (Morgan Guaranty Trust Co.), New York, March 1995.

3   For an interesting critical perspective on VAR and also on high-frequency and algorithmic trading, readers may refer to Wilmott and Orrell's book (see Bibliography).

Bibliography

Ahuja, N. L. 2006. 'Commodity Derivatives Market in India: Development, Regulation and Future Prospects.' *International Research Journal of Finance and Economics* 2: 1450–2887.

Baer, J. B. and O. G. Saxon. 1948. *Commodity Exchanges and Futures Trading*. New York: Harper & Row.

Bakken, H. H. 1966. 'Futures Trading: Origin, Development and Economic Status.' *Futures Trading Seminar*. Wisconsin: Mimir Publishers.

Black, F. and M. J. Scholes. 1973. 'The Pricing of Options and Corporate Liabilities.' *The Journal of Political Economy* 81(3) (May–June): 637–54.

Blau, Gerda. 1944–45. 'Some Aspects of the Theory of Futures Trading.' *Review of Economic Studies* 12(11): 1–30.

Brennan, M. J. 'The Supply of Storage.' In *The Economics of Readings Selected*, edited by B. A. Goss and B. S. Yamey. London: Macmillan.

Damodaran, Harish. 2013. 'The Marwari Business Model I and II.' *The Hindu Business Line*, 7 and 8 April.

Das, Satyajit. 2006. 'Traders, Guns and Money: Knowns and Unknowns in the Dazzling World of Derivatives.' *Financial Times*, 261. New Jersey: Pearson Education.

Goss, B. A. 1972. *The Theory of Futures Trading*. London: Routledge & Kegan–Paul.

Goss, B. A. and B. S. Yamey. (eds.) 1978. *The Economics of Futures Trading: Readings Selected, Edited and Introduced*. Second edition. London: Macmillan.

Government of India. *Indian Accounting Standard 113*. Accessed on 22 May 2017. Available at http://mca.gov.in/Ministry/pdf/INDAS113.pdf. New Delhi: Ministry of Corporate Affairs.

Gray, R. W. 1977. 'The Characteristic Bias in Some Thin Futures Markets.' In *Selected Writings on Futures Markets*, Vol II, edited by A. E. Peck, 318. Chicago: Chicago Board of Trade.

_____. 1984. 'Commentary.' *Review of Research in Futures Markets* 3(1): 80–81.

Hicks, J. R. 1964. *Value and Capital*. Second edition. Oxford: Oxford University Press.

Hieronymus, T. A. 1977. *The Economics of Futures Trading*. New York: Commodity Research Bureau.

Houthakker, H. S. and P. J. Williamson. 1996. *Economics of Financial Markets*. New York: Oxford University Press.

Houthakker, H. S. 1968. 'Normal Backwardation.' In *Value, Capital and Growth—Papers in Honour of Sir John Hicks*, edited by J. N. Wolfe. Edinburgh: Edinburgh University Press.

Israeli, D., C. M. C. Lee and S. A. Sridharan. Forthcoming. 'Is there a Dark Side to Exchange Traded Funds? An Information Perspective', *Review of Accounting Studies*. Accessed on 14 May 2017. Available at https://papers.ssrn.com/sol3/papers.cfm?abstract_id=2625975.

Jorion, P. 1997. 'In Defence of VAR.' *Derivatives Strategy* 2(4) (April). Accessed on 25 May 2017. Available at http://derivativesstrategy.com/magazine/archive/1997/0497fea2.asp.

Keynes, J. M. 1930. *A Treatise on Money*. Volume II. London: Macmillan.

Knight, F. H. 1921. *Risk, Uncertainty and Profit*. Boston: Houghton Mifflin.

Lokeshwarri, S. K. 2016. 'Interest Rate Futures Lose Steam in 2016.' *The Hindu Business Line*. Accessed on 14 May 2017. Available at http://www.thehindubusinessline.com/money-and-banking/interest-rate-futures-losesteam-in-2016/article8490493.ece.

Luttrel, David, Tyler Atkinson and Harvey Rosenblum. 2010. *Assessing the Costs and Consequences of the 2007–09 Financial Crisis and its Aftermath*. Dallas: Federal Reserve Bank of Dallas.

Mayes, Timothy. Lecture Notes (Chapter 15), Course No. 3600 on Investments. Denver: Metropolitan State College of Denver. Accessed on 24 December 2016. Available at http://slideplayer.com/slide/6895061/.

Morgan, J. P. March 1995. 'Introduction to Risk Metrics.' *Risk Metrics*. Third edition. New York: J. P. Morgan (Morgan Guaranty Trust Co.).

National Stock Exchange of India. 2010. 'Products'. Accessed on 15 December 2016. Available at https://nseindia.com/products/content/derivatives/irf/irf.htm.

_____. 2011. *Indian Securities Market Review 2011*. Mumbai.

_____. 2015. *Indian Securities Market Review 2015*. Mumbai.

Natu, W. R. 1962. *Regulation of Forward Markets*. Bombay: Asia Publishing House.

Pavaskar, M. G. 1976. *Economics of Hedging*. Bombay: Popular Prakashan.

Pavaskar, R. 1977. *Efficiency of Futures Trading*. Bombay: Popular Prakashan.

Rajan, Raghuram G. and L. Zingales. 2003. *Saving Capitalism from the Capitalists*. New York: Crown Books.

Reserve Bank of India. 'Comprehensive Guidelines on Over the Counter (OTC) Foreign Exchange Derivatives and Overseas Hedging of Commodity Price and Freight Risks.' Accessed on 15 December 2016. Available at http://rbidocs.rbi.org.in/rdocs/notification/PDFs/APR32281210.pdf.

_____. 2007. 'Comprehensive Guidelines on Derivatives.' *RBI Document*. Accessed on 15 December 2016. Available at http://rbidocs.rbi.org.in/rdocs/notification/PDFs/76926.pdf.

Reuters. 2007. 'ETFs aren't Derivatives.' Accessed on 15 December 2016. Available at http://blogs.reuters.com/felix-salmon/2010/10/01/etfs-arent-derivatives/.

SEBI. 2016. *Securities and Exchange Board of India Annual Report 2015–16*. Published on 19 August. Accessed on 20 August 2016. Available at www.sebi.gov.in/cms/sebi_data/attachdocs/1471609638850.pdf.

Shah, Ajay. 2009. 'How Useful Are the New Interest Rate Futures?' Accessed on 16 December 2016. Available at http://ajayshahblog.blogspot.sg/2009/09/how-useful-are-new-interest-rate.html.

Somanathan, T. V. 1993. 'Commodity and Financial Futures Markets: An Economic Analysis.' Unpublished Ph D Dissertation, Calcutta University.

Somanathan, T. V. and V. Anantha Nageswaran. 2015. *The Economics of Derivatives*. New Delhi: Cambridge University Press.

Stanyer, Peter. 22 April 2010. 'Guide to Investment Strategy: How to Understand Markets, Risk, Rewards and Behaviour.' *The Economist*. Second edition. New York: Bloomberg Press.

Stein, J. L. 1986. *The Economics of Futures Markets*. Oxford: Basil Blackwell.

Stoll, H. R. 1969. 'The Relationship between Put and Call Option Prices.' *Journal of Finance* 24(5) (December): 810–24.

Tomek, W. G. and R. W. Gray. 'Temporal Relationships among Prices in Commodity Futures Markets: Their Allocative and Stabilising Roles.' In *Selected Writings on Futures Markets*, edited by A. E. Peck, Vol II. Chicago: Chicago Board of Trade.

Varangis, P., T. Akiyama and D. Mitchell. 1995. *Managing Commodity Booms and Busts*. Washington DC: World Bank.

Williams, Jeffrey. 1989. *The Economic Function of Futures Markets*. New York: Cambridge University Press.

Wilmott, P. and D. Orrell. 2017. *The Money Formula: Dodgy Finance, Pseudo Science, and How Mathematicians Took Over the Markets*. Chichester: John Wiley and Sons.

Working, H. 1949. 'The Theory of the Price of Storage.' *American Economic Review* 31(December): 1254–62.

_____. 1953. 'Hedging Reconsidered.' *Journal of Farm Economics* 35(4) (November): 544–61.

_____. 1962. 'New Concepts Concerning Futures Markets and Prices.' *American Economic Review* LII(3) (June): 438.

Index